tickled

tickled

A COMMONSENSE GUIDE TO THE
PRESENT MOMENT

DUFF McDONALD

HARPER

An Imprint of HarperCollins*Publishers*

HarperCollins books may be purchased for educational, business, or sales promotional use. For information, please email the Special Markets Department at SPsales@harpercollins.com.

FIRST EDITION

Library of Congress Cataloging-in-Publication Data:
Description: New York, NY : Harper, 2021. | Includes bibliographical
 references.
Identifiers: LCCN 2021018635 (print) | LCCN 2021018636 (ebook) | ISBN
 9780063036895 (hardcover) | ISBN 9780063036901 (ebook)
Subjects: LCSH: Self-actualization (Psychology) | Mind and body. | Creative
 ability. | Conduct of life.
Classification: LCC BF637.S4 M237 2021 (print) | LCC BF637.S4 (ebook)
 | DDC 155.2—dc23
LC record available at https://lccn.loc.gov/2021018635
LC ebook record available at https://lccn.loc.gov/2021018636

ISBN 978-0-06-303689-5

21 22 23 24 25 LSC 10 9 8 7 6 5 4 3 2 1

For Joey
You were right.

For the Lady
You are magic.
You are possibility itself.
Thank you for your love.

For Bob
Thank you for your multitudes.

For JK
Thank you for reintroducing me to my daughter.

For JC
Thank you for reintroducing me to my brain.

For Hugo
Thank you for helping me say what I was trying to say.

For Hollis
Thank you for believing in me.

For Betty
Thank you for Joey.

For Now
Because now is all there is.

Not Yet Tickled

How did those priests ever get so serious
and preach all that
gloom?

I don't think God
tickled them
yet.

Beloved—hurry.

—SAINT TERESA OF AVILA (1515–1582)

CONTENTS

tickled

Chapter 0

It is the greatest of lies that we are mere men;
we are the God of the universe.[1]

—Swami Vivekananda

I'm going to begin this book in a way that's probably a little different than most books you've read. It's certainly different than any
book that I've written. What I'm going to do is tell you about the
book that I had every intention of writing but *didn't* end up writing.
It was about a subject so perfectly suited to what I believed to be
my core talents and strengths that I thought it would turn out to be
the best thing I had ever created—the pinnacle of my career, what
it had all been leading up to. My publisher agreed with me and,
armed with a sense of optimism and a generous advance, I sat down
in May 2020 to do just that.

Nothing turned out the way I planned. The original idea, you
might say, didn't tickle me anymore; I ended up writing something
else entirely.

Before I go into all the reasons why that happened, I want to
let you in on the vision for that original book. Because it's really

important to understanding how I ended up where I did. Please don't think that I'm asking you to read something that didn't make the final cut. Because it did: You're reading it right now. And I still believe every single sentence you're about to read. The difference is that I believe them on a much deeper level than I realized when I began to write. And because of that, I ended up writing a different book than I'd intended.

So here we go.

This is how this book was supposed to go. Rather, this is how it went. I wrote this introduction before I realized what I was doing wrong.

THE PRECISION PARADOX

How Our Obsession with Measurement Has Led to the Decline of Common Sense

There are two kinds of people in the world: those who think we can measure everything, and those who know that we can't. It's remarkable (terrifying, even) that the former group—the one that has it wrong—has somehow wrested control of society's decision-making apparatus away from the latter. It's less remarkable that they've held on to it—if the people in charge think that measurement matters more than it should, then measurement will matter more than it should.

We have handed too much control over our collective decisions to self-described experts who seek *truth* about vital matters of human importance in a place that it cannot be found—in the data.

What do you get when you *count* something? A number, of course. What is contained in that number? Nothing but itself. Are numbers always right? Well . . .

Ask three people to count the number of logs in a woodpile:

Person A: "There are 200 logs in the pile."
Person B: "There are 198 logs in the pile."
Person C: "I don't have time to count them, so I will just average the
first two guesses and call it 199."

Is it possible that one of those numbers is right? Yes, it is.

Is it possible that all of those numbers are right? Of course not.

Is it possible that none of them is right? Absolutely, especially considering that the third person didn't even bother to look for the answer on their own and tried to get at it via mathematics—by averaging two data points—instead of seeking to experience it (that is, to count the logs) directly.

So . . . to summarize . . . a number may or may not contain truth. It depends. Not only that, we all know that the person doing the counting—of anything, really—wields enormous power in setting the terms of a discussion and the apparent importance of that number, even though they may have no clear purchase on truth itself.

Everyone wants to be right. So it's an understandable inclination to want to suggest that one's facts come carrying the weight of truth, even when the facts are wrong. We all do it, all the time. But here's the problem: Somewhere along the way we began to confuse and conflate purported facts and truth. And then, over time, we came to believe, on a very deep level, that numbers were no longer just pointing to facts but pointing at truths. Not only that, we gave them seniority over words as well.

Some people deal with actual people and actual things—let's call them specialists. And then there are those who deal with the data that we generate to try to keep track of those things—let's call them experts. In other words, specialists deal with reality, and experts deal with models of reality.

Look, I know there are other kinds of experts. But if you open any newspaper in 2021, when they say *expert*, they are really talking about analysts. Analysts *count* things. Think about that for a second. In 2021, you get to call yourself an *expert* if you spend your time *counting* things. Three-year-olds know how to count. But it takes someone who knows how to use their words to help a three-year-old understand what they are counting.

The counters want to measure and rank everything.

Are more people dying here or in Europe?
What is the cost of all this death?
Which is the most expensive virus in history?
What does that poll say about that number?

I'm not just talking about COVID, either. I'm talking about *everything*. The reason that we can't stop counting is that counting is easier than understanding. But truth hides in the essence of a thing. If all we want to know is *how many of something there are*, then counting usually does the trick, provided that we can first agree on what we're counting and then come to some agreement about the count itself. But when the question isn't *How many?* but *Why?*, it doesn't matter how often you update your totals. They won't be able to answer your question. The only thing that numbers contain is themselves. There is nothing else there.

And still, we keep trying to measure and count our way to answers about things that cannot be quantified. *What is the worth of a human being?* The experts tell us to evaluate each other based on the numbers that can be assigned to us: our annual sales performance, our IQ, or our influencer rating. But such numbers can't get anywhere close to telling us who we really are or anything at all about those things that make us human, such as our level of awareness and our attitude. Or, put another way: our *state of being*. It is only through awareness of your existence that you are ever going to get to Truth, or Absolute Reality. But there is nothing *precise* about awareness; it just *is*. Because awareness is not *a thing of thought*, it cannot be comprehended by any mental process. It lies entirely outside the domain of the intellect.

We are in the grip of a misguided obsession with the *precision* offered by numbers and a quantified worldview. For the most part, that precision is a mirage. There are some things about which we can be very precise: our height, our age, the number of fingers on each hand, or the total number of people in the room. There are others about which we cannot: intuition, mood, harmony, or the reasons that people do the things they do. And once you measure one thing, as the theoretical physicist Werner Heisenberg would tell you, you've given up context. When you pin down location, you lose your hold on velocity. And when information becomes decontextualized, understanding bleeds away.

When did this happen? The Czech economist Tomas Sedlacek has an idea: "Perhaps the most important characteristic of the modern era has been the change in emphasis from the question *why?* to the question *how?*" he writes. "This shift is, so to speak, from essence to method. The scientific era has tried to demystify the world around us, to present it in mechanical, mathematical, deterministic, and rational garments and to get rid of axioms that cannot be empirically confirmed, such as faith and religion."[2] The shift from *why?* to *how?* is also what happens to most people as they age: Children want to know *why*; adults want to know *how*.

Social scientists are particularly culpable of trying to quantify the unquantifiable. In a grab for respectability a century ago, they dressed themselves in the garb of scientific method, and we've been listening to nonsense about percentages of teamwork and average estimates of optimism ever since. Why do we not stop and address the sheer absurdity of these measurements? Because we are too busy trying to count our way to enlightenment. But the answer to the mystery of existence is not a number.

Nor, for that matter, is the answer to the mystery of COVID. If you simply count what is happening with COVID, all you are doing is describing the surface. That's missing the point. No one needs to be told what this virus is—it's a killer. What's more, all the *experts* seem to be doing is telling us *what* is happening—how many infections here, how many deaths there, how the virus appears to be transmitted. The answer that we should be aiming for is *why* this is happening. Because that's the only way we can get to a meaningful decision not just about how to react to it but about what we might do to prevent it from happening again. We need to ask why so that we can *understand*, and not just *describe*, what is happening to us. We already know *what* is happening, and despite a staggering amount of *expert advice*, we have shown ourselves to be woefully incapable of understanding it.

But this book is not about COVID-19. It's about something much bigger than that. It's about miracles. What is the most miraculous thing that ever happened? For each and every one of us, miracle number one is that we exist. Without that miracle, there is nothing. So existence is the thing. But here's the thing about existence: You can't count it. Or quantify it. It just *is*. It's also ever-changing. Existence is flux. There is not, and never will be, anything *precise* about being alive. And yet we count and count and count away. What are we at risk of losing? What have we already lost? Nothing short of our humanity. Man invented numbers, and, intoxicated with that creation, man wants to measure everything, up to and including trying to calculate *essence itself.* Put differently: Drunk on our success at building machines, we have begun trying to build *technologies of the soul.* And we are risking our souls by doing so.

I am not interested in rehashing the age-old debate of quality versus quantity. What I am interested in is the paradox at the heart of modern life. Everyone can agree, for example, that it would be better to be happy than to be rich. But our obsession with measurement has led us to try to count *quality itself.* The most recent incarnation of such: the utterly absurd *science of happiness* and the vast industry dedicated to the quantification of something as unquantifiable as contentment.

We are trying to use measurement to answer questions including:

Who am I?
Why am I here?
What makes me happy?

The more we try to measure our way to answers to those questions, the less we will ultimately know about our true nature. There are simply far too many moving parts, or variables, that cannot be accommodated when we try to calculate our way to a conclusion. There are too many aspects of humanity, about what we value, and about things we cannot control, to try to jam it all into a formula.

If we want the answer to all answers, we will need to step back from the measurements we have chosen to rely on and try to grasp reality in a different way. As has become clear in recent years, what we thought of as truth isn't quite the immovable object many of us thought it was. That's because Truth—with a capital "T"—sits outside our thought processes. The measurers may be able to count how many of us there are, but they cannot put a number on the only Truth that there is, which is *our state of being.* That is up to us, and the answer is not a number. We cannot, and should not, trade the elusiveness of our spirit for the efficiency of a simple count of the population. The former is all that we are; the latter is simply one way, and a meager one, to describe us.

I have long argued that putting too much control of society into the hands of a very narrow group of thinkers—the analysts—has deprived us of a richer kind of mutual existence. The analysts think that we can measure our way to *truth*. But truth is not a number.

What's more, we have confused what we think of as "objectivity" with *truth*. Objectivity, as most people understand it, is nothing more than process. We measure, we measure, we measure, and we engage in an orgy of process. In doing so, we have exchanged wisdom for exactness, humanity for mathematization.[3] We are, as my friend Chris Wink—one of the cofounders of the Blue Man Group and the mastermind behind Las Vegas's Wink World—describes it, engaging in a frenzy of "statsurbation."

Consider the concept of the Quantified Self. In a culture of self-improvement, measurement gives you a goal in the absence of meaning and purpose. The idea that you can measure your way to a better life is well suited to our mechanized, reductionist, and analytical world. We are constantly measuring our progress. Marketers sell us beacons to help us explain ourselves to ourselves, and they profit while we count.

But while the numbers we use to describe ourselves make us feel like we're in control, we are not. We are stressing over our data. We are intervening when we shouldn't. And then we rely on the people that gave us the numbers to give us the solutions to the problems that the numbers helped create.

Most important, we are not getting closer to *the answer*. We are confusing ourselves with measurements, comparisons, longitudinal studies, and predictions. We need to stop counting everything and start *looking* at it. We need to stop counting our lives and start *living* them. We need fewer measurements of something that has already happened or might happen and more focus on *what is happening right now.*

If we can stay focused on whatever it is that is happening now, the rest will take care of itself. "The wise train the mind to give complete attention to one thing at a time, here and now,"[4] says the Buddha. I agree with that guy.

I hope readers are nodding their heads in agreement to at least some of the above. How did we get to this moment? We got here because numbers changed the world, seemingly for the better, when man learned to control the physical environment around him with the help of the hard sciences. But we have let our dependence on numbers get away from us. A mistaken belief that the scientific method can lead to truth has led us to extend quantification into realms where it does not belong.

The more faith we put in numbers to describe anything beyond *how many is that?*, the more we delude ourselves into thinking that certainty is almost upon us. It is not. Certainty—about pretty much anything—is an illusion. The only thing we can be certain about is the infinite. Meaning, that it *is* infinite, and that we will never be able to count our way out to the edge. Well, that, and our own existence. You exist now, and anything can happen next. Ergo, you are infinite. You are the universe.

This is not a dispatch from the anti-math poetry department. My first intellectual loves were quantitative—coding, chemistry, calculus. I studied finance because I was attracted to its mathematical underpinnings. I am a fan of Jorge Luis Borges, the great Argentinian writer and poet, whose fictions are built on foundations of philosophy, mathematics, and logic.

In recent years, though, my love of mathematics has turned into concern about mathematization. Two of my books, *The Firm* (about

McKinsey & Company) and *The Golden Passport* (about Harvard Business School), sound the alarm about the analytical forces that are increasingly dominating our society.

The result of that adulation is a society of what cultural critic William Deresiewicz labeled *Excellent Sheep*—a desperate population of miseducated elites that can count with the best of them but are nevertheless "adrift when it [comes] to the big questions: how to think critically and creatively, and how to find a sense of purpose."[5]

That elite has eschewed mastery in favor of performance, because performance is more easily measured. And that has had predictable results: Instead of finding satisfaction in the journey, we are focused on the goals. What's more, when we overprioritize the goals and then miss those goals, we get depressed for not hitting them, maybe even lower them, and then get depressed all over again if we miss them again. There's a case to be made that our most frequent experiences of failure emanate straight from the numbers we use to measure ourselves. (You should consult the statistics on depression if you'd like the snake of that thought to eat its own tail.) In other words, you don't know something is wrong with you until someone (perhaps you) tells you that you don't measure up.

Don't get me wrong: The Cult of Measurement has been valuable to us. The hard sciences allowed us to force nature into submission on countless fronts. And early statisticians delivered humanity from an existence based on guesses to one based on prediction, with massive and long-lasting positive effects in realms extending from being prepared for the weather to scheduling trains. But our obsession with trying to put a number on the future has taken us away from ourselves in the present. Even when we are not daydreaming about tomorrow, we are constantly trying to pin ourselves down with numbers, and in doing so, we let the present moment slip away. We have distorted our experience of reality by trying to measure it.

In other words, when we approach a situation seeking under-standing, but our method of doing so is to *measure* something, the odds are good that the only thing we will learn from our inquiries is the result of our measurement itself. If you mistake that for *the answer*, you lose sight of the larger search for truth. That applies to both a particular situation—*Why is this happening?*—and the ulti-mate situation—*Why am I happening?* And there just isn't a single number (or even a handful of them) that is a sufficient answer to ei-ther question. As the author Nathan Hill puts it: "Seeing ourselves clearly is the project of a lifetime."

This book is intended to be an intellectual history of measure-ment. It will document our futile and misguided quest for certainty through numbers, fueled by our persistent (and also futile) hope for a black-and-white world that doesn't exist. Somewhere along the way, we went from trying to understand ourselves to trying to control ourselves, optimize ourselves, and categorize ourselves. In doing so, we created an orthodoxy and a point of view that has be-come so powerful that most of us can't even see behind the assump-tions and presumptions that were put in place to hold them up. We are prisoners of a system—many systems—of our own design.

Just to be clear: This is not a modern problem. I do not trace its roots to social media. Nor do I trace them to the algorithms that underlie much of our modern, technology-heavy existence. Rather, this is a central human intellectual quest that has been playing out for centuries. Plato, one of the early heroes of Western thought, believed that we could calculate ethics using a formal, abstract ap-proach; Aristotle took a look at all the human variables involved and concluded that mathematical precision (in realms like ethics) was a chimera. So we've been arguing about this since we've been arguing at all.

Turn your gaze farther east, to ancient Indian philosophy, and you will find exquisite—and still palpably relevant—articulations of our elaborately constructed prisons of the mind. We live in "temporary and small universes of safety and relative order which [provide] a haven of security at the price of keeping the [self] entrapped in its own constructions of ignorance."[6] Having stared into the abyss of infinite possibility, we chose, instead, to hide behind a mirage of calculable probability.

Over the course of that multicentury argument, we got a lot of stuff right. But we also got a lot of stuff wrong. Lately, though, it's been more wrong than right. We are teetering out of balance, weighed down by all of our numbers. By my *calculation*, the most powerful paradigm shift occurred when capitalism tightened its hold on us, and the numbers people rose to the top of the power hierarchy. That's when measurement for the sake of measurement became widespread, leaving us with the tail wagging the dog phenomenon that we consider progress today.

The capitalist drive to quantify everything in search of ways to *capitalize* on opportunity has led to our imprisonment in a numbers-based reality *that isn't actually real*. When we need to understand something, our gut instinct is to start by measuring it and then frame all further understanding and action around how we might manipulate either the thing being measured or the measurements themselves. It's a system that undervalues that which cannot be measured, disadvantages (to our collective detriment) the less mathematically inclined, and, most important, limits the scope of our total understanding of ourselves.

*   *   *

So there you have it, the book I was all set to write, starting in May 2020. I still think it would have been pretty great. It was the best proposal I ever wrote. It felt clean, inspired, right on point. I'd been selling the idea to friends for months, and everybody was intrigued by it, with most people saying it made intuitive sense to them. So I knew that the timing was right in a broad cultural sense—we *are* living in a quantified era—and I was excited to get down to writing what I was sure would be my breakout book.

When COVID hit, I ran through the same gamut of strange, unfamiliar emotions that hit everyone I know, and probably you, too. But I was lucky in the sense that the project I was about to embark on seemed to take on greater relevance. The blizzard of data that has been heaped on us every waking hour hasn't clarified anything. COVID revealed the Precision Paradox at its pinnacle—a society hypnotized by and searching for meaning in numbers. In other words, *searching for meaning where it does not exist.*

This is not to say there haven't been interesting things to learn in all that COVID data. There surely are. But there probably isn't a single piece of COVID data that you have read that has any relevance to how you should live your life. Yes, wear a mask if you find yourself in the midst of a pandemic. But no, we didn't find that idea in the COVID data. We knew about it already. If you are unhealthy, try to stay out of the way of a deadly virus. We knew that, too. Nothing in the near-infinite array of numbers and statistical analysis that we have been subjected to in the last year and a half tells us anything that you or I or the guy down the street really needs to know. Not only do the numbers not *mean* anything—they are simply a tally, otherwise known as counting, otherwise known as pointlessness—they are a distraction from the matter at hand, which is *your life and whether you intend to keep on living it.*

And yet.

And yet few of us have been able to turn away. Despite the fact that COVID is nowhere near as lethal or terrifying as something like the bubonic plague, it has captured—and kept—the attention of the world in a way that is so unprecedented as to defy comparison. The numbers have hypnotized us, and they have mounted a hostile takeover of our attention. The Counting of COVID has stifled discussion of all the other things that matter, including why COVID is happening at all. At the same time, they have anesthetized us. Large numbers may fascinate but they likewise elude our grasp, leaving us with contradictory phrases like "an incalculable death toll." A death toll is *not* incalculable. What a large death toll can be is *difficult to grasp.* But the wording lays bare our confusion: Our language is so infected by the desire for precision that we use *incalculable* when we mean *ungraspable,* as if understanding *could* be counted. It can't.

Let me be clear: I am grateful that COVID has to this point spared those close to me. The loss of a loved one is as hard as it gets, and nothing I have said or am about to say here should be construed as an attempt to minimize the real pain felt by real people who have suffered exactly that. Nor do I mean it to be provocative. I do not wish to make light of death. What I want to do is to suggest that we have still gained something profound in the midst of that loss.

For much of March and April 2020, I did what everyone else did, and watched things unfold over the Internet while trying to distract myself by watching *Tiger King* on Netflix. By May, I managed to pull myself out of the quagmire and began to write. The Precision Paradox was playing out before my eyes. My timing was *perfect.*

Is it too early for me to introduce another *there are two kinds of people* idea into this book? I hope not, because I'm going to do it anyway. There are two kinds of people in the world: those who can sit comfortably in now, embracing the essential uncertainty of life, and those who cannot. Those who cannot do so end up trying to seek control, to reduce *risk* by calculating *probabilities.* Those who are comfortable with uncertainty ignore *probabilities* and spend their time seeking out *possibilities.* When COVID hit, the population cleaved into these opposing tribes. The first group lost their minds a little bit, and then became more and more desperate for *expert guid-*

ance about the numbers that will show us the future, while the second group settled in for a contemplative and quiet time at home.

The *New York Times*, like most media entities, tries to "make sense" of events on behalf of "the reader." And in a matter of weeks, the newspaper of record went all *expert* on us, claiming in almost every story it ran for weeks that *only the experts* knew what to do. (As I sit here in March 2021, that hasn't changed. They are all expert, all the time.) But the *experts*, who might be better described as *analysts*, didn't know anything other than how to point to some numbers as if the mere invocation of those numbers meant something. It turns out that most "experts" don't know anything we didn't already know—this is a virus, and it kills some people, and it spreads rapidly in some places and less rapidly in others. Yes, masks do help slow the spread of viruses. But no, that is not news. We already knew that.

But just because we already know something doesn't mean that the experts will stop making predictions. Consider the following April 18, 2020, story, called "The Coronavirus: The Year Ahead." In a five-thousand-word story, the word *expert* is used nineteen times.

> *"'There will be no quick return to our previous lives,' according to nearly two dozen* **experts**.*"*
> *"Most* **experts** *believed that once the crisis was over, the nation and its economy would revive quickly."*
> *"The next two years will proceed in fits and starts,* **experts** *said."*

Experts, it seems, predict the future. Which is impossible, because anything can happen. But there's the rub: The reason that numbers people think that they can see into the future is that their numbers told them so. But numbers don't even exist in the present—have you ever bumped into a number walking down the street?—they are nothing but a mental construct. How can something that doesn't even exist point the way to a future that doesn't exist, either? What has happened to us?

My book wasn't due until the fall of 2021, but having realized that I had to start writing immediately, I sat down in May and wrote the introduction, which you have just read above. So far, so good.

But then, to my surprise, I couldn't go any further.

I had just begun to write the best book I would ever write, with the best timing I could have ever hoped for, when I realized that I was about to make a huge mistake.

I realized, in an instant, that I needed to rethink—completely—what it was that I did for a living. I realized that I was part of the problem. Because I was pointing my finger at other people saying, "You people are the problem!"

I realized that I had to turn the focus back on myself. Because I am the only problem that I am responsible for. I realized that the thing I had been doing for much of my adult life—writing about something that I thought we (you, me, everybody) *shouldn't* be doing—was the wrong way to go about it. What I should have been doing was writing about what I *was* doing. "It is only when you 'quote' from your own experience that your words have weight," writes Swami Satchidananda.[7] I finally understand what that means.

*　　*　　*

What should I have been doing? I should have been focusing on the things that I love, not the things that anger or annoy me. I should have been focusing on things that *tickle* me, taking joy in what Sri Aurobindo calls "the favorable touches of life."

My daughter M. (aka The Lady) tickles me. My second wife,

Joey, tickles me. Reading good books tickles me. Listening to Bob Dylan tickles me. Making kombucha tickles me. Building great fires in my airtight stove tickles me. Looking out the window of my office into the woods tickles me. Lying on the roof with Joey and M. and looking out at the stars tickles me.

I will pause here and address my choice of the word *tickle* as part of the underlying philosophy of this book. It's a funny and awkward word, isn't it? In one context, it's as innocent as can be: We tickle our children. M. loves being tickled. In another context, it feels a little dirty. More than a few people have asked me whether a fifty-year-old man using the word *tickle* might evoke the wrong kind of image. And here is what I have to say to that: Let us keep our minds out of the gutter. Just because something *could* be offensive doesn't mean it *has to* be.

The first definition of *tickle* in Merriam-Webster refers to what you might call a surface tickle: to touch (a body part, a person, etc.) lightly so as to excite the surface nerves and cause uneasiness, laughter, or spasmodic movements. When people say that we can't tickle ourselves, this is the definition that they are talking about. It's hard to cause yourself uneasiness with your own touch, after all. You can't tickle the bottom of your own foot or your armpit. If this was the only definition of the word, it wouldn't be incorrect to conclude that it's pretty much impossible to tickle yourself.

But the second and third definitions of *tickle*, per Merriam-Webster, run a little deeper: *to excite or stir up agreeably*, as in to *tickle* your sense of rhythm, and *to provoke to laughter or merriment*, as in to be *tickled* by a clown's antics. Can you excite yourself? Can you make yourself laugh? I can, and I do. Ergo, I *tickle myself.*

So let's talk about the difference between those two definitions. The first describes a *physical* kind of tickling, whereas the second is more of a *spiritual* kind of tickling. The first is about *tickling* some part of you, while the second is about tickling *the whole you*. And tickling your whole being—your soul—is a much more profound act than tickling some part of your body. My friend the photographer Jeff Holt came up with another way to think about it, too: He suggested that the tickle is *the tuning fork of truth*.

Now that I've taken a stand for the right to use a word the way the dictionary defines it, I'm going to take a step back and say that I'm also talking about the full spectrum of the word, all the way from the sacred to the profane. Not only that, I am also talking about tickling yourself *in the present*. Because you cannot tickle yourself (or someone else, for that matter) in the past or the future. Tickles can only happen in the *now*. Following that logic, if something tickles you, what is that telling you? It's telling you that you are *alive*.

You could also say that the act of tickling yourself is a message of love from you to you. When something tickles you, you are experiencing presence. You are alive and you are doing something that you love. So the suggestion that we cannot tickle ourselves is akin to suggesting that we cannot love our own existence. And that's ridiculous. More important, if you are not good *with you*, then how can you possibly be of use to others? If you don't know how to tickle yourself, how can you possibly tickle someone else?

And how can you learn to tickle yourself? The great meditation masters will tell you that you just need to learn to pay attention to what is happening to you. We all know what happiness feels like. The trick is to tighten your focus on it when it comes, to grab hold of it and try to sustain it as long as possible. You don't want to *lose yourself* in the experience. You want to *find your Self* in the experience. Do what brings you joy. It is the means by which you will discover the splendor of the Self.

So what does the *experience* of joy *feel* like when you fix your mind on it?

It tickles.

Suddenly, I realized that I had spent much of my life writing about things that most certainly did not tickle me and covering up that feeling by cracking jokes along the way. I thought that I was doing my part toward trying to understand the business of the world and justifying it by telling myself that these were important matters—that is, of the non-ticklish kind. But the act of doing so was not helping me to live the life that I wanted, to focus on those things that had deep significance for me. Au contraire: It was taking me *out* of my life and into *my ego*. It was taking me out of *now*. I wasn't writing about what *was* but about *what should be* (according to me) in a state of righteous anger. That is the opposite of tickling oneself. When you focus all your energy on resisting what is—say, by insisting that other people should be acting differently—you are introducing friction into your own existence. I was making myself angry *on purpose*, intentionally not writing about the things that truly mattered to me. What was I thinking?

It's not that I have ever been unclear about the things that I love. But I suddenly realized that I'd spent my entire career writing about the things that I *don't* love. More to the point, I realized that I had spent most of my life—not just my writing life—taking the low road, calling people (and ideas) stupid because it was easy. I suddenly realized that I still needed to do the work that had been waiting for me, all along—I needed to dive into a real discussion about the truly meaningful things in my life. I needed to talk about what mattered to me and why.

So let's get back to those two kinds of people. The first group includes those who are comfortable embracing the essential uncertainty of life. Those are the ones who are open—open to love, open to everything. The second group is made up of those who are scared and seek control. For almost fifty years, I had been telling myself a story in which I was one of the people who could deal with uncertainty. I was a maverick, the guy who jumped at possibility and ignored the risks. But then, in an instant, I realized that I wasn't that guy at all.

The discomfort with how I'd been going about my life and work had been building for many years. Rather, it had been building until it had stopped building, at which point it began easing, sometime in 2018 or 2019, thanks to my wife Joey's influence. But it wasn't until COVID put the brakes on all of life's distractions that the last piece of the puzzle fell into place.

Clarity can be like that; it can come in a flash. Like Harry Potter casting a spell. When a paradox resolves itself, it all seems so obvious, even when everything had been so confusing in the moments leading up to the revelation itself. That's what happened to me. I suddenly saw myself clearly, for the very first time in my life. It was destabilizing, to say the least. Why? Because in that moment, I realized that I was precisely wrong about who I was. The paradox wasn't something I was going to write about in a book. The paradox was me.

There are two kinds of thoughts. There are the ones we construct ourselves, in our own minds, on top of the twin edifices of our identity and our intellect. These are entirely *subjective*. And then there are the ones that spring up spontaneously from the depths of our being, the ones that don't need any help from the mind. These aren't *concepts* or the products of *thinking*; rather, they are instantaneous and characterized by their relative *lack of subjectivity*. You don't need to *think* about them; you simply know them to be true. If you spend your life focused on the first type, what you are doing is buying into a single, biased point of view—your own. That's what I was doing, even though I didn't realize it. But it's when you get access to the second that you can tap into something much more important, which is Truth itself.

I recently watched a YouTube video in which Eckhart Tolle describes thinking as an addiction. He's got a point. We are addicted to thinking, because we love the feeling of being right. But right and wrong are always relative. We should focus more on what we *know*.

Do you want to know how you know when you *really* know something?

It tickles.

PART I

The Great Awakening

"He hasn't got a clue who he is,
or where he is, or who we are."[1]

—Ron Weasley, *Harry Potter and the Chamber of Secrets*

CHAPTER 1

Be Here Now

If you find him, ask him why he disappeared.

—*Suspense* radio show, May 12, 1952

In the quiet of the quarantine, all locked up with nothing to do, the control freaks of the world pretty much lost their minds. I know that because I was one of them. Between April and May I started bouncing off the walls of our house in Hurley, New York, talking Joey's face off, telling her over and over that I had to start writing my book. I was suffering a loss of control, which I mistakenly characterized as something outside me—the news was coming at me too fast, the Precision Paradox being ratified too quickly, and it was other people's confusion that was overwhelming my mind. That's what I thought, and that's what I said, over and over again, trying to reassure myself that I could manage the task of sorting through other people's insanity so that I could get the book done.

But that wasn't what was happening.

What was happening: With my daily distractions reduced to almost nothing, my brain was suddenly able to take control of me back from my mind. The mind is where your ego lives, and it is the thing that tells you that you are right. It is the collected content of *your* experience. That's where most of my work has come from.

Your brain, on the other hand, is the thing that connects you to the universe, otherwise known as the ocean of consciousness. That's where all the good ideas come from. When your mind overrides your brain, you lose your connection to that ocean, and the best you can come up with is the best you can come up with. When you stay connected to the ocean, though, you can come up with anything. If you don't believe me, just ask David Lynch. His oeuvre is testament to the fact that he has a direct line to the ocean itself.

CONSCIOUSNESS = THE UNIVERSE = INFINITE POSSIBILITY

If you can tap into that, anything can happen.

So when things got quiet, and I wasn't rushing off to God knows where, I found myself settling a little deeper into *now*. That's the Holy Grail, right? Because now is all there is. I have spent most of my life running away from now—clinging to the past or desperately hoping for some specific future. The goal is to *be here now*. We've known that at least since 1971, the year I was born, when Ram Dass told it to the world. I've spent some of my life in now, but I have never stayed there. Why? Because that's where the toughest questions live:

Why are you acting this way?
Why are you so angry?
Why are you doing what you're doing?
What is your purpose?

Did I want an answer to those questions? I thought I did. I mean, I knew about the questions. But I didn't know how to answer them. Because I didn't know how to stay present long enough to do so. Had I tried to meditate? (Anyone who meditates is trying to get into now.) Sure, but without much success. (Actually, without *any* success, but I didn't know that until I knew it.) I have been practicing hatha yoga, also known as a moving meditation, for nearly a decade. Yoga takes you inside your body, but I hadn't gone *all the way inside*. But I didn't know that, either.

It took a quarantine to get me there. Why? Because what I thought of as resolve was nothing more than stubbornness, and change *really is* hard. When I needed to quit drinking back in 2012 because I'd become a full-fledged alcoholic, I couldn't manage it myself. It took my first wife threatening to sue for full custody of our daughter (because of the alcoholism) to make it happen. So the solution came from without. That's what happened this time as well. That's the curse of people who think they know too much. If you're closed off—disconnected from the ocean of consciousness—you don't have access to new ideas and keep trying all the old ones. And the old ones are what got you in trouble in the first place.

You've probably heard this one: A popular definition of insanity is doing the same thing over and over again and expecting a different result. But here's another one: To be insane is to be *in a state of extreme distraction*. Let's close that loop, shall we? If you are extremely distracted, which most of us are, every single day, you will not be able to stay connected to the ocean of consciousness. So insanity is simply being disconnected from the universe.

What is the universe? You are the universe. So insanity is being disconnected from yourself. Specifically, your *big Self—your Self*. That's what tips most of us into our moments of insanity—when our small self—our ego—disconnects us from the big Self—which is the entire universe. That's why we do the stupid things that we do. Because if you are disconnected from the ocean of consciousness, you are left with nothing but the ideas that your mind (that is, your *small self*) can come up with. And if that's all you've got, you will end up trying some of them again. On the other hand, if you can eliminate all that distraction—say, with the help of a quarantine—you might be able to reconnect to the universe, and, hopefully, begin to see things as they really are. Indeed, you might be able to see what is really happening, *right now*. And if that happens, it can stop you from doing something insane, like writing another book that you didn't really want to write.

If you are the universe, you are God. I consider this the loophole of all loopholes. Is life bringing you down? Well, don't forget that you are God, and then everything will be okay again. Another way to think about it: When you are caught in the mesh of worldly concerns, you are, by definition, hamstrung by subjectivity. You can only see things from your own point of view. The way around that is to focus not on what you *think* is right, but on what you *know* you are a part of, which is the universe, which is God. The former is always debatable; the latter, not so much.

This might be a good time to make something clear: I don't think I'm more enlightened than you. I'm simply saying that I have become more enlightened about me. I'm saying that the quiet of the quarantine let me settle into now, and see, quite clearly, what I had been doing wrong my whole life. COVID locked me down, and then it woke me up. In the quiet of the quarantine, I remembered how to tickle myself again.

What's more, when I talk about the importance of the Self, I am not promoting or proposing selfishness but rather the opposite. If you accept that God lives within each and every one of us, which I do, the implication is that we are all connected. We are all one, with the only thing separating us from each other being the ignorance of our true nature. Nor should you confuse my arguments on behalf of personal choice with some kind of antisocial libertarianism. I believe in the collective. But I can also see, quite clearly, that there is no such thing as collective action outside of storytelling. There is only one thing that any of us can do, ever, and that is to decide what we are going to do right now. That's the only option available to you, to me, or to anyone. Add them up, and it can sometimes appear as if we all did something together. But those actions were not *connected*. It is *we* who are connected, not the choices we make.

Finally, it is true that I am a white male who has had a relatively comfortable life. There's no denying it. But if anyone sees fit to lob an accusation of privilege my way, I will reply the only way that makes sense to me, which is to point out that we can only speak from our particular point of view. My goal in this book is to tell the truth about myself and what I have come to believe. If you're not interested in my point of view, then you are in the wrong place. Because it's all I've got.

If you do want to lash out at me, I can empathize. I am very familiar with the instinct to criticize. The bulk of my career has been spent pointing out what other people are doing wrong. It's a waste of time. I'm not saying that I was wrong about what I thought was wrong, but there is no enduring value in such an exercise. Imagine if you bought something and the directions simply told you *How Not to Use It*. While there have been bright spots along the way, much of my writing adds up to one big manual of *How Not to Do Stuff*. Please do not put that on my epitaph.

In case you hadn't guessed it yet, that is not my plan with this book. This time, I'm going to do it the right way, the way my neighbor Skip described it to me recently. Skip is an artist, a car collector, and an evangelical Christian. But his message isn't about Christianity per se; it's about kindness. "When you're talking to someone," he says, "there is no middle ground. You are either bringing them up or bringing them down. You should always try to leave someone feeling as if you lifted them up." (Skip reminds me of my late father. Like my dad used to do, Skip doles out sage wisdom almost as if in passing. "If you find happiness," Skip told me, Joey, and M., "guard it like a pot of gold. Because if you lose it, it's hard to find it again. So guard it like a treasure.") We have several of Skip's beautiful paintings of the Ashokan Reservoir on the walls of our house, and they make us happy. Skip is a man of his word.

I'm writing this book for myself, most of all. I am also writing it for M., who doesn't really need my help figuring things out, but because I am her father, I am going to pretend that she does. Because I love her.[1] I am doing it for my wife, Joey, because she saved me. And I am doing it for everyone else I love, which I have belatedly realized is . . . everyone. So this book is for me, for M., for Joey, and for everyone else as well.

At various points in the pages that follow, I will argue that we cannot be certain about anything other than what is happening to us *right now*. The past doesn't exist anymore, and even if we think we remember it, we can't be sure: Memory, as we all know, can be faulty. What about the future? Well, it's never even existed at all. What you and I think of as "the future" is nothing but guesswork, ideas of things that may or may not come to pass. How can we be certain about a guess? To claim to know the future is to commit the sin of pride. I'm going to amend my original claim, though. The only thing that you can know with anything approaching certainty—the *only* thing that you *do* know—is that you exist. Following that, in a close second, is what is happening to you *right now*.

I have written many things in my life, but they were rarely about what was happening to me at that very moment. (Or, if they were, they were not labeled as such. That's how mirroring works.) That is what this book is—the first long-form expression of what is happening to me, right now. The result is that I feel wide awake—

aware of my Self—for the very first time in my life. Not only that, I have also realized how I'm supposed to do this thing from here on in, with a focus on expanding my own consciousness. Yes, I realize that's somewhat self-evident: Who wants their consciousness to shrink? But I'm talking about priorities. Henceforth, expanding my awareness is job one.

Do you know what happens when you really start paying attention? You start to notice *everything*. In September 2020, I came across the Henry James novella *The Figure in the Carpet*, written in 1896. Early on, the protagonist is telling a novelist that he doesn't quite believe the novelist has hidden a singular and profound message throughout his life's work of novels. The novelist scoffs in reply: "That's only because you've never had a glimpse of it," he says. "If [you'd] had one the element in question would soon have become practically all you'd see."

The language James is using here is unmistakable. On a superficial level, he's referring to the content of the fictional novelist's works. But what he's really getting at is something deeper. He's talking about what happens when you get a glimpse of the Big Picture, when you realize that you are one with the universe. From that point, there is no turning back—*the element in question . . . becomes practically all you see*. Like most people, I'd been looking for *the answer* my whole life, sometimes with intent, sometimes without. But it wasn't until COVID brought change from *without* that I was finally able to isolate and act on the necessary changes *within*. I don't think I am the only one. Indeed, I would go so far as to suggest that a Great Awakening is upon us.

Why do we do the silly things we do? One of the reasons is that it's the way we've been doing them. Another is that we're too distracted to decide to do otherwise. Have you ever had a loose doorknob in your house? Why do they take so long to first acknowledge and then ultimately fix? Because we have other things to do. Because the clock is ticking and we have someplace to be. When life is lived in linear fashion—with a direction and *goals*—a lot of changes-in-waiting are neglected due to a perceived lack of time.

But what if you had nowhere to go? What if you had nowhere to be? Before COVID, such questions would have seemed absurd to most of us. Everyone *eventually* has somewhere to go, right? That is, unless you're under quarantine. In that case, you are where you are going, you are where you need to be. And when your entire calendar gets canceled, you have no use for time. Rather, you have no use for *linear* time. As you approach the present—meaning, when your calendar is empty save for *now*—time goes *cyclical*. While the seasons still exist, the day-to-day opens up into the infinite. What are you going to do today? Well, what do you *want to do* today?

I'm not saying that nobody had things they had to do when COVID came out of nowhere and scared us into our homes. I am saying that for almost everybody, once quarantined, we had *fewer* things to do than we did before. At least for a few months. In the space that opened up, I figured a few things out. I made a bunch of decisions. I started doing some things and stopped doing others. My ability to focus skyrocketed. Most of my relationships deepened— noticeably so. The ones that did not had their problematics laid bare and accepted. For me, at least, the forced confinement in a state of *nowness* led to both *awareness* and *consciousness*. Joey had already brought tickles back into my life, but the quarantine allowed me to fix my mind on them.

And I know that I'm not alone. Practically everyone I know has a similar story. So from where I stand, *everyone* has started doing at least something—and typically a lot of things—differently. When was the last time that happened? Never? Yes, I know. It's been a tough transition for a lot of people who aren't even dealing with death itself. But I think that's just because they've focused on the challenging parts of COVID and not the wonderful ones, on the things happening to them and not the things they have happened upon. (Some might say this divide lines up quite cleanly with those who have the additional burden of children at home and those that don't. Perhaps. But that's always the case.)

In any case, this book is a true story about one man's ongoing journey of self-discovery. It started a long time ago, but, left to my own devices, I didn't get very far. It took the removal of choice, via quarantine, to open my eyes up to infinite possibility. If that sentence seems a little odd, try this one on for size: It was only when I couldn't do whatever I wanted to do anymore that I realized that I could do whatever I wanted to do. And one of the things I decided to do was write this book, instead of the one I had started to write.

And it tickled. Figuring stuff out always feels good, right? You might even say that it tickles to feel your understanding of something deepening in real time. That's the whole reason to immerse yourself in a thing—because immersion leads to a deepened understanding, which tickles. And while this may not come as a surprise to you, it did to me: When the thing you immerse yourself in is the task of figuring *yourself* out—when you focus on the Self—things can go full-tickle pretty quickly.

When the tsunami of COVID data washed over us all, I saw it for what it was: an altogether perfect manifestation of the paradox itself—the most frenzied orgy of counting the world has ever known. But then something happened: I began using the found time of the quarantine to increase my focus on a few of my favorite things, my tickles. And you can't count a tickle—any part of it. It's ineffable. You can't count love, either. If we're going to talk about the love of our own existence, there are no numbers that are up to the task. Ever. Put another way: If you're talking about a number, you are *definitely not* experiencing the splendor of the Self. We are conditioned to believe that any increase in precision is a step toward truth. But that's just flat-out wrong. I realized, in a flash, that a book seeking the truth should not contain any numbers at all. If I'd written the book as planned, it would have reinforced the Precision Paradox rather than resolved it.

A quick aside: Yes, I know that it would be nearly impossible to make one's way through modern life without dealing with the mountain of numbers that are thrown at us every day. A facility with mathematics comes in handy in that regard. But just because we must deal with numbers does not mean we need to put our faith in them. Instead of treating numbers as things containing meaning, we need to learn to see them for what they are—empty. These days, when I see numbers, I immediately step back and wonder if I need to care about them, in any way. More often than not, I don't. That exercise renders numbers powerless against me, but the ability to practice regularly has been hard-won through constant focus. Meditation works both ways—you can use it to find yourself, but you can also use it to lose things that you don't need, with most numbers ranking very high on my list of things that no longer have power over me.

Instead of writing about numbers, I decided to write about how I could suddenly feel myself as something other than the sum of my own experiences. Like most people, I have spent too much time hung up on or emphasizing a particular experience or expectation that I once had, when the fact of the matter is that we are simply what we are. If you can shed all the baggage—identification with things that have happened or that could happen—what you end up with is the seed of everything anyway: consciousness and intention. You know that you exist and you are aware in this moment. So what are you going to do with it?

We are, every single one of us, faced with the opportunity to make a choice—to do something—in every single moment of our lives. When we do so, we engage in the creation of our own reality. When we don't, we become observers of our own lives, passive players in the game of existence. You are the total of every single choice you have ever made. That is how you got where you are today. But you are not the choices themselves. You are simply what happened as a result of them. And you get to keep making choices, as long as you stay in the game.

When we hear the phrase "everything is connected," most of us tend to think of linear time. We tell ourselves stories as if life happens sequentially—this happened and then that happened. But sequential timelines only reveal the most rudimentary of connections. The fact of the matter is that everything is connected across both time and space, all at once, and in every direction—the center to the periphery and the parts to the whole. It's easy to measure a line. But you cannot measure interconnectedness. It's not some number; it's not *data*. It's everything, all at once. If you're talking about *now*, precision has no purpose.

CHAPTER 2

There Is No Equation for Enlightenment

"Anyway, where's the fun without a bit of risk?"[1]

—Fred Weasley, *Harry Potter and the Goblet of Fire*

So when I figured out that I didn't want to write the kind of book I used to write, I immediately realized that would be a problem. "Who can I point fingers at if I'm not pointing them at everybody else?" I wondered. Because if everyone else was out, that left only me. And an entire book about my own failings doesn't sound like something I'd want to write, let alone something you'd want to read.

And so I have landed on a compromise. In order to protect the innocent, I am going to start the body of this book by telling a story about no one in particular. That way, I can be talking about you, me, and those other people without having to name any names. I am simply telling a story of how I think we ended up in this predicament, and then I'll get to what I think we should consider doing about it all.

* 　 * 　 *

This is a story about how a people got lost. It was an accident, and it wasn't their fault. But they got lost anyway. It is also a story about how one guy got lost, almost found himself, and then got lost again, and then almost found himself again, ad nauseam. But it is also a story of hope. Because that guy eventually began the long process of self-discovery. And maybe those people can, too.

That people is humanity. That guy is me. I got lost by accident, as well, but I finally made it back to where I was supposed to be. I made it back to *right here, right now*. It took a lot of help, from a lot of people, to find my way home. But I did. And I am hoping that my story might help some other people on their own journeys. This is the story of how I *realized* how to use my *real eyes*—the ones that look *in-side* and offer you *in-sight*.

If it sounds like I'm planning to tell two stories at once, I assure you that I am not. I'm telling *my* story in order to tell *our* story, which is the exact same thing you'd be doing if you told *your* story to tell *our* story. They are all the same story, because we are all connected. There is only one story, and it is the story of *right now*.

A caveat: If you tell someone else's story, you are not telling the only story that there is. Because you cannot tell someone else's story. You can only tell your own. If you try to tell someone else's, you aren't telling any story at all. You're just writing words on a page. I know what I am talking about because it's something that I did for years.

Most writers make the mistake of thinking that they need to write about someone else, because they are worried that their truth might not be enough to fill a book. But that is a mistake. Because your truth is *everywhere*. How is that? Well, consider the fact that everything that you think you see and feel and smell—everything that you *perceive*—is actually generated by your brain, when it mingles all your sense data together and *reflects* them in a place called common sense. So everything that you "experience" is, on one level, a creation inside your own mind. In other words, the entire universe has been created by you. And the universe contains some pretty interesting stories. You just need to pick one. And they're yours for the taking, because *you created them*. In modern society, you sometimes hear people talking about establishing boundaries in their interpersonal connections, especially when they are upset with someone. But that's got everything inside out. The universe contains everything, right? So when you are mad at me, it's not *you* being mad at *me*, as if we are separate entities. It's *you being mad at me*, which is all one thing. In other words, we are all connected. So you are everywhere you look and everything you see.[2]

So let's get back to those people and how they got lost. It was because of hubris. Instead of letting the universe—also known as: love, truth, nature—show them the path, they decided that they would build the path themselves. In doing so, they got separated from nature, from the rest of life, from each other, and even from themselves. The irony, of course, is that they *were* looking for the right path. They just ended up on the wrong one.

When they couldn't find the "right" path, they built their own. It looked very promising, but it was the wrong path. Not only that, they didn't realize it for a long time, until after they'd walked *way too far* down it. Which path were they on and where did it lead? It was the pathway through *time* and into *the future*. I know that sounds a little silly but stay with me here. I promise that it will be worth it.

The way you know that it was a man-made path is that the universe doesn't do the future or the past. The universe only deals with now. Everyone who has said this before was right: There is only now. There is nothing else. But a large portion of humanity—call it Western society—decided that it knew better, saw the future just up over the edge of the horizon of now, and figured, "Let's just get a move on. If you just give us a little more *time*, we will get to where we need to be."

Western society decided that the best thing to do *right now* was to *start thinking about the future*. Western society was wrong. Why did the people want to leave the present—the *now*—and head into the future? After all, they had each other and they had nature. They had food, they had wine, they had dance, they had art. They even had the stories they were able to tell themselves, because somewhere along the way, they'd figured out how to speak to each other. All of those things were languages, which allowed them to communicate. What was the rush?

Because despite having all of that, they never knew what was going to happen next. Not only that, but as often as not, whatever actually did happen turned out to be something difficult—a storm, a war, a famine—so they *figured* that they might as well get the hell out of now and start heading into the future. They called the direction *progress*, packed up their stuff, and started heading on down the road. It was there, they told themselves, that they would finally be able to exert some control over their lives. They called their destination *success*.

To summarize: Uncertainty led to fear, which led to a desire for more control. To find that control, they decided to leave *now*, head down the road of *progress*, right into the *future*, to a place called *success*, where everyone was going to be *successful*. (Yes: The future was *full of it*.) This, as they say, is the American Dream.

Control, that was the thing. The problem with the present was that it wouldn't sit still. It just kept moving—every time they turned around, something else was happening. The future, on the other hand, didn't move at all. It just sat there, almost as if it didn't even exist. The reason for that is simple: because *it didn't*. The future is an illusion.

The people got suckered by the fact that it's easy to control something that doesn't exist. You just say things like, *"Tomorrow is going to be better than today"* and who's the wiser for it? Tomorrow hasn't happened yet, so you *can't be wrong*. If today was too slippery to be *controlled*, tomorrow practically put its hands out the way they do in movies, so you could put the handcuffs on it without a fight. Tomorrow did what it was told.

Alas, we are stuck in the here and now, which is always unpredictable and occasionally violent. That's why the path to the future seemed like the obvious way to go: Because no one ever seemed to know what was going to happen, it was hard to prepare, not to mention a little scary. That made it hard to relax into the present, to simply be there, to enjoy things like flowers and rivers and oceans and birds and sunsets and rainbows and fruit.

How did they keep track of their progress down this path? They measured it, of course. This is where numbers come into our story. The main problem with numbers is that, like the future, they only exist in our imagination. Quantities exist in nature, but numbers don't. What do I mean by that? I mean that you might see three apples sitting in front of you, and yes, those apples exist. But the number *3* does not exist. People invented numbers so that they could keep track of things. Sometimes things went wrong, and the numbers looked bad. But when the numbers looked good, they called that *progress*, meaning they were still on the right path, still headed in the right direction, into the future. It didn't matter if people weren't feeling so great about today; if today's number was better than yesterday's, then today was better than yesterday, and tomorrow was probably going to be even better. Because everyone knows that numbers don't lie. (That last part is actually true, but not for the reason that most people think. The reason that numbers don't lie is because they don't exist. People lie, though, and they often use numbers to do so.)

You know how bad it got? In December 2020, people wrote stories with titles like "The COVID-19 Pandemic Ruined Time,"[3] as if it were a bad thing. There's a scientist quoted in that story who studies "trauma and time perception." She argues that a sense of the future is central to our ability to get up in the morning and confidently go about our day. But is it, really? Or is a sense of the future the thing pulling us out of now? Another scientist—this one studies "uncertainty and well-being"—tells us that researchers are "starting to understand how the circuits involved in feelings like surprise, fear, or stress" interact with "a network of regions in the brain" that govern "how we feel the seconds tick by."

I said that I do not want to pick fights in this book, but this is a primary source of our societal malaise, folks: Everything is upside down. There is no clock in the brain. We do not need the future to get out of bed. The writer of the piece is correct in noting "the disintegrated state of time," but she sees it as a bad thing, instead of what it really is, which is a blessing. The quarantine challenged the central illusion of our existence, the idea that we need a clear view of the future in order to comfortably inhabit the present. We don't. The experts won't (or can't) tell you that, of course. On the contrary, they're busy assuring us that they are almost done getting that illusion back in shipshape, as soon as they're done with a few final calculations. But why do we believe that they can predict the future, when it's quite obvious that they can't even predict the present?

Another term we use interchangeably with progress is *positive change*. Positive change is supposed to be good. (See: the hockey stick graph.) Well, it isn't. Wait, I take that back. If something gets better, that is obviously good. Maybe. I'm thinking now of the phrase "It is what it is." So change might be an illusion, too. Anyway, *keeping track of change* is definitely not good . . . for you.

How is keeping track of change not good for you? Because it

tricks you into leaving *now,* retreating into your mind, and *thinking* about the past or the future. The future was such a great place to spend time that the people developed a language that was pretty much designed to be used in the future. They called it mathematics. (It was also for the past, but not really the present, because it required the use of the imagination, which is not real, and therefore cannot be present.)

I do not mean to make this complicated. Rather, I am trying to make a very important point: Mathematics is a language of change—*If this, then that.* People realized that they could use it to take numbers out of the *present* (*how many is that?*) and put them in the *future,* at which point they could start talking about the things that they didn't have today but that they most definitely were going to have tomorrow. Mathematics let them plan things. It even let them store things in the *future* ("We're going to be rich by the time we're thirty!"), which meant they didn't have to worry about not having them in the *present.* All the good stuff was just up ahead, waiting for them, right around that corner of time. Happiness was just a couple of tomorrows away.

Because numbers seemed so at ease in the future, people decided that they offered a superior means of figuring out which path to take as compared with words. One reason: because they were much more *precise,* as if everyone had already agreed that precision was the goal. It isn't. Indeed, precision is actually a hell of a trap, so powerful that it can lure an entire species into thinking that it holds the answers to life itself. Which it doesn't. I'm talking about the problem at the center of it all—*the Precision Paradox*—but we don't have to get into the particulars quite yet.

If you're going to tell the story of humanity, there are *no numbers* that will do it justice other than, perhaps, zero or infinity. Just kidding! Neither of them is a number! Zero is absence, the singularity, the state of being that allows for the process of becoming. It is the place from which becoming arises. Infinity isn't a number, either. It's *an idea*. Wrap your head around it, and you have understood the whole point of now. Now is infinite possibility. Now is everything, all wrapped into . . . one. Okay, maybe *one* is an important number. But that's it—just the *one* number, *one*.

Other than that, numbers are kind of useless. We don't need them as much as we think we do. At least not when we're looking for the answer to the only questions that matter. Numbers do a horrible job of getting at essence. Rather, they *can't do it*. So why do we keep trying? Because it's easier that way. Rather, it *seems* easier. And that is why despite their obvious limitations, large parts of humanity have concluded that numbers, and not words, are the best tool with which to grasp our individual and collective realities.

How old are you?
How many are there?
How many do you want there to be?
How much money do you have?
How much money will you have?
How many calories have you burned?
How many likes did that selfie get?
How many times can I start a question with the word how?
How long is this list going to be?

When the answer is just a number, it's easier to find. And easier to remember, even if it doesn't mean anything. Because of their ease and simplicity, numbers won the war with words. Not only that, they made words their slave. Think about it: It is not unusual in the slightest to see words being used as nothing more than a way to describe some numbers that we think are interesting. Most newspaper stories about COVID, for example, are nothing more than numbers wrapped in words.

And, having reduced the value of words to mere packaging, we have rendered ourselves incapable of communicating with each other. That is why it always feels like people are talking *at* each other, not *with* one another. We have given up on the great power and promise of words—to facilitate *communication* between us, so as to achieve *harmony*—and have chosen to use them as marketing copy for our individual quantified desires instead.

When they realized the power of numbers, the people decided to try to use them to build the best path ever made. Some even suggested that maybe they should try *living in the future* once they got there, because if they did that, they wouldn't have to focus on the difficulties of the present. You don't have to be here now if you live in tomorrow. If you're in tomorrow, now is yesterday. You have moved on. The trick was to speed through it all so that the present (and maybe even the future) became the past, which seemed, at least superficially, to be the place where everything got locked down, once and for all. Yesterday will always seem a little more certain than tomorrow. (It isn't, but you get my point.)

Most of the people agreed that was a good plan, in part because it also held out the promise of a benefit today. Everyone does it, at some point: We worry about the future, about this thing or that. But if we move out of the present and into the future, then we can stop worrying about the future. And who isn't interested in that?

Of course, they later found out that they'd been wrong about the worrying thing. The problem with the future is that by the time you get there, it is no longer the future, it is the present, and that old future has been replaced by a new one that you have to start worrying about anew. You can never cancel out tomorrow. It is always there, waiting for you, cloaked in the garb of uncertainty. Even worse, the future is the thing that manufactures all worries in the first place. It is like a factory of worry, running at capacity, never out of stock.

Worried about the future, the people decided that the best bet was to follow the numbers people through the thickets of time. Consider the following headline: "When Can We Start Making Plans? We asked Dr. Anthony S. Fauci and other experts when they thought life would start to feel more normal." The mathematicians certainly seemed to know where they were going, as they used the swords and scythes of measurement and certainty and precision to cut through the thick undergrowth of the present.

At some point, some super-practical mathematicians, who called themselves scientists, began doing "experiments," which they kept track of using numbers, to figure out solutions to practical problems. Nature had been beating everyone up, and they wanted to turn the tables. With *science*, humanity finally brought nature to heel. Chemistry allowed them to manipulate material things. Physics showed them how matter moves through space and time, which they later found out were the same thing. The list of scientific fields seemed never-ending: industry, medicine, a new kind of communication, when you didn't have to be in the same room as someone to talk to them. They even figured out how to cross-pollinate. The marriage of chemistry and physics, for example, gave us guns. And bombs. Bombs weren't for nature, of course, but to bring other humans to heel. But that's a story for a different book.

Science made life *easier*, or so it seemed. Because from that point forth, the *present*—aka *nature*, aka *now*—seemed a little easier to endure. When I say *seemed*, I mean that science could only do so much. After all, there are only so many things that can benefit from its tools. Health care seems to have gotten better, although it's not entirely clear that's the case. We've certainly been able to make better materials and do some crazy stuff with transportation and communication. But science hasn't really done anything for mental health except come up with pills that numb the brain to the point it can't feel anything. And even if science does seem to have made us more protected from the elements, we are still vulnerable to surprise attacks from the likes of typhoons, floods, and droughts. And let's not even go into viruses. We have been talking about them far too much of late.

Wait, I know what science has done for us! It has made us more comfortable. But comfort is a double-edged sword. If you get too comfortable, you will forget how to act. And if you forget how to act, you can't make choices. That leaves you unprepared for a future that you didn't see coming when it arrives, and is the cause behind headlines like this one, which actually happened: "Is It OK to Take a Walk?"

Or maybe not! This is where the sub-specialists, known as the statisticians, come into our story. They started using *their* tools—averages and probabilities and extrapolations—to cut a swath through the uncertainty way out there on the horizon, right on the very edge of time. They claimed to be able to *predict* the future—they *figured* (there's that word again) that they knew how to tell us what was *probably* going to happen.

It took a while, but science eventually became the official religion, and scientists the new priests. Whenever there was a question that needed answering, the people took it to the scientists first. The scientists themselves agreed, and said that God was dead, and that he was actually a number, something you could find in an experiment.

The present is scary because anything can happen. But not if someone draws a straight line between the present and the future. In that event, you just follow the line and get where you need to be, with no decisions—*What should I do?*—required. Science is for people who want to know *what will happen*, as opposed to those who want to take stock of *what could happen*. Why do people want to know what *will* happen? Because if you know what *will happen*, you no longer have to make a choice. You can just sit back and enjoy the ride. If *anything can happen*, you have more responsibilities. You have to decide what you're going to do.

At one point, the people marching down the road of *progress* decided to name themselves after it—they called themselves *Progressives*. They also claimed that science would solve all of humanity's problems. But could it? Eventually, someone asked the toughest of all the questions: *"Why are we on this path?"*

Ask *why* you are on a particular path, and you are asking a moral question. But moral questions can be difficult to answer. So difficult, in fact, that the scientists tried to make the case that their work took place outside the bounds of morality. They were just doing *research* for the benefit of everyone. But the scientists were wrong, because the question of which path to take is always a moral question. *Always.*

As everyone knows, it's always easy to *start* down a path. But even the most obvious of paths can eventually become obscured. The past disappears, the present is pure fog, and the future is nowhere to be found. (It's always hard to find something that doesn't exist.)

Before long, no one seemed to know where they were headed anymore. Were they lost? Who the hell knew? All the numbers the scientists (and economists, and managers, and consultants, and pollsters) were sending back from the front seemed to point too far into the past or too far into the future for anybody to make out *where they were today.*

A general state of hysteria set in. Everyone began running so fast from this path to the other path that they didn't have the ability to just look down and see that every single path led back to where they already were, which was *now.* They were *too distracted to notice.* They had gone *insane.*

How crazy were they? Crazy enough to think they could find the one true path using numbers. And crazy enough to think that they could be certain about it when they did. Here's the problem with that: Knowledge comes from uncertainty. If you know everything, there is nothing left for you to know, and so the act of seeking new knowledge becomes defunct. At that point, you are effectively out of the game, and before long, you will lose your ability to use your brain at all.

When everyone knew how to speak coherently, words had been a powerful tool. But no one knew how to use words anymore. Fate had infected language with the disease of certainty, and no one knew how to say anything anymore other than, *"You are wrong! I am right! I am certain of that!"*

Even in the midst of all the confusion, the Church of Science continued to insist that their rituals were the only ones that worked. "If we're ever going to find our way back to normal, we are going to need the tools of quantification. We need to get the data and analyze it. Let's start by figuring out just how far down this wrong path we've gone. I bet you that if we *count our steps*, we will be able to find our way back."

Here's the problem: There is no *returning* to anything. The present is all that there is. And all the data and analysis in the world isn't going to help us figure out what's gone wrong with us, because the problems don't lie in front of us, they lie inside of us. We are afraid of everything. We are addicted to the idea of control. We forgot how to be vulnerable. We forgot how to *play*. We forgot about *now*.

* * *

An equation means nothing to me unless
it expresses a thought of God.

—Srinivasa Ramanujan

Look, I know that the invention of numbers and mathematics and ultimately science did wonders for humanity. It allowed people to manipulate matter, make predictions, and play in fantasy football leagues. But numbers also led us astray. They took us *way too far* down the path into the future, and they're the thing that's keeping humanity from finding its way back to the present. Numbers can be useful. But they are also the most destructive thing that man has ever invented. Mathematics asks you to divide things. It is contrary to unity, which means it is contrary to divinity, which means it is contrary to *you*. Because you are God. We need to let the numbers— and their lies about the future—go. We have everything we need right here, in the present.

> *Mathematics is just a language, one of the ways we try to overcome*
> *the challenge of indeterminacy to communicate with each other.*
> *In that sense, it is the same as music, art, cooking, sex, or the spoken*
> *word. All are expressions of the human spirit, a way to connect.*
> *They are a way for human beings to* be.
> *Human be-ings. Get it?*
> *But mathematics is different than the others in a very profound way:*
> *It is the only one of those languages not endorsed by the universe.*
> *What do I mean by that?*
> *I mean that it is the only one that cannot be appreciated through*
> *the senses.*
> *It is the only one that exists only in our minds.*
> *We hear words and music.*
> *We see art.*
> *We smell and taste cooking.*
> *We smell and taste and touch each other during sex.*
> *What would a number even taste like if you could eat it?*

How does the brain do what it does? I like Aristotle's idea: We take in as much information as we can through *the senses*, dump it in a place called *Common Sense,* and our brain feasts on it. That said, none of your other senses is able to cognize anything without what you might call a *sense of presence,* or *consciousness* itself. It is *consciousness* that seeks to *feed your brain,* which then goes ahead and does its thing. There is no work involved in this process. Indeed, the best way to feed your brain is to *play with it.*

Humanity invented numbers and math and started playing with them. They used them to come up with *statistics,* which led us to the idea of *probabilities.* But instead of remembering that they were *toys,* something to *play* with, humanity got all impressed with its own inventions and decided that they were part of something else, something more important, something called *thinking.* They *thought* statistics could be used to *reduce uncertainty* and *exert control.* They got really serious about *thinking* and weren't *playing* anymore. They were *working.*

THINKING = WORK

Everyone who wants you to be impressed by their minds wants you to be impressed by the quality of their thinking. But *thinking* is our invention. *Numbers and math* are our inventions. *The brain* is not our invention. The brain doesn't *think.* The brain doesn't need *numbers or math.* The brain only needs to be fed, via *the senses.* As often as not, when you *think* you understand something, you don't. Intuition happens when thought takes a vacation. Direct perception doesn't require thought, either. Do you *think* that you are alive? No. You *know* that you are alive.

I was talking about the future with my friend Rupam Das, a *physicist.* He thinks we pay too much attention to thinking, and that's the disease. It gives us a false sense of control over reality.

How's that? "Our minds are not under the control that we think they are," he said. "Have you ever considered the fact that you can't predict your next thought?" No, I hadn't. He's right: How on earth do we think we can predict anything having to do with people, when we can't even predict what we're going to think of next?

In the West, we are in love with our analytical powers. We are in love with the act of *thinking* more than we are the act of *doing*. But throw a little humanity—*life itself*—into the mix, and things get complicated. Trying to solve human problems using numbers is a dumb idea, and always has been. Some of you may be thinking that's crazy talk, and that's fine. I'll return to it in a later chapter. For now, let's just agree that people started using numbers to try to exert control over their unpredictable lives.

It may just be the biggest mistake humanity has ever made.

What do I mean by that?

One of the central arguments of this book, if not *the* central argument, is that there is only one question that matters to each and every one of us, whenever and wherever you or I or we happen to be:

What are you going to do right now?

If you think about it, the question is the only way of engaging with the essential uncertainty of existence. We use our senses to try to grasp our reality and then our brain decides what to do. That's the human condition, in a nutshell: *What the hell is going on and what the heck should I do?*

The wrong way to grasp reality is to try to exert some kind of control over it. When humans seek to exert control, they go inside their minds and do some thinking. Increasingly, they won't even do so themselves; they will just ask an "expert" to do so on their behalf and give them their marching orders. The experts will invoke numbers and mathematics and probabilities. They will try to narrow the field before stepping onto it.

The right way to grasp reality is to embrace uncertainty, to start with *possibilities*, not *probabilities*. You do that using your senses, not your mind. And when I say that *you* do that, I mean *your brain* does that. You simply need to feed it, at which point *your brain* will make a *choice*. We need to let go of the mind and its assertions, which requires *surrender* instead of *control*.

Success isn't control.
Success is freedom.
Freedom isn't a number.
Freedom isn't something you can calculate.
Freedom isn't something you can model.
It is a state of being.

A caveat: I am not talking about the freedom to fulfill one's desires. Desires come from the ego. Save, of course, for virtuous desire—the desire to be good to others. I am talking about the freedom to do what is right, in the moment, without constraint. That is true freedom—the freedom to simply *be*. "Being is openness and beneficence that overflows from the timeless into creation," writes the Vedantic scholar David Frawley. "This is offering the mind into the flame of awareness that delivers us beyond time and sorrow."[4] On another note, there is nothing shameful in surrendering to fate. She's going to win the last battle with your existence anyway, and the earlier you cease fighting, the easier life will be.

How is it that we have gotten ourselves into a state that whenever something confuses us, we try to *model* our way to some kind of understanding? We can get to understanding by a much simpler route. Find me an equation, any equation, that does not quite explain the phenomenon it seeks to explain—economics, physics, behaviorism—and I will show you that the missing variable is love. I didn't know that until recently. Between now and Chapter 12 of this book, I will show you how I came to understand that it is so. *That's where I will explain the Love Equation, which is my solution to the Precision Paradox. It's my contribution to Science. Just kidding. It's not scientific. It's not an equation, either. You want the Truth? It's just an idea called Love.*

(After telling you all this, I am going to give you one equation to mull over. It's both the equation for enlightenment and the love equation, all wrapped into one. We don't need to dwell on it, because it's a bit of a mind-bender, but it contains the secrets of the universe. So here it is: 1+1=1. Call it spiritual math, the math of the infinite, or just simplicity itself: An equation that only uses one number, 1. It's both breathtakingly simple and as elusive as can be, like all the good things in life.)

Why do you think the happiest people you know aren't the ones with the most control but the ones who are able to exercise freedom of choice in their lives? The ones who do whatever they want to do? The Quantified Self? Are you kidding me? That's like sentencing yourself to life in the prison of your own mind. You want to be an outdoor cat, not an indoor cat. Outdoor cats do whatever they want. They come and go when they feel like it. Indoor cats might lead a life of relative comfort compared to animals in the wild, but comfort is overrated—freedom is where it's at.

We should spend less time trying to calculate probabilities. We should spend less time in pursuit of certainty. We should spend less time trying to reduce risk. We should drop the quest for precision, once and for all. We should spend way more of our time embracing uncertainty and taking risks. You don't need numbers to do either of those. You just need courage. If you don't believe me, just ask Harry Potter.

You just need to be aware of your own existence. During quarantine, I began to realize what a wonderful thing it is to simply *be*. I felt, for an extended duration, what the philosophers of Kashmir Shaivism refer to as "an absorption whose nature is the cognition of that which has one taste."[5] That's *rasa*, which the dictionary will tell you means "essence," but which actually means love. Or bliss. Because of that, I realized, in a flash, that I have everything I need, *right here* and *right now*. I *woke up* from the dream I'd been stuck in, the one that said the future was a good place to live. It's not. The past isn't, either. The only place that you *can* live is in the present.

The reason that we cannot calculate our way out of the mess we are in is that the tools of science and mathematics cannot grasp the concept of possibility. The reason that we can't think our way out of this mess is that we aren't supposed to be thinking in the first place. We are supposed to be living. Everything we have come to believe about the power of our own minds is an illusion. We need to stop thinking that we are in charge of our brains. The brain does not answer to the mind. The only power the mind has over the brain is the power to disconnect, from the brain and, by extension, the big brain, or the True Self.

The brain doesn't need numbers at all. It just needs to be fed. What does the brain like to eat? Pretty much anything. In the end, though, the brain will let you know what tastes good. If the food tastes good, it will taste good. If the ideas taste good, they will taste good to your brain. Everybody knows what that feels like, but we don't chase those flavors nearly as often as we should. We are too busy eating tasteless numbers instead of scrumptious ideas. Feed your body, feed your brain. But play with them, too. The brain will also let you know what kind of play it likes. And your brain only has one way of communicating with you.

It *tickles* you.

Food tickles the tongue, ideas tickle the brain, sex tickles the . . . you know what I mean. If you learn how to tickle yourself, your brain will do the rest. It will take it all in, and decide . . .

What am I going to do right now?

And then you will do it. That is all.

I saved the best for last. Do you want the package deal? The one thing that gets you all of the above, that feeds and plays with all five senses at once, all five for the price of one?

All You Need Is LOVE.
And when it comes . . .
It will come as Light.
It will come in Waves.
It will Flow.
It will Tickle.
Because it's all the same thing.

CHAPTER 3

The Best Book I Ever Read

People are blind to explanations that lie
outside their perception of reality.[1]

—Stephen King, *The Outsider*

I discovered the writer Alberto Manguel in the fall of 2019, thanks to another writer, Maryanne Wolf. I have never been so blown away by a literary discovery in my life. Manguel's *A History of Reading*—surely the greatest ode to the act of reading ever put down on paper—humbled me. In addition to serving up a deep and profound understanding of the influence of reading on humanity, the book made me aware, for the very first time, of the immense power of the craft to which I have dedicated much of my adult life. I mean, I knew writing was powerful, but I hadn't thought about it *that* much. With respect to myself, that is. I had been underestimating the powers I had at my disposal.

I've recently realized that the way to remain present is to tackle the challenge in three ways: (a) try to be present, (b) talk about trying to be present, and (c) read about trying to be present. The last two lead to the first one. Who knew? Well, when it comes to books, one of the best ways to be a better reader and writer is to think about what it means to be a better reader or writer. Yes, I know that's obvious, too, and I have thought about how to be a better writer a lot. But I hadn't really *thought about reading*. Thanks to Manguel, I began to do so. It's like reading Borges on the infinite or J. K. Rowling on casting spells. If you're going to take the job seriously, you need to consult those who have taken it even more seriously than you.

It's not that Manguel is the only one to have valuable thoughts about reading. But it's his passion, and what he did with that passion was to search high and low for the most insightful things people have ever said about reading over the centuries and then to weave them into the most beautiful tapestry on the subject that's ever been created. It is, in short, his labor of love. Have you ever heard the idea that Aristotle might not be the origin of everything he is supposed to have said all by himself but simply had been a collector of the greatest philosophical hits of his day? If that's true, then Alberto Manguel is the Aristotle of reading.

Consider the following, which he wrote about the emperor Constantine:

> What Constantine discovered . . . is that the meaning of a text is enlarged by the reader's capabilities and desires. Faced with a text, the reader can transform the words into a message that deciphers for him or her a question historically unrelated to the text itself or to its author. This transmigration of meaning can enlarge or impoverish the text itself; invariably it imbues the text with the circumstances of the readers. Through ignorance, through faith, through intelligence, through trickery and cunning, through illumination, the reader rewrites the text with the

same words of the original but under another heading, re-creating it, as it were, in the very act of bringing it into being.[2]

When I finished that passage, I realized, in an instant, that I have been writing too much for me, the writer, and not enough for you, the reader. When my brother Steve, an artist, published a series of coloring books a few years ago, he expressed surprise to me about the feeling he got when he realized that other people were helping finish works of art that he'd initiated. I marveled along with him, envious of that opportunity while being blind to the fact that I have always had the exact same opportunity at my disposal. As a writer, I create something. Anyone who reads something I have written creates their own work in the process of reading. We are all engaged in one long daisy chain of creation, provided that we bring an open mind and the right intention to the situation.

Anything can happen, if we are open to it, and that includes the possible futures that my writing can open up in the lives of someone who reads it. All action comes from thought, and all thoughts are but appearances in consciousness. So anything *really can happen*. It just needs to be conceived of and then brought into manifestation. After I write something, you, the reader, can then think of something, and then off we go. That is a far greater responsibility than I had ever recognized for myself. That doesn't mean I should start telling you what to do—I've done too much of that already—but what it does mean is that it's finally time that I pay attention to the raw power of words and what they are able to achieve when written with purpose. I realized that I needed to tell true stories—which can really only be about what I am thinking and doing *right now*—about amazing things and see what kind of reaction that prompts in my readers. Hopefully it tickles.

*   *   *

Before the Internet, there were encyclopedias. I remember, as a child, being envious of families with the *Encyclopaedia Britannica*, which seemed to my young mind to be more sophisticated than *World Book*. I was even more envious of families who subscribed to *National Geographic* and displayed their collections alongside their favorite books in built-in bookcases. We had a built-in in our house in Don Mills in Toronto. I don't remember many of the books from that house—we moved to the Middle East in 1979, when I was seven—but I do remember that my father's magic collection was in one of the cupboards and *The Rise and Fall of the Third Reich* sat on one of the higher shelves. I finally read that book years later, when I borrowed it from my first wife's father, and, to my surprise, found that it wasn't some dense work of history but a page-turner of journalism.

In his book *With Borges*, Alberto Manguel recalls Borges telling him, "I'm greedy for new encyclopedias." I am, too. Behind me in my office sit five books that qualify as reference materials for nothing but diversion: *1886 Professional Criminals of America*, *The Dictionary of Imaginary Places*, *Fabulous Monsters*, *The Book of Imaginary Beings*, and an ancient copy of the *Encyclopaedia of Superstitions*. Joey's mother, Betty, gave me *Quadrivium* as a gift recently. It's an almanac of sorts, about "the four classical liberal arts of number, geometry, music, and cosmology." Those are numbers I can get with. Anything about sacred geometry is all right with me.

*   *   *

I've said that numbers don't exist. Words don't, either, at least insofar as when you are looking at a tree and you say "leaf," that is not a thing. It's a label we have created for the thing. It describes the thing, but it is not the thing—it just points to it. But just because they're both imaginary doesn't mean they're irrelevant. Or equal. Both are very relevant. And words are way more powerful than numbers. If we're going to talk about communication, you should *always* choose words over numbers. Why? Because words do a better job of getting at *essence*.

We use letters to make words, words to make sentences, and sentences to express meaning. But the effect of a sentence is not fixed; it depends entirely on the set of meanings that it conveys. That is the power of words. A single word can make you aware of something that exists a great distance from you. "Toronto" reminds me of the place of my youth, even though I live five hundred miles away. It is because of words that we are able to navigate both our worldly and spiritual lives. Why is that? Because language comes from God— "In the beginning was the word"—whereas the quantified subset of language—numbers—comes from man.

Gertrude Stein told us, "Rose is a rose is a rose is a rose." The reason you have heard that before is that she nailed it. Hers is a much better way to describe a rose than to tell me that it has five petals and one stem. It is, simply, a rose. That's all you need to know. I recently came across a similar idea in a wonderful book called *Scientism*. Imagine if some alien form wanted to know about us and asked, "What is this thing, humanity?" You could, of course, serve up a biochemical assay of a human body—it's got 99 percent of these six elements and 0.85 percent of some other ones—but that wouldn't really get at our *essence*, would it? The problem is not that the answer is *incorrect*, but that it seems to be the answer to a different question. That question, of course, is *What can you tell me about humanity if the only thing you're allowed to use is numbers?* Or something like that. Numbers actually act as a constraint, as opposed to delivering anything close to a complete explanation of a thing.

When we invoke numbers to describe something, we willingly scale back our own powers of description. Why is that? Because you can't quantify everything about a thing. There are only certain aspects of it that will submit to such an exercise. You have two eyes, and two ears, but how many thoughts? If we are going to spend our time building fantasy castles in the imagination in which to live, do you not think it's a better idea to build them out of words than out of numbers? What would a castle built out of numbers look like, anyway? Actually, I know the answer to that question: It would look like a bank. And who wants to live in a bank?

Yes, I know that numbers can be used to get at practical things that can be described using Cartesian coordinates, like how to get from here to there. And yes, you can count some important things—length, width, weight. But just because someone offers to give you a *more precise* number about something, doesn't make it more *true*. It simply makes it more precise. If you use numbers to get at anything that isn't a simple quantity, you are removing yourself from the Reality that is right there in front of you.

Why are some things about nature so appealing? Like the leaves on a tree blowing in the wind? Or the waves in the ocean? Why do they seem so much more majestic than the things that we have made ourselves? It is because they are uncountable—so obviously so that we don't even try. That is why you can appreciate a tree for what it is, no further explanation necessary. That is why people love the ocean. That is why people surf.

This point is going to come up a lot in this book, so let's just get it out of the way now: Bob Dylan gets it. I don't need to explain that all at once; here's an example referring to the whole uncountable thing. There was a moment in Dylan's mid-career where he went all Christian on us—three albums in a row, *Saved*, *Shot of Love*, and *Slow Train Coming*. Most people didn't know what to make of the move. Some of the songs were great—"Slow Train Coming" is a masterpiece—but the whole thing seemed a little off point. What was Dylan doing?

The reason it seemed off point is that this was the 1980s, when science had pretty much triumphed over religion. (The whole equivalence of science and religion is absurd, but people can be silly, so there you go.) Dylan, a seer, as . . . a Christian? Was he going to be thumping his Bible *onstage*?

Here's my theory of what Dylan was up to: He was adding his voice to the long list of artists who've warned us against going too far down the path of progress. The only things we need are truth and beauty and love, and we already have them in the present. The path of progress leads nowhere. We need to remember that some things are inherently good, and some things aren't. That there really is a connective tissue between all things. That's what C. S. Lewis was talking about, by the way. It is the undercurrent of his entire oeuvre.

Dylan's song "Every Grain of Sand" is one of his countless attempts to solve the human equation. (Without using math.) At one point, he sings that he doesn't have the inclination to look back on any mistake—that is, he's in the moment, not carrying around baggage. When he refers to the "fury of the moment," he's talking about infinite possibility. And then he says he can see the master's hand "in every leaf that trembles, in every grain of sand." The master is you. The moment is now. When Jim James sings "all in the moment, no hesitating" in his song "In the Moment," he's singing about the same thing. Everything is contained in now. *Everything*.

It's all there, people, in one single stanza. Or, if you will, in every grain of sand. It's a great song. But Dylan's Christianity never really caught on. If the people wouldn't listen to the language of God—the one that lays it all out so very clearly—maybe he had to use another one. I wrote a paper in college comparing a Bob Dylan concert to a religious revival. What I was really getting at, of course, was that he was a messiah, someone pointing us to the truth, which is love, in every possible way he could think of. Jim James is also a messiah. Go see him perform, and you will understand what I mean.

And just so that no one starts thinking that I think my people know more than your people—your favorite poet, or analogy—that's not it at all. I only know what I know—what I have learned. So I can only reference the things *that I know* to make my point. You will know other things that make this exact same point to you.

*   *   *

Before I started writing this book, I tore through a string of other people's books that contained remarkable insights and also happened to be beautifully written. Those two things do not always come in the same package, so when you find them, you cherish them. I somehow read a bunch of them *in a row*.

I was, as they say, in *flow*. I always thought that being in *flow* had to do with something you *worked on*, not something that could simply happen to you. Man, I was wrong about that. As Deepak and Oprah try to tell me *every single day* when Joey and I start our morning by meditating with them, if you find your way to *flow*, it literally takes over everything around you. *Everything flows.*

Do you use Waze? One of the things I like to do is fantasize about what would happen if everybody used Waze and it dynamically solved all traffic problems at once, just because it knew where every car was and where it was going, so it could immediately adjust when traffic jams started to happen. Well, when you're in flow, it's as if Waze were directing traffic for your life. It's pretty awesome.

Why have I written an entire chapter about reading? Because when the quarantine hit, and we all went into lockdown, we were all faced with a question: What am I going to do right now? My answer to the question, at least in part, was to start reading. Rather, to resume reading in the way that I love doing, which is to devour books, one after the other.

Every time I finished a book, I would tell Joey that it was *one of the best books I'd ever read*. I'm not alone in having said that about a book. Everyone does it, right? But when I realized I was saying it one after the other after the other, it occurred to me that I was being fickle. Did I no longer have any standard for what constituted the best book I'd ever read? How could every single one of them be the best of them all?

And then I realized what I was actually saying. *Any* good book you are reading is quite literally the best book you have ever read. Because it is the latest thing you have fed to your brain. It's your most recent gift to yourself. Learning is cumulative. You need to keep doing it. The latest book is *always* the best book. It's what keeps you in flow. What's more, when you are in flow, you can see the love in everything around you. It turns out that my standards really have fallen. I no longer think some things are great and some things are horrible. I have found, inside myself, a capacity for appreciating almost everything. It's a remarkable way to live— without complaint. I had no idea it was even possible. But it is, and it's entirely liberating.

Let's talk about metaphors. They're the way we communicate anything and everything important to each other, because we need to be able to meet in the middle, between two (or more) people, to understand each other. In doing so, metaphor is the most important tool at our disposal; it is what allows us to suggest to each other that one thing is similar to another. Similar to metaphors are *idioms* or *figures of speech*. I used to think that the metaphors and figures of speech we use were all *figurative*—that is, not literal, just . . . imaginary or something. What I have realized of late is that most of the things that I thought were merely figurative were actually literal.

I offer you a few of them, just for fun:

Love conquers all.
The only thing you have to fear is fear itself.
Enthusiasm is contagious.

Somewhere in mid-April, I realized what I had been doing to myself. I had stopped paying attention to *words*. I had let numbers shove them aside. I'm not saying I didn't use words, I am saying that I used words to talk about numbers. *I was about to write an entire book about numbers using words.* But then I read a bunch of books that weren't about numbers at all, and I suddenly snapped out of a trance that I'd been in for most of my life. In that moment, I realized that I had been asking myself the wrong questions. I had been asking myself the easy questions.

On more than a few occasions, when listening to Bob Dylan sing the words *every grain of sand*, I'd wondered, to myself, just how many grains of sand there might be in the universe. What I should have been doing was wondering what it meant to see the Master's hand in everything.

Having been chastened by my reading of Alberto Manguel, I have thought a lot about books in the last six months, and I think I have an interesting insight to offer about the nature of writing. But it starts with one about people: What is an identity? It is nothing but a swirling mass of ideas and memories. Our identities are not stable. They change all the time. So what is a book? A book is what happens when that identity manages to square itself—when a swirling mass of ideas is able to capture another swirling mass of ideas and get them out, in some kind of coherent form, before something—the identity or the ideas underlying the book itself—starts to slip away. It's when flux tames flux. You are both a conceiver of concepts and also a concept yourself. It is no coincidence that they call the moment of fertilization "conception."[3] Considered in that light, the universe (meaning, you) could be described as *a great idea*. That came about because of *the Big Bang*. (Get it?) That works for me. Who came up with the idea of me? God only knows, but I endorse it—as far as ideas go, I can't think of a better one. I would assume you feel the same way about your Self.

*   *   *

I know this guy, Crazy Legs Conti. Crazy Legs is a competitive eater—like Coney Island hot dogs competitive eating. Crazy Legs is also a raconteur nonpareil, a master of storytelling. Actually, he's kind of a master of living, a conjuror who has figured out how to transform his *now* into a fountain of narrative. I've never met anyone like him. Crazy Legs has given M. several books, including Katherine Arden's *Small Spaces*, which blew her mind. There is no greater gift you can give to someone else's child. I don't know if I've ever said this about anyone in print, but there's a first time for everything: Crazy Legs has got a heart made of gold.

In January 2021, he gave a book to Joey with the suggestion that she, M., and I all read it—Erin Morgenstern's *The Starless Sea*. Joey read it first and told me that it put her in a state of bliss. I started it on a Saturday morning and was done by Sunday night. Alberto Manguel wrote an ode to reading. Erin Morgenstern has written an ode to storytelling that, as I sit here and type, is the latest best book I have ever read.

I won't tell you anything about the plot, because it's too good to risk spoiling anything. What I will tell you is that you will probably never read a more poignant love letter to storytelling in your life. I don't throw the word *wisdom* around that often, because it doesn't seem like the kind of thing you're supposed to try to point out. It just is. But it runs deep in *The Starless Sea*.

She didn't put it this way, but this is what Morgenstern made me think of while I was reading her book: You are not your body. Nor are you the swarm of thoughts that make up your identity at any given time. What you are is the crucible for those thoughts—consciousness itself. You are the creative force behind your own existence. When you get trapped in your ego—the knot that ties your consciousness to your body and your mind—you get stuck in what the Eastern philosophers will tell you is the "gross," or least subtle, plane of your existence. That's what makes us feel limited, what confuses us into thinking that we are bound by time and space, when in fact they are mere concepts—cognitive creations—that have tricked us into thinking that they are Reality itself.

If you accept that there are limitations to your story, it won't be long before you're persuaded that other people can *know* your story—that other people can tell you who you are. As a culture, we have bought into the idea of credentials. Credentials are valuable insofar as they tell you that someone is, say, a surgeon. But we have let them define us. We have let them draw boundaries around our unlimited selves.

> There are people without faces standing around me feeding me pieces of paper that have all the things I am supposed to be written on them but they never ask me what I am.[4]
>
> —*The Starless Sea*

The problem isn't just other people. There are also the limitations we put on our Selves, the reasons we offer ourselves why we haven't done something we could have done. Because we didn't have time. Or because it was unlikely to work out. But your life is what you make of it. Your life is the story you tell yourself.

When you feel unsatisfied with some particular situation, you're projecting your own inadequate storytelling onto something out-side you, as if your story were someone else's fault. But it's only you. You are the author of you. "I love you but I will not sit here and wait for this story to change," says one of the novel's characters. "I am going to make it change."[5]

Tell someone a great story, and you aren't simply telling them a story. You're also telling them the ideas upon which the story is based. It doesn't matter if those ideas are implicit or explicit; they're communicated either way. There's an argument to be made that telling stories is the most important thing we do. We feed ourselves food to keep our physical bodies alive. But our brains need to be fed, too, so that they can keep creating the story that you're going to be. When you tell someone a story, you are *feeding their brain.*

> I think people came here for the same reason we came here. In search of something. Even if we didn't know what it was. Something more. Something to wonder at. Someplace to belong. We're here to wander through other people's stories, searching for our own.[6]
>
> —*The Starless Sea*

Of course, stories aren't just for the listener; they are also for the storytellers. They're how we give meaning to our own lives. That's why we use words, because they can contain so much meaning. Numbers don't contain anything but themselves.

Your consciousness—that is, your true Self—is no dummy. It can tell meaning from emptiness, even if your ego can't. But like all crucibles, it only contains what it contains. When all is said and done, it's going to do what it always does and *put on a play,* starring you. And if you fill the script with too many measurements, there might not be enough room for who you really are.

*   *   *

So listen to these *words*, my friends. They are not going to be able to deliver *reality itself,* but with them, I hope to convince you that they are a much more powerful tool to describe it to each other—and to grasp it ourselves—than trying to count it. We need to find a different path. But we can't calculate it. It is not a number. Neither is the destination. We need to use words, not numbers, when we are talking to each other about that path. And we need to use words, not numbers, when we are looking for ideas about what to do. If we start using words again, maybe, just maybe, we might be able to *follow them back to now.*

Of course, in the end, if we are to know ourselves, we need to go beyond words, too. Because true Reality—that which you become aware of if you can slip the bounds of ego, and untether the Self from the mind and the body—lies beyond words. When it comes to the power of communication, words are superior to numbers, but in the final analysis, they are both inadequate, because Reality cannot be described but only experienced.

Why do I feel so confident in saying so? Because it happened to me, that's why. When it was convenient, I chose to grasp my own reality by quantifying it. More to the point, I had fallen for the fantasy that quantification serves up to us, every single time we use a number—I had fallen for the illusion of certainty. And then, suddenly, one day during a quarantine, I snapped out of it and started living my life again. When you think you know something—when you feel *certain* about something—that is you telling you that you know all you need to know. And once you do that, you are doomed. Because that's when you stop listening to other people. It's when you stop listening, period. That is, if you ever started listening in the first place.

Stories About Numbers

We may not have wings or leaves, but we humans do
have words. Language is our gift and our responsibility.[1]

—Robin Wall Kimmerer, *Braiding Sweetgrass*

I'm not sure that I ever really realized it until it hit me like a frying
pan in the face, but I have surely felt it over the years: My entire
adult life has been the setting of a tug-of-war between numbers and
words, between reason and intuition.

It's not just my life, mind you. Since the invention of mathematics and the emergence of science, the very same tug-of-war has
been fought by the whole of humanity. And the stakes could not be
higher: our souls.

Allow me to elaborate.

NUMBERS VERSUS WORDS, THE GREAT TUG-OF-WAR!

I found the coursework of a Western education to be fairly straight-
forward and easy. I never had to work that hard, because most things,

even high school physics, seemed to make sense to me. My grades were excellent, in all courses.

When my high school guidance counselor asked me what I wanted to do when I grew up, I told him, "I want to be a businessman." I'm not shitting you. I'm not even sure what I meant, other than the image that was in my mind and still resides there today: I was going to carry a fancy briefcase made out of soft leather. That, to me, constituted some sort of success. But that was going to take *money. Numbers pulling harder.*

I discovered Bob Dylan in high school when my brother Scott gave Dylan's *Biograph* to my other brother Steve for Christmas one year. I secretly copied it, and began listening to it end-to-end almost immediately. I knew some of his most famous songs, of course, but they weren't the draw for me. The draw was the sound of a man who seemed to *know*. What did he know? I had no idea, but I knew that he knew more than me. Not only that; he was obviously one of the coolest people that ever lived. I never put too much stock in being cool myself, but that didn't mean I couldn't recognize it for what it was. And I did. *Words tug back.*

I also told my guidance counselor that I wanted to go to school in the United States, because Canada was too small. I'd spent part of my childhood in the Middle East—my father was an obstetrician and he worked at the Royal Hospital in Saudi Arabia in the early 1980s—and I had the urge to go somewhere myself. Thirty years later, as I begin to actively integrate into my local community for the first time in my life—we *live* in Hurley now, as opposed to *visiting it* like tourists—it occurs to me that wanderlust has its downside. In any case, I felt the need to get out of Canada.

I had superb grades in high school, and my guidance counselor suggested that I apply to the top undergraduate business school in the United States, considered at that time to be Wharton. I did, was admitted early acceptance, and drove down to Philadelphia with my parents in September 1988. I had no concept of Wall Street at the time, yet had somehow landed a highly coveted spot in the top recruiting ground for future Masters of the Universe. *Numbers pulling harder again.*

Thankfully, my curiosity led to an expansion of my awareness during college. At Penn I met Malcolm, one of my lifelong friends, who introduced me to both Jack Kerouac and the Grateful Dead. He drove a Volkswagen bus, and was about as hippie as one could be at an Ivy League school. In college, I discovered the writers Jorge Luis Borges and Italo Calvino, among others. *Words exert themselves again.*

By the time I graduated, I knew I had made a mistake getting a degree in finance. But the system had a hold on me in the form of student debt. I knew, deep down, that I did not want to work on Wall Street, but I owed something like $40,000 in student loans. I decided to do the "mature" thing, which was to go get a job on Wall Street, make enough money to pay off my loans, and then decide if I was going to stay. While taking a job on Wall Street might seem like a win for numbers, I did so with the conscious intention of leaving when my loans were paid down. *Numbers and words settle in for a long battle.*

The following has always been a delicious irony for me: Even though I didn't *really* want to work on Wall Street, and effectively tanked all my interviews, I got a job offer from Goldman Sachs, the firm that everyone wanted to work for. Amazingly, I didn't get a single other offer, a situation that can't possibly have happened before or since. (On Wall Street, if Goldman wants you, everyone wants you.) I worked at Goldman for two years. It was a pointless job, and I knew it. To work in modern finance is to be a middleman taking a piece of other people's hard work. But it wasn't all a loss: In late 1992, I met the actor Will Arnett, whose sister was friends with my brother. Will was couch-surfing at the time—his career hadn't taken off yet—and he moved into an apartment I shared with a friend on the Upper East Side that fall. That saved me. Instead of spending my twenties in New York hanging out with bankers, I spent it hanging out with actors. *No movement.*

When I'd made enough to pay my student loans back, I did as I'd said I'd do, and headed out to find some real purpose. Even though I knew that Wall Street wasn't for me, I didn't quite know what *was* for me.

"What do I like doing?" I asked myself.

"Reading, I guess," I replied.

"Well, then, maybe you should get a job in book publishing," I replied.

At that point, I had no intention (or even inkling) of becoming a writer. I'd never said, "I want to be a writer," out loud. Why? Because I didn't. It had never even occurred to me. But I was a reader, so I figured maybe I could get into book publishing and help create books for people to read. I sent my resume to every single fiction publisher that I could find in New York. It was 1994, before they had all been eaten by corporate monsters, so I'm talking about a few hundred resumes.

I had an economics degree from an Ivy League school, but the publishing industry wouldn't even consider me for an unpaid internship. One memorable interview took place at Doubleday in Times Square. After asking me if I knew how to use spreadsheets, the recruiter suggested that while I was not qualified to work in "editorial," I might find a good fit in the inventory department. I stood up, thanked him for his time, and walked out of his office.

I quit looking for a job in publishing entirely after that. That was the summer of 1994. I'd left Wall Street for no job and had no real idea of what to do with my life. Other than reading, listening to music, talking, and smoking tons of weed, I had no real passions.

"What about journalism?" a friend asked. "Writing is just the flip side of reading, isn't it?"

"You might be right," I replied.

I went on a few interviews for journalism jobs, but the same problem seemed to be an impediment to that, too: Everyone seemed to think you had to be an English major to be a journalist. No one seemed to be interested in the quality of my mind. Increasingly disgusted with the close-mindedness of recruiters, I went to Woodstock '94 with some buddies, mainly to see Dylan play as the headliner. I did more drugs that weekend than I had ever done in my life—wall-to-wall LSD, mushrooms, ecstasy, and weed. It was a great time. The day after I got back, I was offered a job at a financial newsletter called *Derivatives Week*. It was a writing job, but it was writing about numbers. I called my parents immediately and told them that everything was going to be all right. I was going to be able to pay my rent.

STALEMATE

The day after I started that job, meaning just three days after I'd returned from the bacchanalia that was Woodstock, I was told that I had a drug test *the day* after that. I passed that drug test, remarkably, using the tried-and-true method of drinking a gallon of goldenseal tea the morning of my test. (I had to make a pit stop to use the restroom at a Harvey's in Times Square on my way there. It was awful.) I did have to wait a few days to find out that I'd passed, feeling all the while that I would surely fail it. But I guess the drug-testing regime isn't interested in catching people who use psychedelics.

I left *Derivatives Week* after three months. It was, as they say, not a good fit. I landed at *Money* magazine, where I spent five years. I made some great friends there, especially my lifelong pals Peter and Pablo. We had fun. In the early 1990s, Time Inc. was still a little bloated from its decades on top of the corporate media heap, and that meant that I was paid relatively well for not working very hard. And a job in journalism, when done right, is all about finding things that you're interested in, learning about them, and writing up your thoughts after you've done so. There are worse ways to spend your time. The only problem was that even as I was becoming a real journalist, I was still writing about money.

Money magazine was always the ugly stepchild at Time Inc. The golden son was *Fortune*. That never made sense to me—*Fortune* is like the marketing arm of capitalism, constantly kissing the ass of capitalists like Bill Gates, Warren Buffett, Eric Schmidt, or Steve Jobs, whereas *Money* was trying to help real people deal with their real financial issues. Of course, I also couldn't process why *Money* needed to be a monthly magazine rather than a book—there's not a lot you need to know about personal finance on an ongoing basis. The lessons are kind of timeless. But I'm digressing.

In 1997, I convinced the editors to let me write the first-ever investing feature that was exclusively focused on technology stocks. At the time, companies like Microsoft, Oracle, Intel, Cisco, and Dell were changing the very fabric of our society. If I wasn't exactly going to write about things that lit my soul on fire, I wanted to at least be writing about things that seemed to matter to other people. And I was arguably helping shape the direction of the magazine's editorial itself.

I would have stayed there quite some time if a coup hadn't taken place atop the masthead. The editor, Frank Lalli, was out, replaced by Bob Safian, who wasn't much older than me. Not long after that, one of Safian's deputies told me to write another investing feature on technology stocks. I agreed, but soon found out that they wanted me to write the *exact same story* I had written the year before. A personal service magazine is always going to be repetitive, but that doesn't mean you have to write *exactly* the same story every year. That wasn't enough to make me quit, mind you. What was? Money, of course. When I found out that Safian's new writer hires were making $75,000 or so versus my $50,000, I asked for a raise. At the time, I was one of (if not *the*) most productive investing writers on the staff, so I knew I deserved to be paid with the top tier. He came back to me with a $3,000 bump. I decided to quit when I could find a new job.

It didn't take long. *Red Herring* magazine, one of the San Francisco publications that covered the first Internet boom, was looking for a New York editor and had approached my colleague Jim Frederick. But Jim liked his prospects at Time Inc., so he passed the inquiry on to me. In 1999, I left *Money* to be the New York bureau chief for *Red Herring*. Alas, I was still writing about numbers, but numbers seasoned with technology. So it wasn't all bad. But it was still numbers. *Inertia setting in.*

Internet 1.0 was your classic boom-bust, and the fortunes of *Red Herring* mirrored those of the industry. We were on top of the world for a few years—Jon Stewart performed at a Christmas party, before he was *Jon Stewart*. But when the bust started, I had to lay a bunch of people off, one of the worst experiences of my life. (I know it was worse for them than for me, but still. It is thoroughly unpleasant to tell someone that their income and security are gone. Everybody cries.)

Red Herring closed its doors in 2003. At that point, I somehow finagled an interview with Graydon Carter at *Vanity Fair*. Graydon is one of the gods of modern journalism. He asked me if I knew about Paul Frank, the designer and creator of Julius the monkey. I did not. He assigned me a story about him anyway. He also assigned me a story on the rise and fall of Conrad Black, one of the great all-time white-collar villains. That story, when it came out, ran about twelve thousand words, and it changed everything. Whereas before Conrad, I couldn't get anyone to return my calls, after Conrad, it was my phone that started ringing. *Words make their move.*

Around that time, my buddy Owen Burke called me and asked me if I'd like to write a book with him. Owen had lived above me on Hudson Street in New York City for a few years, and Will Arnett and I had taken him to his first show of the Upright Citizens Brigade. He later took improv classes at the theater and ended up becoming the artistic director sometime after that. Then he went to work for Funny or Die, making the world laugh with Will Ferrell and Adam McKay.

Anyway, he called me in 2004 and said, "Do you want to write a book with me?" I did not see that one coming. He explained: He'd pitched a Choose Your Own Adventure about the excesses of the CEO class at the turn of the century. And now he had to find someone who actually knew the "language" of CEOs to write it with him. So Owen called me.

A Choose Your Own Adventure is all about infinite possibility. Instead of just reading a book, you get to make choices. You know, just like existence itself. Your life is always all possibility in the moment, which is actually all there is. The book contained multitudes: We even managed to get llamas that grew bulletproof wool into it. In case you're not sensing a theme here: Owen was working with one of the great improv groups in history at the time. Improv is all about . . . infinite possibility. Life is about infinite possibility. The more you can embrace it and weave it into your daily existence, the better off you will be. It took fifteen years for me to write another book that was anywhere near as close to the spirit of existence than that one. That book, *Frictionless*, which I co-wrote with another old friend, Christiane Lemieux, came out in June 2020, and it's about the same thing—staying open to possibility. Of the five books that had my name on them before this one, the two that came closest to grasping the nature of reality are the ones that I wrote with my friends—the first one and the fifth one. So while it may seem in the pages that follow that the years in between include some kind of forward momentum, you could also characterize it as a lot of marching in place.

For a while, I wrote for Adam Moss's *New York* magazine, mostly about Wall Street. Early in 2008, Adam invited me to his office to talk about whatever story ideas I had for the year ahead: "If we were only going to do one feature on someone on Wall Street this year, who would it be?"

My brain went into high gear, leafing as quickly as possible through what meager files it had on "*interesting people to profile on Wall Street.*" The best I could come up with was an idea that someone else had already had. Only a week or so before, I had read a profile of JPMorgan Chase CEO Jamie Dimon in *Barron's*, a financial newspaper. Dimon had built Citigroup with his mentor Sandy Weill, and now he was doing the empire-building thing again at JPMorgan Chase. The fact that *Barron's* had written about him in no way precluded *New York* doing a story on him, so it didn't feel like I was pitching a story I shouldn't have. Let's not forget about the fact that not a single other name had come to me in the moment. I went with what I had.

"Jamie Dimon," I said.

"Why?" he replied.

At that point, I simply regurgitated whatever I could remember from the *Barron's* story. He told me to start work on it immediately. And then, as the world's luck turned bad, mine turned good. On Sunday, March 16, 2008, Bear Stearns collapsed. JPMorgan stepped in, at the behest of the government, to buy it, to prevent the financial system from melting down. At first, I thought I was screwed. After much pleading and cajoling, Joe Evangelisti, the JPMorgan communications czar, had agreed to schedule an interview for me with Dimon, but a mid-February interview had been postponed until Monday, March 17. Now every news organization on the planet would be calling JPMorgan that night and the next day, and there would be a million stories written about Dimon by the end of the week. I hadn't even started writing mine.

Then I got a call from Evangelisti. Not only were they keeping my rescheduled appointment with Dimon, he told me, but Dimon wasn't going to be talking to anyone else. My story wasn't just alive, it was also going to be the cover of the next issue of *New York*. It was quite the exclusive for a magazine that wasn't a real player in financial media. The most in-demand CEO on Wall Street wasn't talking to *Fortune*, *Forbes*, *BusinessWeek*, the *Wall Street Journal*, or the *New York Times*. He was talking to me, and to *New York* magazine.

In the years that followed, people from the profession often asked me, "How did you get that exclusive?" What I didn't say then but I'm happy to admit now is that it was pure dumb luck.

I'd written a timely and interesting story about the new king of Wall Street. And that little piece of luck was the start of a book career that continues to this day. A week or so after it ran, my future agent David Kuhn called to ask me if I wanted to write a book about Dimon.

Duff: "I don't want to write a book about a fucking banker."

David: "Why don't we see how much money we can get first?"

I reluctantly agreed, telling myself that like everyone, I probably had a price. Publishers fell all over themselves bidding for the book—it was a biography of America's most powerful banker in the midst of the financial crisis—and it turned out that I did. Have a price, that is.

*   *   *

If I'm to be honest, I will admit that I didn't just write about numbers, I embraced them at every turn. At almost every stop along my journalistic journey, I toyed around with numbers in ways that went well beyond stock prices or sales figures.

I created indices for three separate magazines: *The Money 30, The WIRED 30*, and *The Red Herring Portfolio*. At *Portfolio* magazine in the early years of the millennium, I wrote a monthly column called "How to Value It." The point of the column, ironically, was to show how you could put a number on anything if you really wanted to, even if those numbers were more fiction than anything else.

The art department asked me if I could break all of my valuation challenges into three parts, to make the design consistent. "Sure," I said, knowing that when you are making something up, you can break it into whatever number of parts you want. You want three parts? Not four? No problem. That become part of my challenge, to pretend that every "It" that we valued had three components.

Some examples:

What would the New York subway system sell for if they privatized it?

After New York governor Eliot Spitzer got busted using prostitutes, I calculated the size of the Escort Economy in the United States.

When Britney Spears entered into a relatively unstable period and shaved her head, someone in an editorial meeting noted, "She's crazy."

My reply: "Yes, but she's still big-money crazy."

Joanne Lipman, the editor of *Portfolio*, turned toward me. "That's your next column," she said.

By my calculation, Britney Spears had a $110 million economy around her. It might have been the silliest thing I have ever written with a straight face. It also turned out to be the most popular story I have ever written. I went on NPR, CNN, *Inside Edition*, seemingly every radio program in the country, and was cited everywhere you looked.

When my wife was pregnant with our daughter, I sat in the waiting room of her OB/GYN's office during an ultrasound. Leafing through *People* magazine, I found my $110 million quoted in a story as if it were cold, hard, incontrovertible fact. But numbers don't lie, do they?

In the spring of 2020, mid-pandemic, I got an email from a filmmaker who had done projects for HBO and Netflix. Could I talk, she asked, about her newest one? Of course I could talk, and wondered in the interim what it was about: McKinsey? Harvard Business School?

Nope. It was about Britney Spears. They wanted to interview me on camera about the Britney Economy.

"Look," I said, "I don't want to be rude, but I am going to be direct. That was not a serious piece of journalism. What I mean by that was that I was making those numbers up. It wasn't complete nonsense of course—we really did figure out her record sales and her effect on tabloids—but the very idea of a 'Britney Economy' is absurd. There is no such thing. It doesn't exist."

Silence.

"Well, that was one of the most interesting conversations we've had so far," the director replied. We agreed to speak again at a later date. We never did.

*   *   *

I spent fifteen years as a magazine writer. And then in 2009, I started writing books. I never really looked back, because my timing could not have been better. The combination of the Great Recession and the Internet served to decimate the market for freelance journalism, and if I wanted to keep both my freedom and my current level of income, then writing books was, somewhat ironically, the way for me to go. What about the fight between words and numbers, you ask? What happened to that? Well, I took it with me. And the battle raged on.

Does any of this sound familiar to you? Do you ever find yourself pulled between these warring camps? On the one side, there is quantification and all of its apparent simplicity. Counting things is pretty easy, especially if the numbers aren't that big—we even have calculators attached to ourselves in the form of fingers. On the other side is understanding, which requires things like words and experience.

When we count something, we deny ourselves the chance to tickle ourselves, because counting takes us inside our mind and out of presence itself. So why do we do it? Why do we squander so many precious opportunities to feel the glory of existence in favor of compiling a tally of this thing or that? I don't know why you do it, but I'll tell you why I did it—because of the erroneous and misguided assumption that I was doing my future self a favor by running the numbers right now. But my future self never needed the favor, because my future self was imaginary. Unable to live in the moment, I invoked an imaginary person—future me—who needed me to count something, thereby excusing me from the act of living itself.

Future me, of course, never showed up to take responsibility for being so distracting. It's quite the head fake we are pulling on ourselves, is it not? We're all being distracted by imaginary versions of ourselves. They ask us for something and then vaporize. Before long, that old unsatisfied feeling rears its ugly head again—the one that whispers that you are not living to your fullest potential. So who's to blame? Imaginary you? Imaginary me? In the end, we are left holding the bag, shafted by our own phantoms, with nobody but ourselves to blame. Unless, that is, you could find someone to pay you to write entire books about other people's failings.

Books About Numbers

There are also of course, disadvantages to rationality.
Among modern historians, for example, the rigorous
principles that are applied in order to determine causes
too often exclude the role played by accident in history.[1]

—Don LePan, *The Cognitive Revolution in Western Culture*

I did not write a book about Jamie Dimon because I wanted to write a book about a banker. I wrote a book about Jamie Dimon because the money was too good to pass up. *Last Man Standing: The Ascent of Jamie Dimon and JPMorgan Chase* came out in June 2009 from Simon & Schuster. It was well received by the business crowd, but the liberal intelligentsia lambasted me for having the audacity to write a positive book about a banker when the entire country was angry at the financial industry.

Indeed, during the time I wrote the book, a lot of people decided to let Jamie Dimon be a stand-in for everything that is wrong with our financialized society. He was, after all, one of the most powerful bankers in the world, as well as the most outspoken of his peers. But let me tell you what I think: Despite the desire of people for him to be a bad guy, he is nothing of the sort. I have looked into his eyes and seen his soul. Yes, Jamie used his powers to become King of a Mountain of Numbers. That's what a bank is, in case you were wondering—a *mountain of numbers*. The way we've organized ourselves, we need mountains of numbers just to keep everything straight. And Jamie is better at it than anyone else has ever been. But no, he is not the devil. He is just another person who lives in our quantified reality. He just knows how to quantify it better than most.

* * *

Not long after I'd turned that book in to my editor at Simon & Schuster, he asked me what I wanted to write about next. I had no idea, so he gave one to me. There's a passage in *Last Man Standing* where Dimon criticizes CEOs who rely too much on management consultants. He was withering in his remarks, but made one exception: "Except for McKinsey," he'd said. "They're different." I'd put those words in the book without knowing much about management consultants, and that notwithstanding the fact that one of my brothers ran a large consulting firm himself.

"What do you know about McKinsey?" my editor asked me. "Nothing," was my reply. That wasn't entirely true. I am quite sure that I'd interviewed with McKinsey for a job out of college. I didn't receive an offer, but I wasn't exactly holding it against them. I'd have taken the offer I got from Goldman Sachs over an offer from McKinsey anyway. Fifteen years had also passed, and at that point, I really *didn't* know much about them. He told me to look into the legendary consulting firm and tell him what I found.

What I found was surprising: McKinsey was one of the most influential professional services firms in history, but it wasn't really a household name in 2009. If you'd asked somebody whether they knew McKinsey at the time, there was a good chance that they'd mix them up with the Kinsey Report, the scandalous midcentury research about sexuality. But that didn't mean they weren't powerful. Fast-forward to 2019, when the firm was in the press due to former presidential candidate Pete Buttigieg's history at McKinsey, and to 2020, when it was raked over the coals for its role in the opioid scandal. Even then, most people *still* didn't know who they were. And that's because they want it that way. They operate behind the scenes, by design.

In one way, McKinsey is what IBM used to be: a terrifying mass of conformist overachievers. I was intrigued enough by the fact that no one had written a history of the century-old firm to write a proposal in which I told S&S that McKinsey was far more influential than anyone really knew. (That is, other than *BusinessWeek*'s John Byrne and *Fortune*'s John Huey, both of whom had written excellent stories about McKinsey.) Various writers had discussed McKinsey in books about elite northeastern financial institutions over the years, but no one had written a book about McKinsey itself. The reason seemed clear enough: McKinsey is highly secretive and denied access to any writers who they couldn't control. I told Simon & Schuster that we should do it anyway, with or without McKinsey's cooperation. They agreed, and I had my next book contract. We decided that I would start working on it without telling McKinsey, and I waited a year before approaching the firm. They eventually cooperated, and gave me significant access. I later found out that they'd known I was working on it almost the entire time, but instead of penalizing me for the secrecy of it all decided to bet that I could be persuaded to write a book that didn't cast them in an entirely negative light. My book about Jamie Dimon had been largely positive, after all, and there was also the fact that both Wharton and Goldman were on my resume.

What did I think of McKinsey? In my heart of hearts, I felt that they were well-dressed charlatans. But I didn't write that book. I wrote something that you could describe as "fair and balanced," a term that was all the rage at the time thanks to Rupert Murdoch, Roger Ailes, and Fox News. Just as I had done in my first book, I wrote *The Firm: The Story of McKinsey and Its Secret Influence on American Business* as a chronological history. Ask any nonfiction writer: It's a difficult job to write a serious book about a serious topic, especially when you're still a rookie. If you have something like the calendar to use as the skeleton on which to hang the whole thing, it takes some of the stress of organizing all your thoughts away. Like the first book, *The Firm* was what you might call well executed. I hit all the big moments in McKinsey's history and put them in the context of what Henry Luce called the American Century.

But I pulled my punches. When *zeroing* in on the essential question—*Was the world's most expensive consulting firm worth it?*—I chickened out, and decided to answer the question with a question. *Was it worth it to whom?* I asked, and then wrote the answers.

It's worth it to a CEO who hires them with someone else's money.
It's sometimes worth it to a company that hires them, but that depends what advice they give, whether the company follows it, and what happens as a result. In short: it depends.
It's usually not worth it to the employees of said company, who are immediately at risk of being laid off. McKinsey is what I referred to as "the greatest legitimizer of mass layoffs in history," so when McKinsey shows up, employees should always be afraid.
Was it worth it to society itself? I asked. On this one, I chickened out again. It's worth it if you value efficiency and rationality above all else, I said, but maybe not if you value things like beauty, truth, creativity, fairness, and the like.

For some reason, I couldn't just come out and say that I valued truth more than efficiency. I simply settled for: It depends on what you value.

That book sold okay, especially overseas, but the reviews were split down the middle. The business press seemed to enjoy a history of such a powerful and secretive institution. But some reviewers called me out for being wishy-washy on the central question. I was right that the question of something's value depends entirely on the follow-up question: To whom? But I could have just answered the big one—McKinsey's value *to society*—in the negative and called it a day. McKinsey is not good for society. They focus us on the things that we can count, at the expense of the more important things that we cannot. And we are poorer for it.

*　　*　　*

If you don't count books that I have ghostwritten, I can count four serious books to my name: *Last Man Standing, The Firm, The Golden Passport,* and *Frictionless.* In every single one of them, I entered into the project somewhat hesitantly. I never told any of my editors as much, but the fact was that I wasn't sure that I really wanted to write any of them. The only problem was that I had no idea what I really wanted to write, so I wrote what they would buy from me. (If the best reason you can come up with for writing a book is that someone will pay you to do so, then numbers are definitely getting the better of words in the battle for your soul.)

The good news is that in every single one of those books, once I began digging into the subject, I realized that it was, once again, much more interesting than I had thought. My book about McKinsey is no different in that regard. I pitched a book about hidden influence. I had no idea about the extent of that influence. It's not that they weren't influential; rather, I had underestimated the influence of McKinsey significantly, not just in business but in society itself.

One of the things I always told myself when writing about people I didn't particularly admire who were nevertheless successful was that I was not there to judge. (What a crock! I was judging every which way but loose and any which way I could.) If someone wasn't breaking the law, or acting in a blatantly unethical or immoral fashion, I gave them a pass. That is, until I was working on *The Firm*. That's when I realized that you don't have to break the law to be a corrosive influence. You can do it right out in the open, right in front of our faces, all while insisting that you are just a *servant*, doing the bidding of a *client*.

Of course, I didn't write *that* in *The Firm*. Why not? Because I was scared. I mean, I wasn't scared enough to completely hide my poor opinion of them, but I was scared enough to write the book as if we could evaluate their influence using a ledger of pros and cons. In retrospect, it is clear to me that no one should be pro-McKinsey except a CFO looking to wring costs out of their business model or a CEO who hasn't the faintest idea how to make a decision. The rest of us should be anti-McKinsey. They don't have society's best interests in mind. They are parasites who have somehow convinced us that they are good for our health.

Not only that, but McKinsey is a force for capitalism's worst impulse, the ceaseless desire to commodify every single thing, down to our thoughts. Under the guise of spreading *best practices*, McKinsey steals that which it cannot come up with on its own and then sells it to someone else as if it were its own creation. It's quite the business model, and the firm spews out the most overconfident kind of unoriginal people you have ever seen. And yet people keep hiring them. Why? Because we are scared, and McKinsey knows how to scare you talking out of one side of its mouth while promising to take care of you with the other. McKinsey sells advice, but they give the fear away for free.[2]

*　　*　　*

When that book was finished, I was solidly established as a business author. When casting around for a new idea, I had dinner with one of my sources for *The Firm*. "I don't know what I'm going to do next," I said. "Isn't it obvious?" he replied. Exasperated, I said, "Not to me." But it was, at least if you thought that there was some through-line to my own choices. "You should write about Harvard Business School," he said.

He was right. It *was* obvious. Dimon went to HBS. McKinsey & Company has hired more graduates and exercised outsize influence over HBS since the 1930s. My first book was about an individual. My second was about a private organization. And my third would be about an educational institution. A very obvious thread ran between them—the string the pearls were strung on—and it shocked me that I hadn't seen it myself. In retrospect, I know the reason why: I hadn't really wanted to write about the first two, so why would I have been able to see *the third book I didn't want to write*? It's hard to find something that you don't want to look for. I never put it this way, but I didn't want to write another book about numbers people.

But I buried my misgivings and soldiered on. I was confident that a publisher would bite. There have been many, many books about HBS over the years, but most of them have been by insiders drunk on the Kool-Aid of capitalism. Chafing a bit from the criticism of *The Firm*—it bugged me that the reviewers hadn't been able to read between the lines and feel my disdain for McKinsey—I decided that I was going to do it right this time. I was going to say *exactly what I thought* about the influence of HBS and that which it has created, the MBA Industrial Complex.

I already knew what I was going to say, because MBAs and consultants are just two sides of the same coin: analysts who think that the best way to grasp our reality is via quantification and abstraction. Meaning: Neither of them likes to actually *do* things; they'd much rather *analyze* things and leave the dirty work of *doing things* to others. I was going to take HBS to task for warping the minds of our youth and our nation.

(They're not *all* bad. Ron Nahser, provost emeritus of the Presidio Graduate School, told me recently that he wants his school to be the Hogwarts of business schools. I endorse that ambition.)

Four years later, *The Golden Passport* came out. The critics loved it, because I ripped the school to pieces. The self-described school of leadership was nothing of the sort, I wrote. Rather, it was a seedbed of greed and amorality. When one of my favorite writers, Matthew Stewart, wrote a glowing review in the *Wall Street Journal* the week before the book came out, I thought that everything was finally going to come up roses for me. *The Golden Passport* was going to be my bestseller. My publisher even ordered up a second printing before we went on sale. Alas, it turns out that books about HBS don't exactly fly off the shelves.

One of the most startling things I learned while writing that book was about entrenched power. I had bought all that bullshit that America was a meritocracy along with everybody else. I thought I was somehow an example of it, and I was, to a point. But it's much simpler than that: With the business schools acting as outsourced human resource functions for corporate America, I saw quite clearly how the reins of power were handed from one generation of white males to the next in America's Northeast and, eventually, across the globe.

At the time, I thought I'd finally learned how to be a real writer. I had locked myself in my house for six months to write that book, emerging for yoga and groceries on weekdays and the drive to pick up my daughter every other weekend. Writing *The Golden Passport* was the hardest thing I've ever done, mentally speaking. I crammed a century's worth of American business history into my head, learning most of it just moments before I wrote about it. I thought it was difficult because it was a complicated subject, but I was wrong about that. It was difficult because, deep down, I didn't want to be writing it.

How do I know that to be the case? Well, this is what it took to write it: coffee, four to six Red Bulls a day, a half to a full pack of Marlboro Lights a day, four to six toffee Heath bar crunch cookies a day, two Adderall a day, two smoothies a day (for efficiency—*The Firm* had taught me well), and steak for dinner. Every day for months. When I finished the book, I collapsed with what I can only guess was a budding stomach ulcer. Note to aspiring writers: If you find yourself consuming a diet like that while trying to write a book, you are writing the wrong book. Stop what you are doing immediately.

Another thing I learned in *The Golden Passport* is that even if behavior is despicable, it's possible for the writer to be too mean in describing it. I had convinced myself that writing in a righteous anger was okay as long as the recipient of that anger *deserved it*. But I was wrong about that. I spit too much venom on those pages. I'm not saying that I don't stand by the gist of what I said, because I do. I'm saying that I think I could have used a slightly less hostile tone. You're never going to get through to people if you are nasty, even if you are saying something that merits being said. I have spent too much of my life knocking people down when I could have been doing it differently, showing people how to enjoy their life by doing what they love with focus and care. I think I'm doing it now, but it took almost one thousand pages of writing about MBAs to make me sick enough to realize that I was never going to do that again.

*   *   *

The next book I wrote was *Frictionless*, with Christiane Lemieux. Christiane is a superstar, one strong enough to pull me out of my own orbit and into hers for eighteen months while we went around talking to interesting people doing amazing things. I didn't realize it at the time, but in inviting me to do that with her, Christiane played her own part in the cracking open of one Duff McDonald. But I didn't know that until I knew it, and when I turned my attention back to the next book that I was going to write on my own, I set out to find another target at which to aim my bazooka, for the good of all mankind. I might write like a nice guy if I was co-writing something, but when it came to the brand of Duff, the gloves had to come off again.

I did plan on making an adjustment, mind you. Instead of targeting *bad people*, I decided that I was going to go after *bad thinking* itself. Which thinking, exactly? Well, to figure that out, I started doing some thinking myself—about what lay beyond my contempt for McKinsey & Company and the Harvard Business School. Here's what I landed on: The thing that McKinsey and HBS shared was a belief in what I might describe as a quantified reality. They are avatars and proselytizers of the idea that the numbers contain truth, when the fact of the matter is that numbers don't contain anything but themselves.

Why do we spend so much time counting things, when the most important things of all defy quantification entirely? I'm talking about beauty and justice and fairness and truth and love. We do it because *it's easier to count things than to understand them*. When something like COVID hits, we engage in an orgy of data collection. Why? It isn't really because we think the answer to COVID is a number. It's because we've thrown in the towel everywhere else and let numbers be our guide. When someone asks you how much something is *worth*, the answer doesn't have to be a number. What's the value of a smile when you need it most?

The reason we let numbers be our guide is that it's easy, and it gives the illusion of certainty. This is also the reason we follow the money into careers that make us sick and numb to our experience. (Numbers and numbness—the two words aren't even that different.) We don't talk a lot about how much a smile is actually worth because you can't count it; you'd have to use words, and to express the value of something unquantifiable, you need to care about what you're going to say. Despite the fact that most thoughtful people know that a rose is more beautiful than a calculator, we have become a society of people who count things instead of trying to understand them or appreciate their inherent beauty. We are counting COVID because we don't know what else to do.

*   *   *

Talking to Joey about the unceasing conflict between numbers and words I have felt within me my whole life, she made a connection that had eluded me during that same whole life: Many of the relationships that have turned sour for me have done so because people mistook me for a numbers guy (that is, a *money* guy) as opposed to a words guy. And this was not their fault: I was flashing the signs of both gangs. To those of you who mistook me for someone else, I am sorry. I played a part in that deception, even if I wasn't trying to do so.

Okay, so back to numbers versus words. I think my story is pretty interesting in that it has been fought right square in the middle of the two. But as I said above, this is not just about me. It's about all of us. We are drowning in numbers, everywhere we go. *Drowning* in them.

Prices, values, surveys, polls, indices, box-office results, scores, salaries, projections, totals, ratings, likes, calories, dollars, cents, world records, timelines, predictions, statistics, analyses, "research," and more. Everything is quantified. Why? Why do we need *big data* at all? What are we looking for in numbers that we can't find somewhere else? We are looking for *meaning*. Why? Because nobody can sit comfortably in the present. If you can't sit comfortably in the present, you head off into your imagination. And that's where numbers do their best work.

Like everyone else, I have been drawn to numbers because they offered the illusion of control. If life is just one big unknown, a rolling series of uncertainties, numbers held out the promise of nailing a few things down. Your financial life, of course, is all about numbers. But your personal life can be, too, if you want it to be:

How much do I weigh?
How many miles have I run?
How many women have I slept with?
How many Bob Dylan albums do I own?
How many times have you interrupted me?
How many days until that movie comes out?
How many books are in the Library of Babel?
How much wood could a woodchuck chuck if a woodchuck could chuck wood?

*   *   *

In April 2020, I read *The Enchantments of Mammon* by Eugene McCarraher, a professor of humanities at Villanova University. When I put that book down, I felt like I finally understood what had happened to the soul of America and, by extension, the world. It didn't occur to me at all that this newfound understanding was actually about myself, but that day wasn't too far off.

I wrote McCarraher a note asking to speak to him. I told him who I was, mentioned *The Golden Passport*, and my plans for *The Precision Paradox*. I intended to feature his brilliant book in my next one. Would he care to chat? No reply.

A few weeks later, I was putting the finishing touches on a new website showcasing my work, and I came across a review of *The Golden Passport*, written by . . . Eugene McCarraher. Now that was embarrassing. I hadn't mentioned his review in my email to him. But it got worse: At the end of said review, which was largely positive, he lowered the boom:

> What is to be done? Here McDonald disappoints. After exposing the fraudulence of the school's pretensions to wisdom at such voluminous length, he looks to it nonetheless to lead a moral reformation of business. In his own way, McDonald reaffirms what he amply discredits: the ideal of a benevolent capitalist elite.

I have weathered a bad review or two in my day. They're never fun. But that one stung. Why? Because he couldn't have been more right. I had chickened out.

The pain only lasted a few weeks, because McCarraher's critique led me to understand what I had done. I think business schools should be abolished. I really do. But when it came to my book, I had concluded (for no good reason) that I should stick to prescriptions that were *probable*. In other words, because it seemed highly *improbable* to me that business schools *would* be abolished, it was a waste of time to talk about that. That was a mistake. Why? Because anything is *possible*. I should have just gone with the scenario that would have been best for this country, for humanity itself—the end of the charade, and the beginning of something new.

*   *   *

One of humanity's great misconceptions—in my humble opinion—is our belief that we are exceptional. Again: I say this because I know it about myself. But I do not think that I am alone. I think the book that captures this idea best is *Ishmael*, by Daniel Quinn. A long-running conversation between a man and an ape about humanity's place in the world, it packs quite the spiritual punch, and should be required reading for the entire human race.

But wait, allow me to reword that: We actually *are* exceptional, just not in the way that we think. We are not superior to all other living things. We are inferior. We are *the exception*—the one organism on this planet that has lost sight of its connection to the whole. Using our God-given brains, we built our egos and fell so in love with them that we got lost inside them. More recently, we have used numbers to build walls around our interior worlds that have separated us from the one outside of us, the one in which everything is connected.

Joey said this to me: "This world has its pants on backwards."

"That's brilliant," I replied. "I am going to quote you on that."

But it wasn't hers; she was quoting Kabir, a "wild, holy man of India." I hope they say that about me one day. (The wild part, that is. Because everyone is holy.)

If I told you the truth about God,
you might think I was an idiot.
If I lied to you about the Beautiful One
you might parade me through the streets shouting,
"This guy is a genius!"
This world has its pants on backwards.
Most carry their values and knowledge in a jug
that has a big hole in it.
Thus having a clear grasp of the situation
if I am asked anything these days
I just laugh!

—Kabir (c. 1440–1518)

*   *   *

Numbers can be useful things. They can, in many situations, help you get a feel for what something is all about. But they never take you all the way.

Consider a sports team. American sports fans, in particular, love to obsess over statistics, studying them like scripture, looking for the meaning hiding behind the numbers. They love it so much, in fact, that they've even created entirely imaginary sports leagues based around the statistics themselves, so-called *fantasy sports leagues*. In those leagues, it's not the actual people or the real-life plays that matter. It's the *statistics* themselves. What has happened to us?

Everybody knows that stats can't always tell you what you need to know about a team. While the best teams often have the best statistics, it is not unusual for the league champion to be the one that came out of nowhere, defying probability to achieve what we often call *the impossible*—the underdog victory. Of course, that's precisely wrong, as those improbable victories are obviously *very possible indeed*, given that they did, in fact, win. I'm thinking Buster Douglas beating Mike Tyson here. If all you had was the man's statistics, you could not have seen the upset coming. Something happened in that fight that the numbers could not grasp. We often refer to that as *heart*. You could also call it *love*.

When I say that words are far more powerful than numbers, I really mean it. But let me offer an example. In his extraordinary 1973 book, *Social Sciences as Sorcery*, Stanislav Andreski uses a single six-word sentence to demonstrate the almost unfathomable power of words when it comes to containing meaning.

For those of you under a certain age, you'll need some backstory. When President John F. Kennedy was assassinated on November 22, 1963, police almost immediately fingered a shady character named Lee Harvey Oswald, who had ties to communists via Russia *and*

Cuba. Oswald, however, was shot by a guy named Jack Ruby before his guilt could be firmly established. Some thought that the vice president, Lyndon Johnson, was involved. Others thought it was a mafia hit, maybe having something to do with Marilyn Monroe. A 2017 poll suggested that only 33 percent of Americans believed that Oswald did it, although polls about what people believe are kind of pointless. Suffice it to say that there was never any agreement on the matter, and there still isn't today.

So here's the sentence I was talking about. Its six words contain multitudes:

Oswald did not kill John Kennedy.[3]

Andreski first points out that the statement is semantically neutral. There is nothing in the word choice to suggest the person saying it is pleased or appalled by the murder of JFK, or whether the person saying it thinks that it's good news or not that it wasn't Oswald who'd done the dirty deed. Sitting there, unexamined, it could be nothing more than an ethically neutral statement, the equivalent of saying, "That ape just ate a banana."

But, as all students of American history know, the question of who killed JFK is loaded with value judgments. Indeed, it couldn't be more loaded. While you might not infer it from the meaning of the words alone, all you have to do is set them in the context of American political discussion and you are instantly thinking that you are dealing with one or more of the following: (a) a conspiracy theorist, (b) someone who might actually be suggesting that the vice president, Lyndon Johnson, was behind it, (c) someone who thought the mafia was behind it, maybe because of a love triangle involving Marilyn Monroe, (d) someone who actually knew something that other people don't about (b) or (c), (e) Stephen King, who wrote one of his best novels (*11/22/63*) about the subject, or (f) someone who just wants to rile you up.

They say that a picture is worth a thousand words, but I have just shown you that a few words can be worth a thousand words, too. When we ask what something *means*, we are asking for essence, which runs very deep. By comparison, quantity is but a superficial attribute. One word can mean *many different things*. Numbers, on the other hand, are just numbers; they mean one thing, and one thing only. It's amazing, if you think of it, that numbers have triumphed over words. Or maybe it isn't: Counting is much easier than understanding. And so we count and count and count. The problem is that we don't have time to count as high as meaning is deep. In the meantime, you miss out on what is happening right in front of your face.

What are you going to do right now?

If it sounds like I'm starting to get a little holier-than-thou, let me reel this thing back in. It's not a coincidence that I lost faith in the rationale for writing *The Precision Paradox* at the same time that I read Eugene McCarraher's devastating conclusion in his review of *The Golden Passport*. In just a few short sentences, he had revealed that I was nothing but an empty critic. I was squandering my intellect by attacking bad ideas without offering any good ones in their stead. But the problem wasn't just confined to my book career. The problem was with myself.

When I walked away from my actual belief—that business schools should be abolished—and just accepted that such an outcome was *improbable*, and therefore not worth considering, I discarded *the possible* for the merely *probable*. Do that in a book, and you can end up with the wrong ending. Do that in *life*, and you end up closing yourself off from the infinite possibility of existence. That's where certainty makes its move and renders you a prisoner of your own lack of imagination.

I know that, because that's what happened to me: Deluded by my own facility in both using and writing about numbers, I let a sense of certainty creep into both my life and my writing. When you are certain that you are right, you run into a lot of people you think are wrong. And when everyone else is wrong, you get angry. And that's why I have been angry for most of my life.

Something cracked open in April.

And you know what happened then?

I started listening.

But it's not quite time to start writing about the new me yet. We are not quite done with the old me. Up to this point, I have mainly told you about how I somehow managed to string a career together by throwing my lot in with numbers, even though, deep down, I hated myself for it. What did numbers do to me? Well, for starters, they convinced me that the past and the future existed, which took my eye off the present. And you know what happened then? My entire life fell apart.

PART II

The Stamp of Reality

Surely, the memory of an event cannot pass for the event itself. Nor can the anticipation. There is something exceptional, unique, about the present event, which the previous or the coming do not have. There is a livingness about it, an actuality; it stands out as if illumined. There is the "stamp of reality" on the actual, which the past and the future do not have.[1]

—Sri Nisargadatta Maharaj, *I Am That*

CHAPTER 6

The Trap of Time

Don't be afraid of tomorrow. God is already there.

—Unknown

There's a running conversation in Stephen King's *The Outsider* that continues through the whole book. It's about whether or not there's an *end* to the universe. Detective Ralph Anderson keeps coming back to it when talking to his friend Holly Gibney. "I was thinking about the universe," he says at one point. "There really is no end to it, is there? And no explaining it?" "That's right," she replies. "No point in even trying."

I disagree. I think that we can try, and that we might even be able to wrap our heads around it—the universe, that is. So here goes:

The universe is now.
That is all there is.
There is nothing else, no past, no future.
There is only now.
So there is obviously no "end" to the universe.
Because now never ends.
It is always now.

There is no such thing as time. There is only now. If you get stuck in the past or the future, you are stuck in your mind, and you are missing out on now. One of the main ways that we get stuck in the past or the future is by trying to quantify our existence. When we do that, the mind naturally latches on to the numbers we have assembled and wonders how we might change those numbers (in the future) or how much those numbers have changed since some moment that's already happened (in the past). So when we try to describe our *present* using numbers, we are immediately opening ourselves up to the likelihood that we will let our mind wander forward or backward in time. In other words, when we invoke numbers, we move into our imagination. If we want to stay in the present, we need to do a better job of trying to grasp our reality using a language that anchors us in the moment rather than sends us inside our own minds, the way numbers, mathematics, and science do. We need to use words.

When we use words, we engage with other people in the effort of transcending the indeterminacy of thought. You can never know, with certainty, what I am thinking, and I can never know, with certainty, what you are thinking. If we want to talk about the number two or the number twenty-five, we can definitely agree that we are both thinking about that. But numbers can't grasp essence, so if all we're going to do is talk about numbers, even in the present, then all we have done is agree to focus on some superficial characteristic of the situation. ("It's been raining for two hours.") Our goal, however, should not simply be to describe the situation in which we find ourselves. For one, it is usually self-evident, and for two, describing something is not the same as deciding what to do about it. For that, we need words.

Words can help us develop, discern, and describe our intentions in a manner that is and always will be far superior to a quantitative measure of our circumstances. "I weigh 180 pounds and I want to lose ten pounds" is not as insightful a remark as "I weigh more than seems healthy and I want to get my physical body into better shape." There's also the problem with the precision. What happens if you only lose five pounds? If we use the ten-pound goal as our guide, we have failed. If we use the second one, we have succeeded. Precision is a trap made of numbers. We have to start avoiding these traps if we are going to get where we want to go.

And where is that? Well, that's the riddle here. The place we want to get to is *right here, right now*, and there are no numbers that can adequately grasp *now*. Why is that? Because now is infinite. It cannot be captured quantitatively. Of all the tools we have created, numbers and mathematics and science are among the most powerful. They can tell us what happened (which doesn't really matter anymore), or what might happen (which will always be a guess), but they can never tell us *what is happening right now*. Because everything is always happening, and that's a lot to count. And as soon as you start counting, the *now* that you were talking about is already gone, leaving you counting the past again. Not only that, but because numbers are inherently empty, they practically scream out for another number to compare themselves to, with the idea that meaning will arise from relativity.

Did you know that medieval people didn't really have the same concept of time as we do? In *The Cognitive Revolution in Western Culture: The Birth of Expectation*, Don LePan points out that if modern man finds it impossible to envisage time coming to a stop, medieval man found it impossible to imagine time as infinite.[1] Think about that for a second. Our sense of time is cultural, not some innate aspect of reality itself. The modern linear view of time is something that we invented. In ye olden days, they grasped time more like Eastern religions do, as a cyclical thing revolving around the continual present.

For centuries, one's sense of time was more of a subjectively defined temporal realm. Everything changed when the exchange of goods and services went from a local thing to an "economy-wide" thing. If you have a meeting with someone you don't know, you need to agree on when you are meeting. Just as money standardized value, clocks standardized time. The only reason you need to know precise time is that you're on the clock. As E. M. Forster writes in *Howards End*, "He lived for the five minutes that have past, and the five to come; he had the business mind."[2]

If you are making your own decisions, on the other hand, it doesn't really matter what *o'clock* it is—at least not nearly as much. You can't be late for a meeting with yourself.

Just kidding. You most certainly can. I didn't arrive at mine until I was forty-nine years old—almost half a century late. How did that happen? Well, the main way it happened, if you must know, is because of alcohol. Like many of my peers, I began drinking alcohol in high school. I drank my way through college, and through my twenties and thirties. Alcohol is a depressant. It slows the central nervous system down. When you drink to excess, your speech slurs, your movement becomes unsteady, and your reaction time goes out the window. In other words, when you drink to excess, you are no longer present. You are a half step (or more) behind, late to the act of existence itself.

This is going to get a little serpentine, so hang on tight: If you drink too much, you eject yourself from *now*. The aftereffects of excessive drinking—headaches, exhaustion, shame—have pretty much the same effect. You can't really be present when you're hungover. You're too distracted by the pain. So . . . drink too much, too often, and you will soon find that you don't spend any time in the present at all. And that's a problem, because that's where everything is happening. If you don't spend time in the present, you don't actually know what's happening in your own life. That's what happened to me.

This is where it gets interesting. I knew, for most of my drinking career, that things were out of hand. Things went wrong for me all the time. People told me I drank too much. *I told myself* that I drank too much. So why did I keep drinking?

I'm going to blame numbers.

You may be wondering whether I am still drunk right now. I am not. I obviously blame myself. I failed to get a hold of the problem at every possible juncture. So when I say I blame numbers, I am not trying to place blame outside of me. I am trying to tell you what was happening *inside of me* that made it so hard to quit.

I speak for myself here, but something tells me I might be speaking for you, too: One of the reasons true peace eluded me in my life is that I let a culture of quantification—of precision, of certainty—pull me into a place in my imagination where things actually *could* be settled, permanently. But that place does not exist. Everything really is flux, including our own bodies and minds. There is no part of the states in which I (or you, or anyone else) exist—identity, thoughts, physical body—that has the kind of permanence that even merits having a name. We *are* change. And that, I would like to suggest, is the source of the problem: The stories we tell ourselves with certainty fly in the face of experience itself. In other words, it's all a recipe for cognitive dissonance, and discomfort of every variety. The source of my unhappiness was that even as I somehow knew it wasn't possible, I kept living as if precision weren't just achievable, but desirable. It isn't. It's freedom that we need, and nothing else.

Numbers don't offer freedom. They offer the illusion of certainty. All through high school, I was the number one student in my class until my final year, when I got into college on early acceptance and relaxed a little. What did I conclude from my performance? I concluded that I was the smartest person in my class. What should I have concluded from my performance? That I had been the number one student in my class. Numbers, as I have told you, only contain themselves. To see more in them is to see a mirage.

The same thing happened in college. As I drank my way to oblivion on a regular basis, I managed to chalk up a 3.93/4.00 grade point average at an Ivy League university. What did I conclude from that? That I was smarter than everyone else.

If you're one of the smartest people you've ever met, you are destined to do great things. In the future. More to the point, I had a great facility with numbers, so I trafficked in certainty a lot. Say, for example, you are writing about percentages of this or estimates of that. When you use numbers, which are *precisely what they are*, you can make precise statements. *That stock fell by 7.5 percent. Those MBAs make 30 percent more than the average person.* And when you spend your time talking about precise things, you can easily confuse yourself into thinking that the certainty you feel about them can be extended into other areas of life. Take, for example, the question of whether you are right or wrong when you are fighting with someone about how much you drink. Certainty is a feeling, right? And if you get too used to feeling it because you use too many numbers, you might just make a mistake and invoke that feeling where it does not belong.

My intuitive understanding of mathematics is better than most people's. I say that not to brag but to point out the source of my sense of certainty I had not just about myself but about the fact that the future held great things for me. I wasn't arrogant to the point of intolerance, except when I was, but I was definitely someone who knew what he thought about the things he thought about. I was usually quite *certain* about them. That is, except for what was happening to me at any given moment. Indeed, very few of my certainties had anything to do with what I was doing *right now*. Because it didn't matter. Because everything was going to turn out fine once I got that little drinking problem under control.

If numbers are real, then predictions are real. And if predictions are real, then planning is real. And if planning is real, then the future exists, and you can be excused for not putting your entire focus on what you are doing right now. Alas. The future does not exist. The only thing that exists is the present, and it requires your full attention. If you choose to spend that time drinking, as I did, you end up squandering your entire existence. Poof!

*   *   *

Before I dig deep into the concept of time, I want to talk, for a moment, about causality. I'll return to it in the next few chapters, but I think it's important to make something very clear from the start. The ego is that which ties your consciousness to your body and your mind. It's the part of you that takes credit for things that happen to you. Without the ego, time doesn't need to exist. What do I mean by that? When you try to take credit for something, you claim ownership of something that happened before some other thing. In other words, you assume the existence of time.

I did this, and then that happened as a result.

That, you might say, is the essence of ego itself, the suggestion by anyone—in any circumstance—that something (or someone) was the *cause* of something else. Trapped as we are within our own bodies and minds, the idea of ownership is seductive. We try to take credit for the good things that happen to us, and we try to blame someone else for the bad ones. But the believability of either—*I caused this* or *you caused that*—is predicated on a contracted awareness that tries to pinpoint *precise causes* when, in actuality, such things do not exist. Everybody knows that life is complicated, but we all forget that obvious fact when we want to take credit for something. In those situations, we see causality as clear as day.

But what if there were a higher order to the universe—a fundamental unity, or wholeness? What if the reason everything is happening is simply because of everything that's already happened? I know that sounds complicated, but I would like to suggest that it's a lot less complicated than trying to be *precise* about anything. When we ascribe *this* cause to *that* effect, we are engaging in a wild oversimplification, because this cause *also* has a cause, and that cause, in turn, has its own. Not only that, things don't just have *one* cause. Things happen because of everything that has already happened. If you're looking for a single cause of anything, there is only one, and that is the causeless cause of creation, otherwise known as God. I don't mean to get all religious on you here, by the way. I am simply pointing out that whenever we try to point to one single cause of something, that's both an *indirect* and *unripe* apprehension of the matter at hand, an arbitrary line in the sand, as if all of existence had just started at the very moment of our preferred cause. The only way out of the quagmire is to reject the notion of causation almost entirely, and just accept that things happen because they happen. Especially when you are talking about creation itself. Because creation has no cause. It just happens, spontaneously and without effort. That applies to the creation of the entire universe but also the creative force that flows within each and every one of us. The moment of conception is the ultimate expression of this force, when two universes get together to create a third.

Of course, the above has not stopped us from trying to model everything down to the very last variable. That's where we get the notion of "complex systems." A machine is a complex system. We understand machines, because we invented them, and because they are "closed" systems. But when social scientists speak of "complex systems" in society as if they understand something that the rest of us do not, they really don't. If they did, they wouldn't be trying to model them. Because life cannot be modeled. The folks who brought us chaos theory were onto something when they thought they saw an order behind the apparent chaos of complex systems, but then they made the mistake of trying to make that chaos submit to mathematics. Why was it a mistake? Because mathematics will never be able to grasp the biggest picture of all, the system behind the system. There is not order in chaos. There is a higher order that only appears to us as chaos because we are trying to grasp it using inadequate means. The challenge isn't to model that system. The challenge is to understand that it cannot be modeled. The challenge is to find that unity *inside of ourselves*.

I was talking to Joey about this—the fact that the answer lies not without, but within—and she pointed out that all of our efforts to *explain* things are really just storytelling. I'm okay with storytelling; it's what I do. Because you can't see inside my mind, and I can't see inside yours—otherwise known as the challenge of indeterminacy—we resort to language in the hopes that we can share our ideas with other people. We use stories to communicate with *each other*. In doing so, we create *systems of thought* that seek to wrangle our experiences into something *shareable*. Language is what allows that to happen.

But there's one thing that lies outside the realm of storytelling and of language—existence itself. There is no *story* that can adequately capture the nature of existence. It just *is*. If you want to get in touch with your Self, you cannot do it with stories, and you have no need for *this is what caused that*. More to the point, when you seek to know the Self, it isn't just concepts like time and causality that miss the mark, it is *words themselves*. Every single thing we tell ourselves about ourselves—either out loud or inside our minds—is a distraction from the matter at hand, which is *be-ing*.

I'm not saying that we should throw all of our systems out the window. They're the means by which we communicate and cooperate with each other, every single day. We wouldn't be able to understand each other without them. When it comes to understanding *our Selves*, though, the systems that we have created—language, science, even religion—can only get in the way. Because you cannot *explain* the nature of existence, even to your Self. You can only experience it. It can't be shared and it can't be *told*, because there is no *story* that will do it justice. The experience of existence also sits outside of time. The former has no need for the latter, because experience, as we all know, happens only in the now.

Am I contradicting myself? First, I spend all this time telling you to choose words over numbers, and now I'm suggesting that we need to let go of words, too, if we ever want to understand ourselves? I see it more as an ongoing process of *involution*. Numbers can't get at the essence of anything, whereas words can get at the essence of pretty much anything but the Self. If we can shake off the urge to quantify our lives, we can start to experience (and to understand) them again. Once we do that, the only thing left is to stop talking to ourselves so much. And if we can do *that*, we might just be able to hear the voice of God telling us that there is nothing to worry about, because everything really is okay, right here, and right now.

*   *   *

I'm about to start talking about time and how it's a trap. And in doing so, I am going to talk about the past and the future as if they are different things. But I am also going to make the case that neither of them exists, and that's why the title of this chapter is "The *Trap* of Time" and not "The *Traps* of Time." Because it's one thing, that doesn't exist, that's such a powerful trap for the human mind.

I know that I am not the first person to be tackling this topic. And while I have, at times, contemplated other people's notions of time, I never really *understood* it in the truest sense of the word. It took a quarantine to make that happen, along with a couple of well-timed books that lit my brain on fire. (In a good way.) What follows, then, is what I have come to understand about time. It is not what someone told me, or what I read somewhere. It is something that I finally figured out, for myself.

So . . . people invented numbers. If you're going to use numbers simply to ascertain quantity, you can do so in the present without having to leave *now:*

How many are there?

There's nothing wrong with that question. Sometimes, you just need to know.

I'll return to a bunch of the good stuff science has done for us in a later chapter, but I would like to set those things aside and ask you to think, for a moment, not about the things that numbers and science have given us, but about the ways that *we think about numbers.* I'm not talking about the fact that it took numbers to build the computer I am typing on. I am talking about the numbers that drift through our minds, each and every day.

The thing that numbers do that traps us into taking our attention out of the present is that they induce us to obsess about change—progress—toward some future that promises to eclipse *this* moment or at least render it less important than some future moment that will surely be worth the wait.

If this, then that.

The simple act of ascertaining quantities can be done by anyone. But if you want someone to really take you out of the present, you need someone who knows the black magic of mathematics or statistics or science. That's when numbers really start to cast their spell, when they are promising you *change*.

You don't *need* numbers to contemplate change. But numbers make it easy, and numbers make it addictive. If I can only add one more to this pile, then I will have *pile+1*. If I can only reduce this crushing debt by a dollar, I will only owe the bank *loan–1*. Things will be better when that happens.

Or they won't. Numbers can also be horrible for your mood, if you let the wrong numbers get inside your head. You want to know the best place to keep your eyes out for a number trap? Watch out for experts. Okay, fine, not *all* experts—just the ones that try to predict things. I think you will be surprised, however, just how many of them there are. Go search the *New York Times* website for the phrase "experts predict." I predict that the results will shock you. I checked in December 2020, and the word *expert* had shown up more than 9,000 times in the newspaper in 2020 alone. That's almost 30 times a day, up from just 17 times a day in 2019. How many experts can one paper cite?

Do you see what happened there? I started using numbers, and my sentences suddenly started to seem as if I was telling you something *real*. But was I? I would have communicated much more meaning if I said that we are watching a great irony play out in front of us. Do you think we can predict the future? If so, you trust experts. But why did the pandemic throw the world into chaos? Because almost *no one saw it coming*. So . . . in the wake of a wrenching societal experience that no one saw coming, the newspaper has done the unexpected itself: Instead of reducing their reliance on an "expert" class of fortune-tellers that didn't warn us about a plague, they have turned to them with even more frequency, including on matters about the plague they didn't even see coming in the first place. Note the lack of numbers in what I just said.

Why are we constantly trying to predict the future? Well, for starters, we got drunk (metaphorically) on our ability to predict things like the weather, because that was helpful, and started trying to predict every single thing that could happen, which is not. But the main reason we do it is that we are uncomfortable in the present.

Consider the person who wants to predict what the stock market is going to do tomorrow. That way, they can place a bet on it, and get rich. At the end of tomorrow. They are not rich today, but if they are right, they will be rich by the end of tomorrow. But what's so bad about today? It's when everything is happening. Life is *now*, not tomorrow. As the saying goes, tomorrow never comes. So why do we keep insisting that it does? Because we have forgotten about today. I blame the numbers here again. Our faith in them convinced us that we could do this. Our faith in them led us to believe that we could calculate *probabilities* and *reduce risk*. But have you ever stopped to wonder what we mean when we say that? Reduce the risk of *what*? Something that *might* happen? Why are we not spending our energy focusing on the thing that is most definitely going to happen, because it is happening *right now*?

Having lost our ability to make decisions in the present, we have outsourced it to "experts" who claim to be able to predict the future. I think that we should stop listening to what all the fortune-tellers *are predicting* and start paying attention to what the specialists *are doing*. Specialists are people with skills. Specialists are people who know how to *do* something in the present. Specialists don't try to scare people with vague warnings about impending doom. That's something that *experts* do. A huge part of our modern predicament is that we are listening to too many *experts* and not trying to become *specialists*.

Another way to think about it: Specialists are people with highly developed *skills*. They have honed their craft and learned something to the point that they know how *to act* when the situation calls for their particular skill set. My friend J. C. Spender recently sent me the *Introduction to the Routledge Handbook of Philosophy of Skill and Expertise*. In the section on "Skill in the History of Eastern Philosophy," the authors write that in the Eastern tradition, "practical knowledge embodied in skill is our principal cognitive achievement." They're talking about *flow*. "Thought and skill are not necessarily at odds," they write, "but skill is necessarily immediate and spontaneous." Skill is craft refined to the point of flow. By comparison, our modern notion of *expertise* is mostly hot air.

If you ask me, Westerners have utterly failed to understand the goal of refining craft into skill into flow, and are inappropriately satisfied with our own paltry version, which is the decidedly less practical *experts talking about something*. We have far too many talkers, and far too few doers in our society, to our collective detriment.

Setting that aside, why do we spend so much time talking about the future when we could be talking (if we should even be talking at all, and not just *doing*) about the things we need to do *right now*, to address the challenges we are facing *right now*?

Worrying about the future is pointless, because it doesn't exist. There is only now. Let's say we will have some problem to deal with down the road. We can deal with that . . . down the road. The whole *preparing for the future* thing is a red herring.

Don't get me wrong: We should obviously prepare for the things that we can be sure are coming, like next winter or the next financial crisis (we never do this, even though we keep saying that we will). But preparing for some theoretical thing that might not happen at all? Why on earth should we spend time preparing for that? Whatever time we do set aside for *preparing for future things* should be applied to the *inevitable*, instead of things that are merely *possible*. Because anything is possible, including the possibility that the thing that you are predicting might not happen at all.

> *"I have heard that anything is possible in God's*
> *creation, and I always bear that in mind."*[3]

—Sri Ramakrishna

On the same day in 1985, the following three things happened to my friend Andy, in this order:

> *He found out that his testicular cancer, for which he'd been*
> *undergoing chemo treatments for five years, was gone, for good.*
> *He proposed to his girlfriend. He'd been waiting until he was*
> *in the clear, because he didn't want to saddle her with a dying*
> *husband.*
> *That afternoon, he found out that he'd gotten HIV through a blood*
> *transfusion.*

How does your worst day stack up against that? Andy and I were talking about the fact that since he was a child, he has lived life like he only had a few years left to live, because *that's what the experts kept telling him.* He's pushing sixty now, and HIV doesn't appear to have slowed him down a bit. Andy lives in the now, in the space of infinite possibility. He lives without fear. Nothing is going to kill him but old age.

Now that we're on the subject, let's talk about prediction for a second. Sure, the universe often complies, and lets us predict a few days out, just for kicks. I mean, why not? It's kind of fun to predict things, even if it isn't quite as fun as simply living in the moment, right here, right now.

But that's where the universe draws the line. What about next year? Nope. Next month? Nope. Next week? Nope, save for things we agree to schedule and a few easier-to-predict-although-still-essentially-impossible things, like the weather. When I say it's "essentially impossible," what I'm saying is that while we might be able to predict some things using broad strokes, we cannot predict, with precision and consistency, the essential attributes about tomorrow's weather today. Why? Because we can't, that's why.

The main reason that people are susceptible to the traps of time is that life is hard, and it would be nice (for all of us) if it were a little less hard. You know, the way it used to be. Or the way it will be at some future date. Thinking about time is simply an exercise in wishfulness, the all-too-human desire for things to be a little better than they are right now.

The current moment is a perfect example of that. On the one hand, you have the people who won't stop talking about the way things used to be, before the virus brought our seemingly predictable lives to a grinding halt. Of course, we now know that they weren't predictable at all, and that's why so many people are in shock.

Our capacity for wishful thinking has always had its most shining moments when things go wrong. When the illusion of predictability is replaced by something utterly unexpected. That's when we get scared enough to start asking questions that are, at root, a desire to turn back the clock and try again. "We don't want this to be happening," we tell ourselves, and then start asking ourselves questions in the hope that maybe the mere raising of such will somehow make the present disappear, to be replaced by the past. When we are startled by the *improbable*, we respond by asking for the *impossible*.

Why can't things be the way they used to be? Because they can't. Rather, because they aren't. Things are the way they are.

Why can't things have turned out some other way? Things didn't turn out another way because they didn't; they turned out this way.

What would have happened if we had done this, and not that? This is known as a counterfactual, and it's pointless. Because we didn't, and here we are.

What about the future? That's where the futurists come in. They're not stuck in the past, like all those poor saps. They are pointing the way to more glorious times ahead. They know the signposts toward Success, and they will take us down the road of Progress.

But it's just the same problem, facing in a different direction. The future isn't here yet. And it never will be. There is only now.

What are you going to do right now?

That is all you need to ask. Because there is nothing else you ever need to do.

*   *   *

Do you want an actual example of what happens when you make a mistake and get stuck on it rather than figuring out what you should do right now? I've got one for you: Once upon a time, I got married before realizing some fundamental incompatibilities, felt trapped, and decided—in a moment of pure genius—that the way out was through alcohol. I then spent nearly a decade coming to pieces and became a drunk. Then we had a child, which should have stopped me in my tracks, but I just kept drinking until my wife finally got so tired of it all that she left me.

Before that, in the summer of 2008, when my daughter was three months shy of being born, my father sat me down one day when we were at the family cottage in Ontario and told me that he was going to die pretty soon, maybe within a few weeks. He'd been sick for a year, and the doctors hadn't been able to figure out what was wrong with him. It turns out that he'd had some sort of blood infection, but by the time they figured that out, he was too far gone.

Anyway, when he told me about his impending death, I was in the midst of another of my futile attempts to stop drinking. When he told me, the next thing I did was crack open a beer. And then, sufficiently buffered out of the pain of the present, I told him that I didn't want to talk about it, that I wouldn't hear of such things. He tried to get me to listen, but I refused. A few days later, my wife and I flew back to New York from Canada. A few days after that, he was dead.

I'd passed on having the last real conversation I would ever have with my father in favor of a beer. There I was, in 2008, about to become a father for the first (and only) time, and I was carrying three crises with me at once: alcoholism, a broken marriage, and a career that meant nothing to me. Wrap them all up and you have a life without purpose. If you've got all that going for you, you might not be able to hear your father trying to tell you that he loves you at the same time that he's saying goodbye.

Where do you even start if you want to let such colossal personal failures go? The answer lies in forgiveness. You need to forgive yourself. And how does one figure out how to do such a thing? Well, you try everything, from Alcoholics Anonymous to outpatient and inpatient rehab to one-on-one talk therapy to dabbling in other kinds of drugs, just in case the mistake wasn't in taking drugs, but simply taking *the wrong drugs*. Science demands evidence, so if you're going to do science on the self, you need to keep on experimenting.

I'm just kidding. Sort of. I have consumed almost all of the drugs in my life, save for the ones you inject and the really addictive ones made by Big Pharma. It turns out that none of them contain truth. But I know that from a process of elimination, aka lived experience. I just had to be sure. Jim James may have done the same thing. He speaks for both of us in the My Morning Jacket song "Outta My System."

But it's not just me. There's a reason that alcoholism is so prevalent in American society, and it's because we are so busy talking about the future and the past—traveling through time—that we've lost our ability to be comfortable in the present. And if you don't want to be present, all you need to do is grab a drink. Some people drink to excess because they can't let the past go. That's what AA will tell you. But there must be just as many who do so because our culture of anticipation has left them so antsy for tomorrow to arrive that they no longer care about being present today. Happy hour on Friday isn't just about wiping the week's work away. It's about telling yourself that your weekend is going to be awesome. As long as that hangover doesn't slow you down too much.

There's a stop along the train route into alcoholism that they call the "Fuckits." That's when nothing seems to matter anymore. You don't want to drink, because you know that drinking has taken over your life. But you also don't see how you're ever going to stop drinking, because it's got you in a straitjacket embrace. That's when you say, "Fuck it. I am going to have a drink." You're close to the bottom when that happens. Because that's when you drink all the time, when you can no longer come up with a reason not to do so. It's when you lose faith in your ability to make the right decision, so you don't even bother anymore.

Fuck it.

In late 2011, my wife told me she was leaving me and moved out of our house in Philadelphia. We both moved into the same building in Greenpoint, Brooklyn. But I kept drinking. I even knocked on her door one night and asked to sleep on her couch, because I couldn't find the keys to my apartment in my drunkenness. "Fuck it," I thought. "What does it matter? Everything is fucked up already anyway." A few weeks after we moved, she served me with divorce papers. She also told me that if I didn't quit drinking, then she would sue for full custody. She imposed clarity on me from the outside. It might be the best thing that she ever did for me. At that point, I didn't care about myself, my relationship, my career, or my life. But I did care about that little girl. I've heard it said that having a child makes you realize that you are not the center of the universe anymore. I'm not sure that's true, but it can feel like that at times. She made me realize that I was making a bad choice. That's when I realized that I needed to stay alive, and I quit drinking on the spot.

So where was I? Oh, right: The past does not exist and the future doesn't, either. Like the past, it's nice to think about. The numbers do always seem to look a little better in the future, too. Unless you're an expert trying to scare us, in which case the numbers look horrible. See what numbers are doing here? They are being used as tools of worry, the weaponry of anxiety and the language of concern. And it's all imaginary.

We don't need to worry or be anxious or be concerned.

We just need to figure out what we need to do right now.

The future will take care of itself. It always has, and it always will. It doesn't need our help. We seduce ourselves into thinking that it does, though, by using numbers that seem to require us to do something.

If I do this, then that will happen.

Maybe it will, maybe it won't.

Again: It's the numbers' fault. Better said: We do it to ourselves, using numbers. Either way, the numbers trick us into thinking that the future needs our attention. Our quantified reality tells us that it needs to be counted. Actually, it *demands* that we count it, under threat that the future *requires* that we do so. But that's a lie. It's the trap. The future doesn't require anything. It doesn't need anything at all. Because it doesn't exist.

The only thing that exists is *now*. And the only thing that *now* requires of you is that you decide something, that you make a choice. If you feel you need to count something in order to make that choice, knock yourself out, I won't stop you. But do it quick, because now won't sit around and wait for you forever. Before you know it, it will be the past, and the opportunity will be lost. And then you'll be thinking about the past again, and wishing you'd just done what you knew you had to do.

The hysteria that has consumed so many of us during the COVID pandemic is one caused by the traps of time. Yes, I know people are dying. And that's a horrible thing. But for the rest of us, the ones who aren't dying, we are spending *way too much time* talking about things past and things yet to come. These are the traps that we keep falling into and, as often as not, it's numbers that are the bait.

The same thing happened during the presidential election, when we got stuck in another of our periodic orgies of listening to people talk about other people counting something, in real time, for days. Consider the sheer insanity of the whole "pathways to victory" conversation. Once we had voted, there was only one thing that was going to happen, and that was that the votes would be counted, someone would win, and someone would lose. But because we cannot look away from the numbers, we agreed on a mass delusion that there were still countless possibilities coming our way. Pre-vote, it was true that anything could happen. Post-vote, though, all of those possibilities collapsed into a single result. At that point, only one thing was going to happen, and all we had to do was wait and see what it was. Once the vote was in, the outcome was fixed. I understand that most people were antsy to hear the result, and, not being able to enjoy the uncertainty, looked to their media personality of choice to drone on, ad nauseam, about their future fantasy outcome. But you can't masturbate to a fixed number, can you? If you want to keep the excitement high, you have to pretend that all sorts of possibilities still exist, even when they don't.

It's scary out there. And when you're scared, you kind of wish you were somewhere else. Rather, you wish you were in some other time, other than the one you are in right now. And so we created the past and the future as a place to hide inside our minds, so that we didn't have to come to terms with the present, which is right here in front of our faces.

Time is nothing but a way of thinking. It is actually a system of thinking, built on top of a number of assumptions, that has manifested into social structures and institutions and ways of behaving in the world. The reason that we measure anything, whether it is time or distance or anything else, is that the very act of measurement offers us a false sense of certainty and safety in the face of the unknown. What we're seeking is unity, the thing that ties it all together, the *equation* that can tell us why things happen and what's going to happen next. But we can't measure everything, no matter how hard we try. We're also looking in the wrong place. Unity isn't outside of us, waiting to be measured. It is on the inside, waiting to be felt.

*   *   *

There's a line near the end of *Harry Potter and the Sorcerer's Stone* when Harry is pondering the lure of the Stone itself.

"You know, the Stone really was not such a wonderful thing," Dumbledore tells him. "As much money and life as you could want! The two things most human beings would choose above all—the trouble is, humans do have a knack of choosing precisely those things that are worst for them."[4]

When it comes to life, Dumbledore is talking about wanting *the future*. When it comes to money, he is talking about wanting *more*. We don't need either of those things. We simply need to be here now. You are the universe, you are the path, you are the destination. It's all happening, right here and right now. There's a reason that the saying "be here now" resonates. Because it's true. Everything that's true *sounds a little heavier* than anything that isn't, and that's because it carries the weight of truth itself. Bullshit doesn't weigh a thing.

I missed much of the first three years of my daughter's life because I was drinking on a daily basis. And I barely even realized what was happening, because I wasn't present at all. As we wait, with bated breath, for everything great that's just around that corner of time, we miss the sheer infinitude of that which is happening *right now*. I quit drinking when my daughter was three, which made it possible to be present for her. But then I replaced the alcohol with certainty and started telling everyone else what they were doing wrong, just because I had finally done something right.

You know the feeling, right? When you figure something out, you feel like you know more than the people around you, when the only person you know more than is the person that you used to be.

CHAPTER 7

You Can't Measure Freedom

Divination is one of the most
imprecise branches of magic.[1]

—Professor McGonagall,
Harry Potter and the Prisoner of Azkaban

I made quite a mess of things, didn't I?

What was wrong with me? What was wrong with my thinking? I am baffled by the fact that I was able to spend the majority of my fifty years on earth thinking that I was right, even when I was wrong. How can a person be capable of that?

I would like to submit that it's because of our culture of precision and our unrelenting quest for certainty. It's because we delude ourselves into thinking that the things we invented—numbers and science—hold the secret to our Selves. I'm talking about the Precision Paradox here, people. We have come to believe our own bullshit.

I'm not saying that my behavior was *society's* fault; I am simply saying that there are reasons that we think the things that we do that lie outside of conscious choice. The most obvious one is that it's what we were taught. But that's just skimming the surface of things. A large part of how we think is embedded in language itself. While it's nice to think that our social institutions are built on foundations of conscious intention, those intentions are just the tip of the iceberg poking out of the water while the assumptions implicit in the language we use to express them hover underneath, gigantic but unseen.

That's what drives philosophers, right? The desire to understand why we see things the way that we do? But it's not just *what* we think that matters. Because that's only the tip of another iceberg, which rests on top of the much larger, but submerged, question of *how* we think. If your grasp of reality rests on the assumption that this is all *one* thing, then you will seek the fundamental unity behind an apparent diversity. Come at it from the other direction, though, and you end up trying to catalogue the universe. If you start with distinctions, it won't be long before value judgments rear their ugly head.

I speak from experience. From my current vantage point, I can see that I spent far too much of my life trying to separate right from wrong. More to the point, I spent my time searching for things to be right about. Why did I think that everything was so black-and-white? Why am I not alone in this? Why are we always arguing—about everything?

Before I get into what you might call the *current* state of affairs in the world, I want to talk a little bit more about how we think. Because it's how we think that got us into this mess in the first place.

There's an out-of-print book called *The Kundalini Experience*, by Lee Sannella. The *Kundalini Shakti* is the *serpent power*, a form of psychospiritual energy. It is the energy of consciousness. A kundalini experience is what happens when you become capable of accessing or harnessing that energy. In other words, when you become *enlightened*.

Sannella makes a very important point, which is that, even as we accumulate *wealth*, the West still can't seem to get *spirituality* right because of certain burdens we have inherited from our forefathers, language being first and foremost among them. "Language structures our experience," he writes. "Once we have accepted a particular model as a faithful reflection of reality, we cease to think of it in terms of a model and instead equate it with reality."[2]

For English-speaking cultures, our language model is effectively *closed* to a kundalini experience, and that's why we are such a disconnected people. Worse yet, the triumph of capitalism is threatening the spirituality of cultures and languages that have historically been more *open* in that regard. As capitalism spreads its tentacles around the world, spirituality is harder and harder to come by.

What I learned in writing about McKinsey and the Harvard Business School is that their models—*any* models—are inherently incapable of grasping Reality itself. They talk of creating *value*, but they do not understand *the deeper meaning of the word*. True value is not something that can be quantified. It simply is. Why is that friendship valuable to you? You cannot count your way to meaning.

But it's not just them. Our entire culture has become *disenchanted* by virtue of our obsession with reductionism. From that flows our obsessive individualism, as well as our refusal to countenance the notion that measurement-based science will never be able to explain the nature of reality. We are trapped in our own egos, individually and collectively, insisting that we are right (and happy) while at the same time desperately seeking the meaning that we have been unable to find.

The reason that we can't find meaning is that our Western values, attitudes, and approaches to life—all of which are embedded in *our language*—have rendered us incapable of contemplating the very nature of existence. If you start by trying to break everything down so that you can measure it, you are never going to be able to see the whole.

*   *   *

I know there are a lot of people out there who call themselves *scientists*. And I don't want to ruin anybody's day. I know that most people have good intentions and that most scientists think they're working on important things. The problem is that we have confused complicated things with important things. So let me be clear about this: I am not making an anti-science argument. I am making an anti-measurement argument. Not all measurement, of course. Rather, I am against our knee-jerk desire to measure things before we have even begun to understand them. I am against data for the sake of data, when it tells us nothing. Good science does not have to rest on a foundation of measurement. Good science can be based on experience, method, and generalization without ever having to measure a single thing.

Why does so much of what modern scientists work on seem so *complicated*? I'd like to suggest that it's because it doesn't have much to do with how to live a life. Existence is pretty simple when it comes down to it, even if it's almost impossible to express it in words. The only things that are really complicated are things that man has created, like machines, institutions, political systems, and delusions.

In the West, we believe that reality, or nature, lies outside of us. That is, it is *external*, and so the means for controlling it are *external* as well. We see nature as a machine, run by laws, and we have embarked on an endless quest to classify the universe so that we can decipher those laws and then do things with them. Our goal: to control external nature, so as to control everything.

Other cultures—particularly the yogis—believe that the external world is just the gross form of the internal, or subtle world. Because the finer is always the cause and the grosser is the effect, the yogi seeks to manipulate our internal world—to conquer the mind—so as to control the external one. Their goal: to control internal nature, so as to control everything.

Ultimately, both are right, because in the end, there is no such thing as internal or external. Those are just boundaries, fictitious limitations that don't actually exist. So both "externalists" and "internalists" will meet at the extreme end of their knowledge, where the distinction between the two dissolves. "Just as a physicist, when he pushes his knowledge to its limits, finds it melting away into metaphysics, so a metaphysician will find that what he calls mind and matter are but apparent distinctions, the reality being One," writes Swami Vivekananda. "The end and aim of all science is to find the unity, the One out of which the manifold is being manufactured, that One existing as many."[3]

And here's the punch line: When the two methods meet, there is one last step to get to Truth. But it cannot be measured. Because you cannot measure the infinite. You can, if you are lucky, experience it. But you will never be able to measure it, because there is no instrument other than the human brain that is capable of measuring the smallest of the small or the largest of the large. There's a reason that we say both "infinitely small" and "infinitely large"— because no matter which end of the spectrum you're looking at, our tools of measurement will eventually lose their purchase on the question at hand. We have built a lot of machines that control some aspect of the external world, but no machine can do everything. The promise of measurement-based science ends at the doorway to the infinite, because the next step is called Unity, which can't be measured at all. It is now, and it contains everything. You could also call it God, or love, with the common *denominator* being that you cannot measure those, either.

In the end, measurement-based approaches to grasping reality can do a lot of things. But they cannot go all the way. We need to rely more on the science of experience—one that acknowledges the subtleties of existence, the ones that we can't and won't ever be able to measure—if we want to do that. The good news is that it already exists—the spiritual masters call it Brahmavidya—and all that's required to "study" it is to learn to look within. The reason that the universe is miraculous is not that it's the world's greatest machine. The reason that the universe is miraculous is that anything can happen. Everything is possibility. Anything is choice. So for anything to happen, everything must always be happening. Thankfully—thank God!—it is.[4]

*　　*　　*

Let me carve out the big exception here before I go any further. When it comes to large groups of people, we can use measurement to our advantage. Jeff Bezos has done it with logistics at Amazon. The medical community has figured out a bunch of stuff about how to extend people's lives when they're flirting with the end. Urban planners have figured out things like sewer systems (very valuable!), train schedules, the right number of subway cars, how to build a bridge that won't collapse (although they don't always get that right), and more. So measurement can be very valuable when it comes to things that have to do with large numbers of people. Say, for example, you were looking for a vaccine to stop a plague. I think the best way to eliminate the devastation of plagues is to live healthier lives, but in the absence of that, measurement-based science might be able to help in the clutch with a vaccine.

Measurement can also be useful when manipulating inanimate matter. All of the materials sciences, in fact, have done much for humanity. At times, they have also hurt humanity—see: plastics—but I don't want to get in an argument with you about that. It's nice to have a house that doesn't blow away in a windstorm, and I do enjoy the clothes that keep me warm in winter. And the containers that

I keep my kombucha in. We use flip-top bottles, so as to keep the carbonation in. Because energy doesn't like to be trapped. We know that, and sometimes use it to our advantage. But sometimes we don't.

Anyway, enough about inanimate stuff. Let's talk about people. The way that science is conceived of and practiced in the West can be helpful when trying to manage the needs of large populations, but it is much *less* useful when it comes to individual lives. We already know how to live a life, and there is nothing in it that requires measurement, calculation, or regression analyses. We don't need any *scientific* rules or laws about choice. We just need to use our common sense. We need to realize that there really is nothing objective about anything we do. Everything is filtered through the lens of our experience.

A science concerned only with quantity and based exclusively on measurement is inherently unable to deal with experience, quality, or values.[5]

—Fritjof Capra, author of *The Tao of Physics*

The measurement community is fixated on the belief that objectivity is something attainable, given the right experimental constraints. But that is simply not true. Everything is subjective. Until we give up the illusion of objectivity, we will never be able to properly investigate the only thing that matters, which is the Self. In the meantime, we delude ourselves into the belief that we are looking outside of us when we look at anything. We are not. It is the act of looking that matters, not the thing we think we are looking at. We need to realize that the seeker is the sought. There is nothing else. It's so hard, because the one thing that the eye is incapable of seeing is itself. The trick, as it were, is to *realize* the Self, to stumble on the only truth worth knowing, which is that we exist. All other valuable insights derive from that. Anything short of self-realization is illusory.

Here's a thought. Have you ever considered the fact that our culture of measurement can't tell us what we *want* to happen? It can only tell us what *seems likely* to happen. We should have been spending far more time on the first and much less time on the second. Because we can *make things happen*, and the more time we spend trying to *predict* things, the less time we spend trying to *create* things. Instead of focusing on the fact that anything can happen, we are trying to predict what will happen. There may be no better way to squander the moment than that. You cannot pounce on opportunity when you are seeking to exert control. The former requires the absence of the latter.

Not only that, but there is also the idea of the causeless cause, the thing that happens because it is in its very nature to happen, a spontaneous occurrence without effort. People act spontaneously when they are in flow. You can call that insight, the creative impulse, or you can call it something else—love, kindness, generosity—but whatever you call it, you can't *predict* it. Some things happen just because they happen, not because something else *caused* them to happen. That includes the universe. And you. Yes, I know, for you to exist, your parents had to, as my daughter likes to say, "do the business." But conception can't be forced, or scheduled. Conception happens when it happens. Remember, you are the greatest idea that anyone has ever had. But great ideas can't be scheduled, either. They just happen when they happen. Are you seeing a pattern here? Every single thing that is amazing about being alive—including the very start of it—is not something you can predict, using some kind of algorithm. Why? Because you cannot quantify the most important variable of all, which is love, which is only available in the present. When you try to predict something, you lose your purchase on now.

Or, put another way, everything is the result of everything that has already happened, and *everything is always happening*. When people aren't trying to *make something happen*, but simply *existing*, they are in a state of receptivity, and make decisions based on *what is going on right now*, not what has happened in the past. The science of measurement doesn't know what to do with *now*, because it's too big to be captured in a formula.

*   *   *

My father was an obstetrician. But as with all doctors, everyone considered him a doctor of everything. One of my favorite things about him was that no matter what your ailment, he had only one piece of medical advice: "Gargle with salt and water."

Sore elbow? Gargle with salt and water.

Stuffy nose? Gargle with salt and water.

When I started getting acne, mind you, he told me that it was because of "impure thoughts."

Neither Joey nor M. ever met Dr. Don McDonald. I have already mentioned that my father died just a few months before M. was born. I dedicated my first book to the two of them.

After he died, things went haywire for a while. My drinking got worse. While the arrival of M. centered me for a short time, before long I was back to drinking heavily. My behavior during that time is the most regrettable of my life. To my ex-wife: I am sorry for putting you through that. You didn't deserve it. You have a beautiful heart, and I stomped all over it. I thank God for the time we spent together and the child that you brought into this world. And I thank you for having the fortitude to endure me for as long as you did.

I'm not exactly sure why I couldn't stop drinking, to tell you the truth. It wasn't like I was trying to kill myself. I mean, it was in the sense that any addiction is the slow road to suicide. I'm just saying that I hadn't thrown in the towel entirely. At least not at first. The best explanation that I can come up with is that I never got to know myself well enough to care about what I was doing to myself. There's a reason that they put a hood on people when they're about to execute them—because it's not fair to make the executioner look into the condemned man's eyes. Well, what if you put a hood on yourself? What if you couldn't see your own face anymore when you looked in the mirror?

Ah yes, mirrors. And mirroring. I have, of late, come to the understanding that pretty much everything that we find fault with in the world is, in fact, just a mirror of something that is not right within ourselves.

But I am not the only one who has labored under the mistaken understanding that the answer (or explanation) lay outside of myself. In an "evidence-based" society—where we don't believe something until someone *proves* it to us, often with *numbers*—we long ago lost sight of the fact that we are the sum of our own decisions. When you don't like the way something is going, the person you should be angry with (if you should be angry at all) is yourself. You are the one who got yourself into every situation that you've ever been in. The person responsible for your predicament is *you*. It's a fundamental part of experience that almost everyone forgets.

(Of course, there are exceptions, including unprovoked violence, and completely irrational behavior. I am talking about our day-to-day here—the things we choose to do and the people we choose to blame when things don't go the way we want them to.)

This might seem like I am going on a bit of a detour here, but I am not. The reason we find it so easy to blame other people for how we feel is that we have fallen for the central illusion of science, which is that we can predict things. While we may actually be able to do so in laboratory experiments, when we apply the concepts of *cause* and *effect* to our own lives, we are engaging in a wild over-simplification. When it comes to human behavior, one thing most certainly does not lead to another. The reason that you did what you did is that you chose to do so, not that someone else *made you do it.* When we choose to believe that we can *blame* someone else for our own behavior, we are effectively arguing that we *had no choice* in the matter. But that's simply not true. You can do whatever you want to do. No one else is in charge of you.

He yelled at me, so I yelled at him.

That's incorrect.

He yelled at you, and then you chose to yell at him in return.

By going all-in on science, we have gone all-in on a way of thinking that allows us to give ourselves a pass on our behavior because someone else did something before we did what we did. At least that's how it always worked for me. When I did something wrong, it was because you did something wrong first. While it may help some people loosen up, what alcohol did for me was allow me to build boundaries around myself. With those in place, I lost the ability to engage in the lives of the people around mc, as if I were walking around inside a force field that let everything in but the one thing that mattered, which is love.

The good news? Don McDonald lives on in my daughter. She definitely has his twinkle in her eyes. And he would have adored Joey. Why? Because she would have appreciated—and laughed at—all of his jokes. She does it every day, when I pass some of his classics on to her and my child. Dr. Duff diagnosed some impure thoughts not that long ago, in fact.

Recently, M. was in the kitchen with Joey. She had a sore throat.

"You know what Dr. Don would tell you to do, right?" Joey asked her.

"Gargle with salt and water," said The Lady.

Thanks, Dad. Your universal prescription is still in force.

*   *   *

Let's talk about history for a second, shall we? Three of the books that I have written could be characterized as *histories*. Looking back, I think I made a fundamental mistake in all: I bought into the notion of causality, and told stories where one thing led to another. They weren't completely off point—those things *were* followed by those other things—but I relied on the idea of causality too much. I am not writing any more books like that.

Of course, that doesn't mean that the study of history can't be helpful in trying to figure out where we took a wrong turn. It works both on an individual level (that is, assessing the outcomes of your own decisions) and on a collective one (when we try to figure out where we all went wrong together). There is a lot in this book about the places where I went wrong, all by myself.

What's the worst decision I've ever made? None of them. I'm still here, aren't I?

What's the worst decision we've made as a group? After much deliberation on this subject, I think I'm going to say it's when we took the measuring tools of Western science and began to use them to try to understand ourselves.

In his delightful book *Balthasar's Odyssey*, set in the year 1665, the writer Amin Maalouf suggests that this has been going on *for centuries*.

> Numerical value! I get angry whenever I hear the notion mentioned! Instead of trying to understand the significance of words my contemporaries prefer to calculate the value of the letters that make them up. And these they manipulate to suit their own ends—adding, subtracting, dividing, and multiplying, and always ending up with a figure that will astonish, reassure or terrify them. And so human thought is diluted, and human reason weakened and dissolved in superstition. . . . A curse on numbers and those who make use of them![6]

Anyway, Western science, as we have discussed, is built upon a foundation of experiments. And scientists gather the results of those experiments, typically in data form, in something called *statistics*. Statistics are just a bunch of numbers.

Scientists scour those numbers and then pronounce their *findings*. In the early days, scientists had freer rein, and just said whatever they wanted and called it science. These days, even if society as a whole kneels at the altar of science, there are more people watching, so they try to bluff their way through it using jargon like correlation, causation, and margin of error.

Again: If you're dealing with things like metal, not people, it's perfectly reasonable to use statistics to find out what the *average* outcome will be. That's how they predict the weather, inasmuch as you want to call what weather *forecasters* do *prediction*. (It's more like educated guessing.) But if you are doing *science* in the context of people, I am going to have to ask you to put down the calculator and step away from the Bunsen burner.

An overreliance on statistics leads to a lack of trust. How so? Well, we all make decisions as individuals, yes? Very few of us consider ourselves *average* in any sense of the word. But when we are persuaded to think of other people in terms of aggregates and averages—you make *more* or *less* than the average person, you weigh *more* or *less* than other people as tall as you, you run *faster* or *slower* than the average marathoner—we replace others' humanity with data. And in modern society, we treat almost everyone that we don't know as data. We know them by their numbers.

What percentage of people from the political party that's not your own are as smart as you?

What's the latest way to analyze other people's failings?

If you believe in the science-by-measurement worldview, *and* you believe that it can be extended into the human realm, then you basically believe, by definition, that other people *are data points*. If you believe in the interconnectedness of everything, other people are *you*. If we all had faith, we'd trust each other, because I am you and you are me. But because we don't, we lack trust. When scientists do experiments, their colleagues and peers *demand* evidence. Why? Because they don't trust each other. We have taken their lead, and extended that lack of trust into society itself. It isn't such a stretch, mind you. The reason it's so easy not to believe others is that we don't believe ourselves. Why? Because we define ourselves with those very same numbers, and numbers are empty. The existential emptiness of modern life has an anchor made out of data.

Of course, you can use statistics to understand population trends. How many people are having babies and such. When the early French statisticians invented the tracking of people using numbers, they were trying to get a hold of the thing called *society*. People in large numbers can be a little . . . unpredictable . . . so it's not such a bad idea to see if there are some things that we can predict. If everybody gets pregnant during quarantine, we're going to need a lot of diapers in nine months. That kind of thing.

Things start to get problematic pretty quickly, though. Before long, the statisticians became complicit in helping the state *control* its people. This is where all the Michel Foucault fans are going to want to put their hands up and start telling us about the intersection of knowledge and power. He was right.

Did you know that the idea of the average person was originally supposed to be a good thing? If you were average, you were . . . normal. Which meant that you were not . . . aberrant. Which meant that you were less likely to . . . prove a problem for . . . the system. Statistics are very useful when it comes to power and control.

But *the average person* does not exist. It is an abstraction that might be useful when thinking in aggregates (for example, how many children will be born this year, per average birth rates) but is useless and degrading when applied to the individual. Every single academic discipline that says it's using *science* to address human problems is doing it wrong. And everyone who calls themself a *social scientist* is just pretending to do two things—science and social work—when they are doing neither.

*   *   *

While I was writing this book, Joey was reading *Braiding Sweetgrass*, an ode to nature by Robin Wall Kimmerer, a professor of environmental biology and a member of the Citizen Potawatomi Nation. Kimmerer warns about the dangers of scientism herself:

> While science could be a source of and repository for knowledge, the scientific worldview is all too often an enemy of ecological compassion. It is important in thinking about this lens to separate two ideas that are often synonymous in the mind of the public: the practice of science and the scientific worldview that it feeds. Science is the process of revealing the world through rational inquiry. The practice of doing real science brings the questioner into an unparalleled intimacy with nature fraught with wonder and creativity as we try to comprehend the mysteries of the more-than-human world. . . . Contrasting with this is the scientific worldview, in which a culture uses the process of interpreting science in a cultural context that uses science and technology to reinforce reductionist, materialist economic and political agendas. I maintain that the destructive lens of the people made of wood is not science itself, but the lens of the

scientific worldview, the illusion of dominance and control, the separation of knowledge from responsibility.

* * *

I'm going to repeat this, because I think it is crucial: The central problem of trying to employ measurement-based science in service of something human is that it is essentially a predicting system. But when it comes to real-life stuff, prediction misses both the point and the target. Not only that, but it also squanders the opportunity for creative freedom. Prediction points us into tomorrow, when we should be trying to stay right here, *now*, in today. Oh, and you can't predict the future. So there's that, too.

Let's talk about that most inane of predictions, the 50–50 split. What is it with people answering a question about prediction by saying they think it's 50–50? I mean, I know I just said that you can't predict the future, but if we're going to insist on trying, saying that you think there is a 50–50 chance is basically a cop-out, the equivalent of saying "anything can happen." We already knew that.

Look, I get it: Measurement has brought us many practical things. The concept of reductionism—breaking things down into their component parts—led us to conduct experiments that allowed us to tame the natural world to the point where we didn't have to worry that someone in the village was going to die every night, or every morning, or just . . . soon . . . because of the things the natural world sometimes likes to throw our way: weather, disease, famine, plagues.

But you can't employ the tools of reductionism when it comes to the realm of love. Or anything else that contains true essence. There is just no point in doing so. All you're going to end up with is separate pieces, or individual parts, of a whole.

"Individual parts"—I guess that's why Western society loves reductionism in the first place: because even though we are all a *part* of something larger, our egos *love themselves so very much* that our egos think it's more interesting to focus on the *individual* parts than on the interconnectedness of the whole.

So we've got another battle on our hands. Actually, it's the same one, the one between numbers and words. On the one side are the forces of reductionism. Its soldiers are the scientists and statisticians who won't stop breaking us down until they have reduced us to the tiniest increments. Of course, what's left will not be human in any way, shape, or form, but it will be easy to organize and put into some sort of table.

The scientists and mathematicians, in their attempts to conquer uncertainty, have focused us on the wrong side of now, the things that are *probable*. What we should be focused on is the other side, the things that are *possible*.

Why? Because anything is possible.

If you take this side, you have much less use for numbers and a far greater inclination to use words. Words like *harmony, interconnectedness, wholesomeness*, and . . . *love*. These are the kinds of things that art tries to show us, and the aspects of reality that the enlightened can see. That we are all one.

The underlying force of the entire universe is one of harmony—not entropy, which the disillusioned would have us believe—and it is so awesome as to be inexplicable. The fact that we exist is a miracle. That is all you need to know. You are a miracle. I am a miracle. When I finally realized that, I realized that I had been letting the small stuff get to me for my entire life. What is the point of arguing about who is right or wrong in the context of the miracle of existence itself? We should be thanking our lucky stars every single second that we are alive. I'm going to go with my daughter, who can't get enough of Harry Potter, and just call it magic.

Life is magical.

Why do we keep trying to get out from under its spell? Why have we lost touch with magical thinking, the idea that we can do anything we want, and that no one else is stopping us? The world doesn't just contain magic; it *is* magic. That is, until we stop believing in it. One reason that happens is that the society we have created seeks to find love when it first sprouts—in the young—and banish it to some deep, dark dungeon. In its place we put *education* and *mathematics* and *science* and *facts*. We think we are doing our children a favor when we tell them to be scientists. We are not. We need to teach them about magic—teach them how to live, which will teach them how to love. Or maybe it's the other way around.

CHAPTER 8

The Precision Paradox

Hogwarts was founded over a thousand years
ago—the precise date is uncertain. . . .[1]

—Professor Binns, *Harry Potter and the Chamber of Secrets*

I've been thinking a lot about the idea of discovery lately. I used to see it the way I think most people do, which is that the act of discovery is about finding something *new*. These days, I'm not so sure about that. The act of creation results in something new. But the act of discovery is something else entirely.

Consider the word itself: *dis-cover*. The Truth is always there, but it's been covered up. When we realize something, we dis-cover that truth, and take the covers of ignorance off of it. Whenever you realize something, it is simply a matter of losing your own illusions. The *thrill of discovery* is not actually about finding *new* things: it is the *thrill of awareness of Self*, which every one of us has had all along. We don't discover *things*; we discover *our Selves*.

This has serious implications for how we look at the whole idea of scientific discovery. When scientists *discover* things, they're not actually finding something that exists outside of themselves. What they're doing is figuring out how they are connected to something that happens, whether that's splitting atoms or creating vaccines. This is a subtle point, but it's an important one: Anything that has been *discovered* needed someone to *discover* it. The former cannot occur without the latter. In a way, then, the former *is* the latter. The seeker is the sought.

Consider, if you will, the *discoveries* made by physicists. Through observation and experiment, they seek to understand and explain phenomena in the physical world. They do that by trying to tabulate and organize things that have happened. In other words, *the past*. And then they try to use that understanding to predict what will happen to something under given conditions. In other words, they try to *predict the future*.

I've already made my case that you cannot predict the future. Because the future does not exist. But that does seem to fly in the face of the fact that scientists do seem to be able to tell us what is going to happen in many situations, right? That's why we place so much faith in their findings. But I'd like to suggest that we've misunderstood what they're doing. Scientists can't tell us what's going to happen in the future; scientists have figured out a systematic means of *altering* the present.

I know it might seem like I'm going rogue here, but stick with me for a second. We have misunderstood what science is all about. It's not about predicting things in the future, it's about doing things in the present. A scientist who is *doing* something is engaged in the act of creation, just like the rest of us. But a scientist who is simply *predicting* is attempting the impossible. You can't predict the future.

What do I mean by that? I mean that predictions don't really amount to much all by themselves. Someone can, of course, say, *If we do this, then that will happen*. But unless someone actually does that thing, then who's to know? They actually *have to do what they say they're going to do,* at which point something will happen. Yes, I know—they might be right. But that's not *predicting the future.* That's *doing something in the present.*

But what if there is nothing to *do*? Consider, if you will, the goal of understanding the nature of Reality, which is arguably the same goal as understanding ourselves. Why are they the same thing? Well, if you're not there, there's no Reality for you to understand, is there? And when it comes to understanding the Self, the challenge isn't to *do* anything; the challenge is simply to understand what it means to *be.* The same goes for Reality. You can't *do anything* to Reality. It just *is.*

Our problem, you might say, is that we forget that *this* contains all of *that.* To get at the very nature of existence—*this that I am*—we make the mistake of looking at something—anything—outside of us, and trying to figure out what *that* might be. But *that* which seems to exist outside of us is actually part of *this* existence we are seeking to understand. *It's all the same thing.* The very act of trying to separate *this* from *that* is an effort to put a limit on the unlimited. We draw boundaries to emphasize those limits. We establish territories, we make distinctions, and we put labels on things. The problem is that when we do so, we lose touch with the unlimited nature of existence that lies within. You can see it outside, too. Look at anything in nature closely enough—a tree, a river, or a snowflake—and you will see no end to the details of its appearance. But look for its limits, and soon that's all you will be able to see. The same goes for existence itself.

"If we pursue the limited we will find it everywhere," writes the Vedantic scholar David Frawley. "We will find boundaries to everything. If we pursue the unlimited, we will also find it everywhere. We will find no end to the beauty, uniqueness and variety of life. If we pursue the limited we ourselves will become limited, trapped in time and matter. If we pursue the unlimited we ourselves will become unlimited. We will open into the eternal and the infinite."[2] I know which one I'm going with. What about you?

Again: Science is useful for *doing* things. In other words, it can be useful for what you might call *downstream* projects, other things that will submit to our intellect as well. But the Self is greater than the intellect, and Reality contains all. An invention cannot explain its inventor. Nor can it explain the context that gave rise to it. It is, and always will be, subordinate to both.

The central quest of modern physics—the hope of discovering the *laws*, or *rules*, by which the universe operates—is premised on the very dubious assumption that we can use intellectual inquiry to understand Reality itself. Can physics explain the context that gave rise to it? The physics community certainly thinks so, because that's pretty much what most of them are trying to do. To that end, in 2021, there are two main theories in physics that seek to explain the physical universe—the *context* of existence itself. The first is Einstein's theory of general relativity. The second is quantum mechanics, also known as quantum physics. The goal of both, to put it simply, is to try to *predict* things that will happen under a given set of conditions. *This* is the explanation for *that*.

Until Einstein came along, Newton's law of universal gravitation was the most revered of all the laws, because he seemed to have figured out why the things that we can see move the way that they do. He wasn't quite right, but his model (which was mistakenly called a law) seemed to explain why things did what they did, whether you're talking about an apple falling from a tree or a planet orbiting the sun.

Newton's "law" of gravity: Every particle in the universe attracts every other particle with a force that is directly proportional to the product of their masses and inversely proportional to the square of the distance between them. Another way you can say that, if you don't feel like getting all fancy: *Everything is connected.*

Newton's idea of gravity did seem to explain why the apple falls from the tree, instead of floating up into space. But Newton himself was deeply uncomfortable with the notion of "action at a distance" implied by his equations. Just because two things were there didn't explain why they somehow *acted on each other* through space and time. Why did gravity happen as opposed to not happening at all? In other words, where did gravity *come from*?

In 1692, he wrote: "That one body may act upon another at a distance through a vacuum without the mediation of anything else . . . is to me so great an absurdity that, I believe, no man who has in philosophic matters a competent faculty of thinking could ever fall into it." But he searched in vain for the "source" of that gravitational force. He failed to find it. In the end, he was reduced to claiming that he was convinced "by many reasons" that there were "causes hitherto unknown" behind it, and that "it is enough to say that gravity does really exist." He just accepted it, and so did everybody else.

That is, until Albert Einstein came along. Gravity didn't come from anywhere, Einstein argued, because gravity *didn't* exist. Nothing can travel *instantly*, he argued, including the pull of gravity itself. Our notion of space and time as separate concepts was erroneous, he suggested. They were, instead, two aspects of the fabric of reality itself—*spacetime*. In his theory, any concentration of mass (or energy) such as a star or a planet bends the fabric of spacetime around it, causing a curvature in that fabric. So objects don't *act on* other objects at a distance, they simply cause a distortion in the geometry of spacetime, thereby altering the trajectory of any other bodies nearby. Imagine a basketball sitting on an outstretched sheet. The sheet is spacetime.

Einstein's theory made more sense than Newton's law, because it seemed to explain not just everything Newton's did, but also more.

If the tree drops this apple, it will hit me on the head.

—That's Newton making a prediction.

I'm moving at the speed of light and you're not. You will get older faster than me.

—That's Einstein doing the same thing: making a prediction.

Einstein's theory of general relativity has been described as "a theory of extraordinary beauty." Beautiful it may be, but even he would tell you that it doesn't explain all that it seeks to explain, and therefore it isn't *true*. I know that doesn't seem like the kind of remark one should write and then walk away from, but I'm going to do just that. I will get back to it in a moment, though. We are going to kill all the sacred cows with one swing of the sword of clarity here, and we need to talk about quantum physics before we do so.

Quantum physics makes its predictions in the realm of the very small—subatomic particles, atoms, and molecules. It differs from classical physics in a couple of important ways. The first is that unlike on the macroscopic scale, at the quantum level, objects appear to have characteristics of both particles and waves. (This is known as the notion of complementarity.) The second is that there appear to be limits to how accurately the *value* of a physical quantity can be *predicted* prior to its being *measured*, a problem that physicists have termed the uncertainty principle.

The problem is that *complementarity* is *contradictory*. Is an electron a localized particle or is it a probability wave? "It is both but it cannot be both," say the scientists. They walk away from that contradiction by claiming that *quantum physics does not have the same level of certainty as classical physics*. Since when do we describe a statement that contradicts itself as having a different *level of certainty* than something else?

Maybe, just maybe . . . it's *wrong*.

For starters, there is no such thing as a *probability* wave. That's a man-made idea, something you create with math. It does not exist outside our minds. It is a *possibility* wave, which is just another way of saying *possibility itself.* Understand that, and you understand that an electron can, in fact, be both: In the wave, the electron is all possible electrons. It exists in a state of *pure subjectivity*, or *potentiality*. When we turn our focus to it, it *objectifies* into *actuality*, as a particle. You can't explain this with physics, because physics seeks to *predict* what will happen, when things only happen when they happen. *And everything is always happening, so the predictions are chasing a ghost, searching the future for the past while letting the present slip away.*

Einstein seemed to have moved the ball forward, but he was ultimately unable to reconcile his theory of general relativity (the physics of the unimaginably large) with the so-called laws of quantum mechanics (the physics of the vanishingly small). He wasn't able to *unify* general relativity with quantum mechanics, and no one else has been able to do so, either.

Both theories seem to have things going for them. They explain some things but not some others. But a theory that doesn't explain everything it seeks to explain can't really be promoted to the status of a *law*, can it? Not only that; the two theories are incompatible in some fairly important ways. So we don't just have one theory that doesn't seem to do the whole job. We have two that can't get it done whether together or apart.

Common sense would tell you that the theories are *wrong*. And here's why: because we are trying to count our way to understanding, also known as *unity*.

Einstein was right to throw out the notion of time as a distinct entity. But when he decided to keep it, attaching it to space, he made the same mistake as every other physicist, of trying to *predict* things, just on different levels and on different scales. He should have just discarded *time* entirely. Time doesn't exist at all. The reason that the theories cannot be unified is that they're all built on top of something that doesn't exist. There is no flimsier foundation than that.

Scientists find it hard to let go of their theories, though. A theory that explains some things but not others isn't seen as *wrong*, it is simply seen as *incomplete*. That way, all the *thinking* that went into it didn't go to waste. Admit that the thinking is wrong, and you have to start all over again. Insist that the thinking is right, just . . . *incomplete* . . . and you can keep doing what you're doing. And that's what physics has done: Instead of throwing out two *incomplete* theories, physicists are now in search of a *third* theory, the one that will fix everything.

This third theory, the one that is supposed to do the impossible, has been called the Theory of Everything, or ToE. This is the big kahuna, the hypothetical, all-encompassing, coherent theoretical framework of physics that would fully explain and link together all aspects of the physical universe. But that's never going to happen, because we cannot create something that will contain everything, including ourselves. Indeed, there is only one tool at our disposal that is capable of doing so, and it isn't really a tool. It is the Self itself. That's where unity lies. It's not outside of us; it's *inside of us*.

The trick is to remove time—aka measurement—from the situation entirely. It is only then that you can see what's really going on—when you can become *aware* of what is happening. Because there is no such thing as time, there is only now. Now is a state of becoming, which means that *anything can happen*. There is no possibility of unifying the incomplete theories of physics with any new one, either, because they assume that time exists, when it does not. All we're left with is *now*, which is not something that you can calculate. You cannot run the numbers on infinite possibility. Because it is everything, at once.

When mathematics attempts to narrow the range of possibility by calculating probability, it necessarily fails to accommodate all the things that can happen, which is, quite literally, *anything*. And because mathematics does try to predict things, it is, by its very nature and design (meaning: *our design*), incapable of grasping all that there is. Not only that, but by assuming the existence of time, it has invalidated itself in the design stage. The same point holds for spacetime, too: Any *theory* that assumes that something can happen in the future is fundamentally flawed. Because there is no such thing as the future.

Albert Einstein was a great scientist because he got physics as far as it's going to be able to go. But the next stop in understanding—unity—will require a repudiation of physics itself. Because the challenge here wasn't to solve a physics problem. The challenge was to solve a problem by removing the physics from it. There is no paradox that isn't destined for collapse when you have the right perspective.

There is no such thing as the future.
Things can't happen in the future, because it doesn't exist.
The only thing that can happen is what is happening right now.

The physicist Werner Heisenberg did a pretty good job of explaining physics' Achilles' heel. "When we speak of the picture of nature in the exact science of our age," he wrote, "we do not mean a picture of nature as much as a *picture of our relationships with nature.* . . . Science no longer confronts nature as an objective observer, but sees itself as an actor in this interplay between man and nature. The scientific method of analyzing, explaining and classifying has become conscious of its limitations, which arise out of the fact that by its intervention science alters and refashions the object of investigation. In other words, method and object can no longer be separated."

Mind you, *method and object had never been separated in the first place.* There was no way to *preserve* or even *strive for* objectivity. Scientists hadn't stumbled on *the potential for subjectivity*, something they could guard against. They had stumbled on the nature of *subjectivity itself.* The universe is *pure subjectivity.* Method and object and science and scientist and particle are all *one.* We do not really have *relationships* with things outside ourselves. There is only one true relationship, and it's the experience of *unity*, when you realize that the universe is but a manifestation of your Self. When you experience that, you don't just feel yourself in everything around you but you also feel everything within yourself.

The challenge is not to keep an appropriate methodological distance from the subject at hand. The challenge is to realize that that so-called *distance* is an illusion. There is nothing to *analyze* or *explain* or *classify*. There is simply awareness. The reason that we find particles where we do find them is not that there was a *probability* that they might be here or they might be there. We find them where we find them *because that's where we have put our focus—because we have become aware of them.*

In other words, it is the act of looking itself that causes something to exist, not the other way around. It's kind of funny, if you consider all the talk about the advances of quantum physics in the twentieth and twenty-first centuries, that we knew this thousands of years ago. The yogi Patanjali put it this way: "The seen exists only for the sake of the Seer."[3] We think we have figured out so much, when the fact of the matter is that we have forgotten more than we have learned.

*   *   *

I read a delightful book in my quarantine binge called *The Blind Spot*, by William Byers. In one passage, he's talking about how humanity responds to the suggestion that we are not in a position to understand the nature of reality. It's dead-on:

> [Our] reaction to the suggestion that our powerful, infinitely subtle, intellect cannot penetrate to the deepest layer of reality is initially to reject it out of hand. The whole thrust of our culture is to map out a rational universe using our rational minds. Science is the cutting edge of this tendency—it promises to make the unknown known, to clearly display the whole of the universe to the mind's eye. Unlimited understanding through science promises to bring in its wake unlimited power to control our environment, eradicate disease, and perhaps one day even defeat death itself. This is the dream of reason—the dominant mythology on which our culture is based.[4]

The ultimate science, yoga, is one of direct experience. I am all for yoga, and uniting of the Self with the Universal Consciousness. So I am not anti-science in all the ways. I am simply anti-science as it has been conceived and understood in the West, which is a study—typically via measurement—of things outside of our Selves. The study of the Self is where it's at. It's the only thing worth studying in the end, because once you figure that out, the rest just falls into place. The best-known "textbook" of the science of yoga is the Yoga Sūtras of Patanjali. They don't involve intellectual reasoning or territorial disputes over one theory or another. They're just a practical treatise on understanding the Self. When you practice yoga, you practice concentration, or the taming of the mind. The ultimate goal is to see your own true nature, which is existence itself. Which is only available in the now.

I asked Joey about *now*, and she replied that it's both the longest and the shortest period of time that there is. But even Joey, who is never wrong, is kind of wrong about that: *Now* is neither of those things, because it sits outside of time entirely. It is simply, *now*.

There's a concept in yoga where they talk about getting rid of ignorance with ignorance. Meaning, it's not such a bad thing to upgrade your relative state of ignorance, as long as you are moving in the right direction. "Take a better ignorance to get rid of a worse one," writes Swami Satchidananda. Considered in that light, Albert Einstein does deserve to be treated with reverence. After all, his guesses are more interesting than anyone else's. But just because something is interesting does not mean it's true. "In the final analysis," says Swami Satchidananda, "only the light of understanding will remove the darkness of ignorance."

I recently saw a clip from the movie *What the Bleep Do We Know!?*, which posits a connection between quantum physics and consciousness. One physicist goes so far as to claim that scientists have "proven" that the fabric of reality is a unified field. But that's ridiculous. The suggestion that physics can grasp unity is akin to proposing to unlock a door with a feather. One of the primary reasons for that is that the mathematics of the infinite do not comport with the mathematics of the finite. The infinite is not simply the sum of all things; it is that which is all things and more. Sri Aurobindo cites the Upanishads on this issue: "This is the complete and That is the complete; subtract the complete from the complete, the complete is the remainder."

The interconnectedness of all things is just another way of saying God. God cannot be understood by the mind, because the mind is matter, and God is much more subtle than matter. The experience of God can only come when we are able to *transcend the mind*. In other words, we cannot *prove* the unity underlying all things. It just *is*. And it must be experienced to be understood.

Awareness of unity, or consciousness, is beyond the reach of measurement-based science, so the filmmakers were being extremely kind to physicists by even letting them into a conversation that their tools do not have the capacity to comprehend. There is no "physics of consciousness"—that's a contradiction in terms. There cannot and will not ever be a Theory of Everything, because you cannot contain everything in anything.

*   *   *

The reach of the Precision Paradox extends beyond physics and into most of the social sciences as practiced today. But it's not really necessary to go through this whole argument all over again, only to make the same point. Models of reality that seek to predict human behavior will never capture all the possibilities. Some might make some pretty good guesses—which direction will the huge crowd run if there is a fire at one end of the football stadium?—but when it comes to individual behavior, science is always going to come up short. Why? Because it cannot account for the variable called love, the creative force of the universe and the x-factor of personal choice.

When economics is practiced as a *science*—using *models*—it will always come up short. I read this book called *Willful* recently, and it tried to make the case that even though *rational choice theory* (that is, the one that says we're all robots) was wrong, maybe it was *right enough*. That's silly. It's physics all over again: *Two wrongs do not make a right*. We need to learn to accept when we don't have the answers instead of trying to figure out a way to be wrong but also right.

If we ever want to make any headway in economics, we need to focus on the reasons that firms even exist in the first place and why the people within them do what they do. Such an approach will center on the imagination and the languages we conjure to engage with the essential uncertainty at the heart of all decision-making, otherwise known as existence. You make decisions every single *now*. The man who could lead that charge is named J. C. Spender, and he's been trying to get everyone's attention about this for decades.

As for the rest of the *social sciences*, including behavioral economics, criminology, or all the other *sciences of the mind*, you will find the same problem anywhere you look. Let's say you saw a blooming garden and thought it was really beautiful. But then you looked closer and thought, "Jesus, I had no idea just how beautiful it really was." Do you think it's possible to measure the difference between those two thoughts? Some things just aren't countable, right? And yet we nevertheless insist on trying to count everything. By doing so, we continue down a fundamentally incorrect path. That way lies confusion, not clarity.

Unable to count things that really matter, we are left counting all the things that don't. Every single day, we continue to calculate and tally pointless numbers that are of no use whatsoever. We have become so infatuated with the notion that precision *adds* to understanding that numbers have mounted a hostile takeover of common sense. Why have we let this happen to us? Because in the absence of *the* answer (which is just *love*, by the way), it seems that we prefer *an* answer to *no* answer.

What would love look like if you put it under a microscope? That's an outrageous question. You know what is equally outrageous? The idea that you can count it. Or happiness. Or intelligence. But that's not even the end of the madness. Enamored with the language of statistics, we've also gone on a causality binge, doubling down on error in the process.

Here's an easy way to figure out what to do with some statistic that someone cites to you as somehow having some *scientific* basis. Ask yourself the following: What if someone wanted to *do something* with that number—what could they *do* with it? An example: "Forty-five percent of people believe in the efficacy of vaccines." What can you do with that number? If there is no obvious answer, then the number is not useful. I'm not anti-measurement. I am simply questioning the value of precision past a certain point. In almost all parts of life, there is a moment when any further increase in precision is met with a decrease in understanding.

It's time to start listening to our common sense again. It's the most powerful tool we have at our disposal, but we have, of late, subordinated it to external tools of measurement. Your brain creates an entire universe every time you open your eyes. Have you ever seen a man-made tool create a universe?

*   *   *

I know how we got here: In the aftermath of the Industrial Revolution, scientists were held in great esteem. Worried that they were getting left behind, the less mathematically inclined academics and *thinkers* among us decided that they should probably use the tools of measurement, too. The social sciences are the result of that decision, large swaths of which engage in endless surveys, measurements of pure nonsense, and misguided attempts to engineer society.

Statistics, by definition, are not interested in individual experience, even if they do hold some allure to those in thrall with the idea of the Quantified Self. I've already argued that a single number, in and of itself, does not contain meaning. It only contains itself—the number *14*, for example, is just that, nothing more. Faced with that paucity, statisticians answered in a way that would, in time, become known as Big Data: *If one number doesn't contain meaning, what about a giant pile of numbers?* In other words, if one didn't contain meaning, maybe we could find meaning in *more than one*. The logic doesn't really follow, does it? Alas, we bought into the notion that *more* was better, when the fact is that only *better* is better.

Before anybody knew what had happened, anyone armed with a pile of numbers and a story to tell about them could find an audience. It wasn't too long after that that everyone began to be afraid to cite personal experience as evidence of anything, because it didn't come with the seeming heft of a data set alongside it. We cannot measure fear, so we ignore it when we try to understand things like viruses. Fear can make you sick, right? And sickness can make you afraid? But we ignore it, because we cannot measure it. Love can also heal. But we ignore it when we engage in science, because love cannot be measured, either. And when we obsess over those things that *can* be quantified, we lose sight of the much more powerful aspects of existence that cannot.

Today, when we talk about social change, it is almost always accompanied by some set of numbers that seek to *confirm* it. But change doesn't happen to us collectively. Change happens to you, to me, to someone else, *on an individual basis*. And yet we don't even consider acknowledging change until it shows up in the data. Talk about living in the past. Once something shows up in the data, it is long gone—*all statistics are artifacts*—and you are no longer talking about the present.

Should we ever use statistics about the many to try to explain the predicament of the few? We like to think we can, but we cannot. In the most important realms of existence—love, life, happiness—we cannot. And yet we continue to try. Henry Buckle claimed in his 1857 book, *History of Civilization in England*, that it "was proven by statistics that human actions are governed by laws that are as fixed as those occurring in the world of physics."[5] That's horseshit.

There will never be a unified theory of physics, only incomplete theories that cannot grasp totality. There will never be a unified theory of human behavior, either, some statistical law that can tell us what a person will or will not do. The *average person* does not exist, and any theory that assumes otherwise is making the same mistake as they make in physics, trying to cram infinite possibility into an equation.

If we are ever going to get anywhere real in this project called humanity, we need to drop the language of statistical precision. It's going to be hard, because it has seeped so far into our cognitive frameworks and language—words like *causality, correlation, average, mean,* and *extrapolation* have come to dominate modern discourse. But the point of those numbers, in many situations, isn't the measurement itself, but the manipulation that it affords. Because it turns out that it's easier to control people and persuade them of the validity of your point of view if you have *data* that supports the reasons you think that people should do what you say. Modern politics and ideology seek nothing less than to measure the pulse of the people and then sell them ideas built around their points of view.

At some point, maybe we will be able to summon the courage to admit that we have relied on wrongheaded ways to solve the problems of living. Math and science can do many things, but they do not know what to do with unity. The irony is that we continue to look to these fields of study for certitude and precision, when they will never be able to deliver the Truth. Physics is useful for figuring some things out. But if you are looking for the biggest answer of all—enlightenment—it doesn't even know where to start.

The only thing that you can ever be utterly, truly certain about is the fact that you exist. That is all. As do I. But we are all just a part of one big thing, individual manifestations of energy in the cosmic field. The reason that one piece of mass can seem to have *action at a distance* on another is that it is all one. We are all floating on the wave (or field, or whatever you want to call it) of possibility, what the scholar and meditation teacher Paul Eduardo Muller-Ortega calls the "blissful, cosmic, creative wave that continually surges at the core of all things."[6] Just as the fish is in water, we are in something, too. You are not *different from it*; you are *part of it*. (Or, as the Vedantic philosophers would tell you: "*That art thou.*")

There's a conversation you can find online between Einstein and a Bengali philosopher named Rabindranath Tagore.[7] They found that they agreed on a number of things but disagreed on one major issue: Tagore said that truth and beauty were not independent of man. Einstein agreed on beauty but differed on truth; he said that although he could not prove it, he believed that truth existed independently of man. Following his lead, all of physics is in search of truth outside of man.

Scientists' tools are made to seek the quantum—that is, the numbered—universe. Those tools cannot grasp the thing that ties it all together, which is possibility. We're talking about the creative force of the universe here, also known as love. And love has no number. You cannot calculate connection itself. It just is. Einstein was wrong. Tagore was right. The truth lies inside you. Because you are the universe.

CHAPTER 9

The Answer Is Not for Sale

There it was again: Choose what to believe.
He wanted the truth. Why was everybody so
determined that he should not get it?[1]

—*Harry Potter and the Deathly Hallows*

As I mentioned, I started my career at Goldman Sachs, an investment bank. You can't get closer to the heart of capitalism than that. And while I had the good sense to leave the finance industry after just two years, I have spent the majority of my career writing about capitalists or their servants. While the following doesn't have to do with me specifically, it comes from half a lifetime spent wondering about this kind of thing. But I am going to stick to the promise that I made earlier in the book and not talk about specific people. I am going to talk about the system that we have created for ourselves.

*   *   *

At some point, a group of people calling themselves the capitalists showed up. It turned out that all this science, applied with human ingenuity to problems practical and manufactured, had also allowed the people to make, buy, sell, and store all sorts of stuff. At which point, they also needed a place to keep all the stuff they were dragging with them through time. Where should they put their *property*? They decided to try to divide the earth itself into portions, and they called that property, too. Everyone could keep their property on their property, or maybe, sometimes, store it on someone else's property. That way, when they finally got to tomorrow, they would know where everybody's stuff was, and they could all then sit down, get all their stuff, and . . .

Actually, they hadn't quite figured that part out yet. But they knew that they were bringing their stuff with them, no matter what. If they needed food in the future, they could sell some of their stuff and buy some food from someone else. But what if no one wanted their stuff anymore? What if stuff that cost a lot today wasn't worth a thing tomorrow? They used to ask soothsayers and fortune-tellers to tell them about the weather, but the scientists had figured that out. So they asked scientists to take on a different task, to tell them what *things were going to be worth in the future*. They called that particular brand of scientist *the economists*, and they treated them with the reverence due anyone who could—rather, who *claimed to be able to*—do the impossible. That is, to know *the future*.

Things got even more complicated after that. They started making so much stuff that no one knew who was doing what anymore, and it was hard to figure out just how much stuff you needed to make if you wanted to be able to meet demand in the future. Stuff was all spread out, to boot—the factory was here, the distribution depot was there, and the mall was over there. That became known as *an economy*. It was complicated stuff, and every now and then fate would show up again, throw a spanner in the works, and the whole damn thing would fall apart. They called that a recession. As Nicholas Nassim Taleb would tell you, the way to distinguish between most man-made things and nature-made things is that the man-made things will eventually collapse. That includes economies, countries, institutions, so-called scientific revolutions, currencies, and other assorted things you buy at Walmart.

Where was I? Right! There was too much stuff to keep track of. One thing that was really hard to keep track of was which *jobs* people were supposed to be doing. Everyone started nominating themselves for the jobs that seemed most important. Some people even founded "schools" that would make you the best person for this job or that one. Other people started selling something called "leadership," which you could apparently just buy at a school instead of looking inside to see what you were really made of. A lot of people believed those people, so it kind of worked, I guess, but it wasn't actual leadership they were selling (or buying). It was nonsense. But everybody was selling it, so nobody really noticed.

How did everything get so complicated? *Now* isn't complicated at all. Tomorrow, on the other hand, seemed quite complicated indeed. Who could explain it all? The *experts*, of course. But what about everybody else? Some jobs were so pointless that it was hard to know who was doing what and for whom. If everybody had to be assigned *a job*, couldn't they make it someone's *job* to keep track of the other people's jobs so that things didn't just come apart at the seams when shit got real?

That didn't seem quite like *science* to the *scientists*, so they demurred, at which point a bunch of people calling themselves *managers* said they'd take the gig. Some of them claimed to be scientists, too, and while no one was quite sure what to make of that claim, there wasn't any time to find someone else. Fate might be somewhere hiding around the corner of the present, and the future demanded some kind of accounting and projection from the standpoint of today. That's what "studies" were for—a bunch of numbers and other "data" that would tell them what to do.

So who was going to be in charge of morale, and how to generate it using "scientific" methods? That's when the messiahs of managerialism showed up. They called themselves managerial consultants, and they were in the business of finding paths to the future, too. They had their own tool, and they called it *strategy*. The thing about strategy, they insisted, was that you could use it to change paths if you had to—once you realized you were on the wrong path, all you had to do was tinker with your strategy a bit, and your strategy would find another path for you.

People were dubious. How, exactly, could you just *tinker* with *strategy*, they asked, given that few people even knew what a strategy was or how to make one, and thereby find the right path again? What did all that mumbo jumbo even mean?

"Listen," said the management consultants. "We are the most talented collection of scientists the world has ever seen. This is easy stuff. All you have to do is *build a model*. That's your strategy—your *model*—and when it seems like the path might not be the right one, you just fiddle with one of the controls, called *a variable*, and you will once again be headed in the right direction."

*   *   *

The problem with capitalism is that it has birthed a monster called money and its counterpart, the *money supply*. The whole concept of monetary stimulus shows the essential absurdity of currency itself. The *economy* freezes up, so the answer is to just start sending money in circles? Take money from tomorrow and push it out to jobless people today? Take money from me and send it back to me? What the hell is wrong with us?

What about a system in which we simply tried to exchange things of value? If everyone did something of *value*, no one would need a *job*. If you want to know more about this soul-crushing aspect of capitalism, read the late David Graeber's *Bullshit Jobs*. Graeber isn't picking on specific people, either. In his classification system, a bullshit job is a bullshit job not because you think my job is bullshit, but because you think *your job* is bullshit—the bullshit jobs are defined by the people doing them. It is just horrifying. How many of us wake up every day and go do something that we think is bullshit?

I did it. I wrote books I didn't want to write. I wrote a column about Britney Spears. In the modern capitalist economy, it is a rare person indeed who does not feel like their *job* is bullshit at least some of the time. How did we get here? How did we come to accept that we should spend precious hours of our time on earth doing things that we think are stupid? Because we have all come to believe that we need *a job*, that's why, when we should instead be focusing on doing the things that we love.

What if we all decided to find our passion and figure out how to do or make something that people find *valuable*? What if we just pursued our passions and traded things of equivalent value? In that scenario, you don't have economic crises, because there is no bubble in anything, because there are no *paper* assets that can be inflated or deflated according to the madness of crowds. If we all just focused on creating things with real *value*, then no one could ever be out of a *job*. You do what you do because you love it and because other people value it. How much simpler would that be? (For more on this, see Burning Man.)

Joey pointed me toward a startling passage in *Braiding Sweetgrass* that describes English as a noun-based language. We are so obsessed with *things* that only 30 percent of our words are verbs, versus 70 percent–plus in the language of the Native American Potawatomi. Think about that for a second: If you see life as an opportunity to *do things*, you need verbs. If you see life as an opportunity to *collect or own things*, you need nouns. Our cognitive framework is created by the language that we use; it's no wonder that the West has lost the spiritual path. We're too busy trying to hoard everything we come across, because capitalism depends on our accepting the premise that everything is scarce, and you'd better get yours before someone takes it for themselves.

In *Harry Potter and the Prisoner of Azkaban*, Harry Potter almost convinces himself that he needs a brand-new broomstick, the Firebolt. It is so exclusive that it is only sold via *Price on Request*.[2] How did we ever fall for that bullshit? That it was some kind of privilege to be told the price of something someone was trying to sell to us? That we had to *request* the price, as if it were *us* asking something of *them* as opposed to the other way around? (The family of Ron Weasley—Harry's best friend—by the way, owns nothing but secondhand goods, and they are as happy as can be. There goes J. K. Rowling, telling us truth under the cover of fantasy.)

The problem with capitalism is that it incentivizes people to rip other people off. When the Harvard Business School teaches strategy, they are teaching fledgling entrepreneurs how to establish a monopoly, from which point one can charge customers whatever one wants.

My friend Billy does the best carpentry work of anyone I know. And he charges a fair price. Why? Because he's not *a capitalist*; he's just a really nice guy who knows how to do some stuff really well (he's a *specialist*) and he trades that stuff with me for money. When people *negotiate* deals, they are always trying to get the most out of the other person at the least cost to themselves. Well, Billy and I have worked out a deal where we both get exactly what we want from the other guy.

The problem with capitalism is that capitalists think they own labor. They treat it as a *cost* of doing business, kind of like owning a machine. That's offensive. We should each own our own labor. Think of it: an ownership society where we all get to own ourselves and the products of our own labors. The idea that *shareholders* are owners is also offensive. It's a perversion of the idea of ownership, in which the *owner* owns the product of the *worker's* imagination.

The problem with capitalism is that it makes us think we have so many *jobs* to do that we end up *multitasking*, which is impossible. You cannot do two things at once. In Harry Potter, Hermione shows Ron and Harry her class schedule for the semester and Ron asks her how she thinks she can take three classes that are all at the same time. How indeed?

The problem with capitalism is that it points you to the future and takes you out of today. In his book *IT'S A FREAKIN' MESS: How to Thrive in Divisive Times*, Richard Gillett makes clear just how much of a danger this is—to both our individual and collective well-being. Because the future isn't just a source of anxiety. It is a frequent source of disappointment as well.

"When there is . . . demand that things *should* come out the [exact] way we want . . . we feel a keen disappointment when they don't," he writes. "We have made an *appointment* in our own minds with an imagined result, with a destiny we cannot control. When this appointment is not met by reality, we feel the pang of *disappointment*. . . . We blame life for not conforming to our wishes, and we feel pain, not realizing that this pain comes from the appointment that we ourselves pre-constructed in our minds. When friends, family, or society in general all share the same expectations, it makes it even harder to let go of them."[3]

The problem with capitalism is that because so many people no longer participate in the actual creation of value, people don't even recognize value anymore, and so they buy shit just for the sake of buying it.

The problem with capitalism is that the numbers people think *value* is something that you can *calculate*. But true value isn't a number. True value is the thing that gets created when you do something *with love*. True value *is* love. When you come across something of real value, it *tickles*. That's the brain rewarding you for engaging in your own existence. All the venture capitalists and bankers and Wall Street types running around trying to tell us the *fair value* of things in terms of dollars really have no idea what they are talking about. The value of something that has been created with love is not something that they teach at Harvard Business School. They teach it at Hogwarts. It's called the Dark Arts. Everything else is a distraction.

The problem with capitalism is that so many people end up doing so many pointless jobs, no one knows how to do anything anymore, and everyone just ends up trying to *copy* everybody else, with counterfeit goods. Copying can be okay, but not when it's *stealing*. The problem with capitalism is that because people don't know how to create value, they just copy each other, all day long.

Americans like to talk about how the Chinese are the world's most egregious counterfeiters, but that's just projection, or mirroring. American capitalism is practically built on the notion that if you can't actually figure out how to do something, you should just find a way to attach yourself to someone else's transaction and suck some value out of it. Now that I'm writing this sentence, I realize that American capitalists are parasites more than copycats. We're all copycats in one way or another, because there are no original ideas, only novel ones. Parasites, on the other hand, live off someone else's energy. You know, someone else's love, or someone else's creative output (which is also love), or someone else's generosity.

*   *   *

All of this brings us to *the news*. Turn on the television or open a paper or Google News today, and you could be forgiven for thinking that *the news* is simply the day's numbers. What temperature was it? What did the stock market do? Who won which game by how much? Because we have accepted a quantified realm during our *workdays*, we have somehow come to believe that anything else that *matters* can also be expressed in a number.

How many people died today?
How many months until that vaccine?
What is the size of my stimulus check?

In that society, the news is a number.

In a society that is centered on things of actual value, the news is something new and valuable that someone has created. There are no numbers required. The news, in other words, is something *new*. In that society, they would study *Tickle-Down Economics*, not its arrogant and offensive real-world counterpart, Trickle-Down Economics.

The journalistic and liberal elite love to discuss artificial intelligence and its limits and possibilities, and to do all sorts of *thinking* about what it all means. A.I. could *never* replace real writing and editing, the writers and editors say, in hopeful yet terrified tones. But haven't we done that already? With each passing day, a larger and larger portion of stories come (a) from the algorithm or (b) simply as a result of analyzing some set of numbers.

We are already *computing* the stories of the day, even if we don't know it yet. A front-page newspaper article from May 2020 announced that the United States had topped 100,000 deaths from COVID-19, adding that the total was "incalculable." We've been through this already. First of all, a death toll is not a *calculation*; it is a *count*. And while 100,000 is a large number, it is entirely countable. What they meant, of course, is that a number that large can be *difficult to grasp*. Even though the paper did go on to say that the enormity of such a tragedy is hard to grasp and that it shouldn't be done with numbers, *they proceeded to do that very thing*. We are so confused about the power that numbers have over us that we use them and disclaim them from one sentence to the next.

It doesn't have to be this way. We can grasp essence by using our words. We can leave the numbers behind.

You know what's fascinating? As someone who has covered the numbers side of life his whole career, it is only in the last few months that I finally realized what had happened to us. Up until May 2020, in fact, I was a subscriber to Bloomberg's online news operation for forty dollars a month. Bloomberg is nothing but a giant computer staffed by people deluding themselves into thinking that they're running the show. The numbers are running the show. Everything about that place, down to the name tags they try to make you wear in the building, says Big Brother. The numbers are winning, my friends.

But I don't want to pick on Bloomberg by itself. I want to point out that the media we love so dearly isn't really the media that we should want or need. I am one of those people who used to spend a ridiculous amount of their Sunday reading hundreds of pages of newspaper in the *New York Times*. I thought it made me smart. But is there any more pointless way to spend one's day than reading about yesterday? Talk about being stuck in the past. Anyone who spends their Sundays thinking that they are getting *smarter* by squandering their *now* is missing the point of living. Yes, you can feed words to your brain by reading. I'm a big fan of reading books, and I hope you are, too. My livelihood kind of depends on it. But your brain prefers the taste of experience. Life needs to be experienced to be understood.

But that's not the end of it. Newspapers do focus on the past, but they also ruminate about the future. The most revered columnists are the ones who are supposedly able to parse through yesterday's news to help us chart a way into an uncertain future. In Harry Potter, the Hogwarts newspaper is called the *Daily Prophet*. Could J. K. Rowling have been any clearer about that? We read newspapers to have them rehash the past and try to predict the future (with the expected results) and we all think we are smarter and better *informed* for it. And all we've really done is waste the time we spent reading them.

*   *   *

Everything that has value needs to be experienced to be understood. Listening to a recording of live music, for example, might point to the experience, but it can't quite get you to the show itself. And if you haven't experienced something, you have only imagined it, which means it didn't really happen at all. A mental model is just the same as any other model—they're not the real thing. As Sri Aurobindo puts it, "the mind . . . represents but cannot truly know."[4] If we buy into life inside the model—that is, inside our heads—we might as well just buy a bootleg copy of our own lives.

You know when one kid is trying to get into another kid's head, and they start copying their movements or things they're saying? It never fails to work, with the tormented eventually exclaiming, "Stop copying me!"

Why do we get irritated when people *copy* us? I'll tell you why: It's because it's a reminder to the ego that we really are all one, and the ego does not like to hear such talk. The ego thinks that it is special, and that anyone else doing the same thing is somehow *stealing* from us. The fact of the matter, of course, is that everybody copies everybody, because we are all just individual manifestations of the one big idea, of consciousness itself, of the universe. We are all love.

Let's expand the frame here a little bit, so that we are talking about life itself. There are no original ideas. There is only one. We just copy each other's versions of it. Some people's versions are more compelling than others, of course. That's how we get great art. And great ideas.

That's where everything great comes from—when someone assembles, through care and attention and focus, a set of experiences that leads to a more realized self. When you do that, your version of the one idea, which is *love*, is a little easier to make out, and people like to be near you. What is it that they feel when you're around? They feel *tickled*. Because that is the sensation of love. Rather, the tickle is the *language* of love. It's how love *gets communicated* from one thing to another, from one person to another, and from one person to themselves. When you love something or someone, it tickles. In every direction. We are going to go deeper into this in a moment, but let's just take our . . . *time*.

When pressed, J. K. Rowling has cited several writers as influences in the creation of Harry Potter. A bunch of *academics* have decided that it would be an interesting idea to try to compile them, instead of just reading the books and noticing them or not. Academics like to do this—they study other people's work—instead of learning by living and making art out of it. Rowling puts it this way: "I haven't got the faintest idea where my ideas come from, or how my imagination works. I'm just grateful that it does, because it gives me more entertainment than it gives anyone else."

I am not so sure about that last point, J.K. You are selling yourself short. (Although I have said that about my own writing—that I enjoy it as much as anybody—so I think you might have been copying me when you said it.) More to the point, I *do* know where her ideas come from: They come from consciousness, the brain, the universe, which Rowling obviously tapped into when she channeled the one story, love, and gave us the most wonderful individual expression of it that we've seen in the form of a story in God knows how long. In a children's book, that is. I mean, a book about children. It's a book about growing up, also known as life. So Rowling wrote a book about life, which is love, which is the same as all the other stories. So she basically copied it from everyone who has already told it. The list on Wikipedia is way too short. She got her ideas from *everyone else*.

I know this might seem like a bit of a non sequitur, but I want to talk about ghosts for a second. Do you believe in ghosts? I always had a bit of a hard time with one thing: the idea that a ghost stays the same forever, even as each and every one of us *is change itself*. But what if a ghost isn't an echo of a *person* but simply the echo of *an idea that that person had*? If you believe me about the consciousness thing, then it's not *supernatural* at all to believe that ideas had by people are still floating around in the places where they used to hang out.

Or, to switch gears a little, it's not *supernatural* to think that your closest relatives (we're *all* related) are still hanging around you in the form of ideas.

Not that long ago, M. was running upstairs to put her bathing suit on and she said, "I'll be down in a jiffy." It stopped me *dead in my tracks*.

"Where did you hear that figure of speech?" I asked her.

"I don't know, from you?" she replied.

She was wrong. I don't say "in a jiffy." But I will tell you who did: my father, Don McDonald. He said it *all the time*. I realized, in that moment, that my father was speaking to me through my child. Or, if you will, my father's *ideas* were speaking to me. Because they are all part of the one big idea, which is *consciousness itself*.

I posted something about that on Instagram and told the old man that I missed him, which prompted my old pal Dave Foster to send me a link that told me that a *jiffy* was actually a unit of time, defined in quantum physics as the time it takes for light to travel one fermi, which is approximately the length of a nucleon.

I have told you that time doesn't exist. So my father was actually making a joke through M. when she said that. He was reminding me that he used the word, all while pointing Dave—and therefore me—to the silliness of the concept of time. My father is not *gone*. He is right here, right now, where he will always be. Because there is only now. My father, just like you, me, and M., is possibility itself. He is infinite. He's also one funny bastard, making jokes about physics through the mouth of a twelve-year-old. I remain in awe of you, Don McDonald. You knew how to do this thing called life, and apparently still do. The reason Dave Foster heard the joke was because he loved my father as much as I did. That's tickle-down humor for you, all the way from the very top of Reality itself.

While we're on the subject of McDonald men, I told you not long ago that I got into Bob Dylan when my brother Scott gave my other brother Steve a *copy* of Dylan's *Biograph* for Christmas. And I *copied* it. The first step on my path toward Dylan was *copied* from someone else's *copy*.

In *Braiding Sweetgrass*, Robin Wall Kimmerer talks about copying in the context of the Windingo, a legendary monster of the Anishinaabe people. "It is said that the Windingo will never enter the spirit world," she writes, "but will suffer the eternal pain of need, its essence a hunger that will never be sated. The more a Windingo eats, the more ravenous it becomes. It shrieks with its craving, its mind a torture of unmet want. Consumed by consumption, it lays waste to humankind."

The Windingo is a case study in the positive feedback loop, adds Kimmerer, in which a change in one entity results in a similar change in another, connected part of the system. The Windingo is a copycat. Negative feedback loops work the other way: You're hungry, so you eat, and then you're not hungry anymore. The Windingo stories were meant to encourage negative feedback loops in the minds of listeners, "to strengthen self-discipline, to build resistance against the insidious germ of taking too much."[5]

The human being is the only animal that can know its maker. That is why we are supposed to take care of everything. We are supposed to see the connectedness of all things. We are supposed to use our power of discernment as gratitude for our good fortune. Instead, we have become Windingoes. As a great guru once said, if you don't know your own divinity, you are nothing but a talking animal.

CHAPTER 10

What Now?
(The Only Thing That Matters)

It is our choices, Harry, that show what we
truly are, far more than our abilities.[1]

—Dumbledore, *Harry Potter and the Chamber of Secrets*

Something cracked open inside me in the early weeks of the quarantine, and it changed everything. I really mean that. I've used the phrase "it changed everything" to describe a few other turning points in my life—when I joined *Red Herring*, when I began writing for *Vanity Fair*, when my daughter was born, and when I met Joey—but the truth is that every single one of the course corrections I have ever made save for this last one has been a change in degree, not a change in direction itself. And by that I mean that I was never too concerned about whether I was headed in the right direction or not. Every now and then, I would tweak my direction a little bit. And every now and then, I would have to swing the steering wheel wildly to keep from driving right off the road. But most of the time, I was pretty much unconscious behind the wheel.

There's a Sanskrit term in the Bhagavad Gita known as *shraddha*. It means "that which is placed in the heart."[2] What does that mean? It means that our shraddha is our substance; it is what we have made of ourselves. More to the point, it is not passive, because what you are points to what you will become. Your shraddha determines your destiny.

Here's the tough part: There is *right shraddha* and there is *wrong shraddha*. Right shraddha is faith in spiritual laws, the unity of life, and the presence of the divine in each and every one of us. Wrong shraddha is ignorance. It is the belief that we are but our physical existence and that happiness is something you get when you pursue your self-interest. Western capitalism is wrong shraddha. Duff McDonald 1.0 was wrong shraddha.

I didn't care enough. I mean, I cared about some things, but not about all the things. I preached the gospel of laissez-faire, which says that as long as you stay out of my business, I will stay out of yours. I subscribed to the notion of common decency, of course, but beyond that, I didn't really give a shit. Until mid-2020, I thought my purpose was to have a career and provide for my daughter. But that was nowhere near specific enough.

I was focused on the wrong things. I spent my career thinking that numbers told the story. I have said, on more than one occasion, "Find the numbers, and you have the story," when that was the worst approach to storytelling that one can take. And because I was focused on numbers, I was rarely, if ever, truly present. My sense of self suffered (see: alcoholism), my relationships suffered (see: divorce), and my potential as a father was at risk. There was only one thing that was going to save me, and that was love. Thankfully, I finally found it.

I do not think that I am alone. Indeed, I think that society itself is stuck looking for truth in all the wrong places.

First, we invented numbers.

Second, we started using them to make all sorts of decisions, some of which were to our benefit.

Third, we started using them to help us with the wrong questions, things about human life and human dignity. We began to define and describe ourselves using numbers. And suddenly, we couldn't stop doing so. I have made this point before: Numbers do not contain meaning. They only contain themselves. If you spend too much time talking to yourself about numbers, you will lose touch with the meaning of your own life. I know this, because it happened to me.

Fourth, we began looking to numbers to tell us the future. We asked experts to look in their spreadsheets and take us to the promised land. And while we wait for them to finish their calculations, the present slips away in a cloud of confusion. "It's not our fault," we tell ourselves. "It's someone else's." But it *is* our fault. When we ask science to bring us miracles, we lose sight of the greatest miracle of all—the fact that we exist. As we try to calculate our way to nirvana, we have lost focus on the awesomeness of the mere fact that any of this is happening in the first place. We have lost sight of the cosmic context of it all. We have lost sight of now.

Our addiction to quantification has made it impossible to grasp reality in the way that is necessary to make decisions about the only thing that matters, which is love. Everything else—all the numbers, every single one of them—is nothing but noise.

So here we are. And the question we each must grapple with— the only one we *ever* need to grapple with—is as simple as can be. It does not require a model or an expert or a businessman to tell you how to make it. And you don't need to yell it at anybody, or criticize anybody else while you're answering it, because it only requires an audience of one—*you.*

What should I do right now?

The modern mistake is thinking that we need numbers to come up with our answer. More to the point, we think that the more precise the numbers we can gin up, the more true will be the answers. But that's a red herring. The path to truth is not lined with numbers; it is lined with love.

Of course, it might be discernible using books about magic. Harry Potter read the following at Hogwarts:

Predicting the Unpredictable: Insulate Yourself Against Shocks
Broken Balls: When Fortunes Turn Foul
Unfogging the Future
Death Omens: What to Do When You Know the Worst Is Coming[3]

Maybe one of those will work. I'm kidding. Just like J. K. Rowling was kidding when she came up with those book titles.

We are using the wrong tools to make the big decisions. We are lost, because we are trying to use the tools of *precision* to answer questions that are really about *love*. That is the Precision Paradox.

*   *   *

How can we do a better job of *being here now*?

We can start by stopping with all the numbers and the quest for precision.

The quest for precision has taken us in the wrong direction, away from the present and into the past or the future. Those might seem like real places, but they're not. If you are not present, you are nowhere.

The quest for precision took us to a false prophet, *probability*, when we should have been looking for the true savior, *possibility*.

We have come to believe that life can be *calculated*, using numbers, when the reality is that the best parts of life lie beyond the realm of calculation. There is no calculation for everything.

Those two words—*probability* and *possibility*—sound almost the same, but they could not be more different.

One of them seeks to narrow experience, to tame uncertainty, to exercise control.

The other seeks to widen experience, to embrace uncertainty, and to imbue the present with the only thing that has ever mattered: *LOVE*.

Probabilities are for looking into *the future*. Possibilities are for looking into *now*. Only one of those things exists, and it is not the future.

The science of probability blinded us to the art of possibility.

We could not have been more wrong. We need to put the numbers down and start heading back to now.

*   *   *

"Okay, then," you might be saying. "So what should *we* do right now?"

I have an idea: Let's start listening to the people who are comfortable dwelling in uncertainty instead of the ones who are always trying to exert control. The people who can sit comfortably in *now*. Because they might have some ideas that you haven't been able to hear in the midst of all the control people yelling at each other about what needs to be done.

I have been pretty calm during this pandemic, and it's not because I have absolute certainty that my number isn't about to come up. It's because as a freelance writer, I made peace with uncertainty a long time ago. It's not that I know for sure that I won't die; it's simply that there are no odds of dying I have to be worried about, just like there are no odds of more work coming in the door that can be calculated to reduce the stress of worrying about tomorrow. The only thing that I—or you—have to do today is to understand that everything is okay, right now. That calm allowed me to write this book.

What has Joey done? She retired from a job she never enjoyed—being a real estate broker in New York City—and has taken over all major projects at the global headquarters we call Rockledge—our home in upstate New York. In May, she ordered a geodesic dome with a twenty-six-foot diameter and has begun growing all the food we need, year-round. She built a chicken coop and got us ten chickens. Five had to go, because we ended up with six roosters, but the eggs started coming in the winter, and four more hens came soon after that.

Have you seen the art that is being created right now? Check out my favorite website of all time, ThisIsColossal.com, and you will see it, everywhere around the world. Artists engage with the realm of uncertainty in order to make art—you must bring presence out of absence—so this is their time, too. The blues singer Paul Reddick put together a concert series, Wednesdays at Sauce, that is nothing short of majestic. The singer known as Bahamas has been putting out a YouTube series called Live to Tape that is sublime. The Barr Brothers took to Patreon to keep an open dialogue with die-hard fans like Joey and me, including uploading the complete recording of a transcendent show they put on at Levon's Barn in Woodstock in December 2018. So the world has not stopped. Lots of people are *creating* things *in the now*, which is what we are all supposed to be doing, every single second of our lives.

What are you going to do right now?

So what should *you* do? I can't answer that for you, but I can tell you that you should do *something* instead of just sitting around, waiting for herd immunity. Return to normal? There is no return to anything. There is only now.

More to the point, we need to stop telling other people what to do. Because if you are doing that, you are stuck up there in your ego, thinking you know something that other people don't. And you can never know what other people think, because you cannot see inside their minds. (If you are so inclined, you might consider it an irony that I am telling people to stop telling people what to do. But that's nothing but a hall of mirrors.)

> Do not give your attention to what others do or fail to do;
> give it to what you do or fail to do.[4]

The Buddha said that, too. Again: I agree with that guy.

This pandemic can go down in history as a transformative moment, if we don't let it slip away from us by engaging in an orgy of pointless analysis when we do come out our doors again. The solution—for everybody—is to simply grapple with what is happening *right now* and make any adjustments necessary. If we don't, we will be stuck in the past, spinning our wheels. If we choose to worry about the future instead, we will get stuck inside our minds, buried under a pile of something that doesn't even exist. Stay open, free from the attachments of memory or expectation, and we can act spontaneously, with *true intelligence*, aka *awareness*. Stay open, and do what the situation calls for, not what someone else *thinks* needs to be done. It's a lot easier than most of us have been led to believe.

> *If you stay aware of the present moment—that is, if you stay conscious of your own existence—things will happen, just like they always do.*

It seems important here to make clear the distinction between *presence* and *the present moment*. Presence is *being*, while moments slip away. The former is what you're after; the latter is already gone.

I watched my daughter's brain growing by the day during quarantine. All our brains wanted was a little peace and quiet, so that they could do their thing once more instead of being smothered under all that noise and all those pointless numbers. It's the mind that gets scared, and makes us afraid, but the brain is and always will be capable of embracing the uncertainty that is inherent in our very existence. That's *what it does*. All we need to do is listen to what it is telling us. We all know that, deep down, but we've confused ourselves into thinking that it's something *we have to do with our minds*, instead of just letting the brain do what it does. And because of that, we are afraid. It's hard to face uncertainty, and so we fill our lives with distractions instead.

As for me, I am not going to turn away from now.
I am going to
Keep feeding my body.
Keep feeding my mind.
Play with my body.
Play with my mind.
There is nothing else I have to do.
It's tickle time.

PART III

————

Anything Is Possible

Be in your beingness and everything
that is to happen will happen.[1]

—Sri Nisargadatta Maharaj, *Seeds of Consciousness*

No Time to Think

He can feel the way the story spreads out from this
point, through space and through time and so much
farther than he ever imagined but this is the beating,
buzzing heart of it. Right here and right now.[1]

—*The Starless Sea*

Why do we like live music? Because musicians know how to tickle
the now, and we get to watch them do it. My friend Kyle Ferguson is
the greatest guitarist I have ever seen. I asked him to describe what's
happening onstage. "Well, I guess the first thing is the know-how,"
he said. "The years of practicing."

And the second? "The ability to connect to something spiritual
or aesthetic."

What else? "One of the things I feel when it's all coming together
onstage is a complete lack of anxiety," he said. "It's hard to describe,
but let's call it *the opposite of anxiety*. I feel like I can't do any wrong."
He's talking about feeling *unlimited*, because he's found his way into
the deep now. That's where the *infinite* lives, and it's where you have
to go if you want to find it.

What does it feel like to play so well? "When you ask me about what I'm *feeling* when I play," he said, "you are speaking my language."

Ah, language. There you are again.

This is Kyle's best story: Once, when he was playing with his long-time collaborator, Paul Reddick, he was so relaxed in a solo that *he fell asleep while playing*. When he came out of it, he was shocked, not sure what had just happened, and also concerned that he'd ruined the performance. Nope. No one even noticed. They told him it had been a great show. Talk about being in *flow*, which is also *now*, which is also *love*. That, my friends, is why we love live music. Because when they get it right, it's nothing short of *magic*.

Thinking kills spontaneity. There's no time for thinking when you are in flow. If you don't believe me, just ask Bob Dylan. He wrote an entire song about it. Mind you, he's written songs about everything. How does he know about everything? That's simple: He spends a lot of time in *now*, too. And you can see everything from there.

*   *   *

Bob Dylan swims in the sea of consciousness. He has been doing so for decades. If you cannot hear that in his songs, then you are not listening. Along with all the other great songwriters, he is constantly reminding us that there is only love. That it is all that matters.

I've had phases in my life where I made everyone sit, quietly, listening to Dylan. It was partly an exercise in self-restraint: Could I, just this once, not get irritated when someone started talking before the end of the song? But I don't do it so much anymore. At some point, I realized that I didn't need people to agree with me about Bob Dylan in order to enjoy him. It would have been nice if I'd realized that same thing about all the other things I thought people couldn't understand. But hey, you can't win 'em all.

Ask any woman who has ever been involved with me, and she will tell you about how I tried to make her understand. At some point, I would invariably play "Last Thoughts on Woody Guthrie," the best spoken-word performance I have ever heard. "You need something special, all right," he says mid-poem. "You need something special to give you hope." For years, when I heard that line, I also yearned for that something. I knew he knew what it was, I just didn't know where to find it.

This would seem like an impossible thing to actually *calculate*, but I don't see how Bob Dylan isn't the most covered songwriter in history. Frank Sinatra, maybe? But that would make sense, too, as Dylan spent five albums covering the master himself in recent years. (It's all one big tapestry, folks.)

One of my music discovery strategies has simply been to check out people who have covered Dylan songs and see what else they had to offer. That's how I first listened to everyone from Sam Cooke to Emmylou Harris to Joan Baez, Ralph Stanley, Nina Simone, Mark Knopfler, Roy Orbison, and, yes, Miley Cyrus. Her cover of "You're Gonna Make Me Lonesome When You Go" is astoundingly good, which led me to discover that the rest of Miley Cyrus is also astoundingly good. I started listening to Jim James, M. Ward, and Josh Ritter because *I could just tell* that they had all inhaled all kinds of Bob Dylan on their way to becoming great artists. All roads lead to Dylan, at some point or another. He is the connective tissue at the center of a certain kind of music. He is the interconnectedness of all things.

You can also look at Dylan's career as an example of the notion of infinite possibility. Take musical genres: He has ranged from rock to country, gospel, blues, folk, standards, and rockabilly. You never know what style he's going to play next. Infinite possibility. Dylan is also famous for slipping new and novel words into his songs when he performs them. Again: infinite possibility.

One of my favorite Dylan songs is "Brownsville Girl," a rambling poem of a song that is like a meandering journey through memory itself. And one of the things Dylan does in that song is shift perspective—it flows—and it's never quite clear who is speaking. It doesn't seem like it's all the same person, but who knows? What I think Dylan was trying to do in that song was to show us that it doesn't matter. It's all the same story anyway. There is only one story, and it is life, and it is love. There's this great part in the song where he shifts from being in the audience of a movie starring Gregory Peck to being *in the movie itself*. It's a stunning piece of art about the self and identity. Infinite possibility.

> Always maintain awareness in all your activities.
>
> —Spanda Kārikā 3.12

The misinformed discuss the idea of buying tickets to see a show on Dylan's Never-Ending Tour as a crapshoot, because you never know what you're going to see when you see Dylan. You've got that right, folks, but you are missing the point: That is what's known as infinite possibility.

He's been doing it right in front of us for decades, and few have ever really figured out what the man is up to. His embrace of uncertainty is more powerful than that of pretty much any performer who has ever lived, including the so-called gods of improvisation, the Grateful Dead. I mean, I love the Dead, but you just need to think about the way the admiration flowed between them: Jerry Garcia worshipped Bob Dylan.

The Dead's *Postcards of the Hanging* is a full album of Dylan covers. (I had the idea for an album of Dead-doing-Dylan covers and then discovered that they'd already done it. So the Dead copied me, in advance.) Dylan hasn't done an album of Grateful Dead covers, although he might. Infinite possibility.

During my brief stint on Wall Street, I managed to secure the entire Goldman Sachs box at Madison Square Garden for a Jerry Garcia Band show. I took fifteen friends to see Jerry Garcia Band play a ridiculous version of "Tangled Up in Blue" at Madison Square Garden. That night, I felt like a bit of a legend myself.

The *New York Sessions* of Dylan's *Blood on the Tracks* album is one of the most unique albums you will ever listen to. It is an entire album, recorded and mixed, and ready to go, and then shelved in favor of a newer version of the album that he recorded in Nashville. Do you really need any more evidence that everything is just a different version of everything else than that? With that album, Dylan *covered himself*.

I saw Dylan play twice in one week in late 2019. Because the two shows were close together, the memory of the first allowed me to watch the second with the kind of attention that you don't often get at a live show. I realized, to my great shock, that a Dylan performance is as choreographed as a ballet. I mean, I know that bands need to get in a groove to put on good shows, and when you're combining the work of several people, it helps to do things in roughly the same way. But I had no idea about the level of precision that they circled around in order to bring their magic. I heard Dylan take audible breaths through his microphone in the exact same spot and with the exact same amount of energy as during the previous show. I guess that's what they mean by great art coming out of constraint. It's possible to lock something down to the point that that's when the real magic happens, when it starts flowing in from the universe and through each person on the stage.

*   *   *

Look, I could write an entire book about Bob Dylan if I had the time. But I don't. I'm too busy working on The Bob Project, which is my lifelong quest to sneak Dylan references into anything and everything that I do.

Why do I do that? Do you really need to ask? Because it's *fun*. It's not even that hard. Like J. K. Rowling, Dylan has put *everything* into his oeuvre. They even let you search his lyrics on www.bobdylan.com. When I'm writing a story about greed, I search for *greed*. This is pretty simple stuff, folks. All you have to do is consult the Bob Dylan Lyric Almanac of life.

In late 2019, I wrote a story for Graydon Carter's *Air Mail* weekly revealing The Bob Project. Graydon also let me write about Dylan for *Vanity Fair*. God bless you, Graydon, for letting me write about Bob not once, but twice. You have my eternal gratitude for that and for giving me a chance to become a real writer. I hope you're proud of me, because along with Hugo Lindgren, you're the only other person in journalism whose approval I ever really, truly craved.

So there's this movie that Martin Scorsese made for Netflix about Dylan called *Rolling Thunder Revue*. The music in it is amazing, with astoundingly good concert footage. I won't ruin anything for you, but I want to point out the fact that while it may seem like your typical music documentary, all is not what it seems. It never is with Dylan. The man has been wearing masks all his life. Just when you think you know what's going on, you don't.

So, anyway, I called that *Air Mail* piece The Bob Project because it seemed like the appropriate thing to do. It was a project, about Bob. What else was I going to call it? It wasn't until later that I realized that I'd made a mistake. You see, my quest is *my project*. Dylan himself is working on *The Bob Project*. What I am working on is *The Duff Project*.

I had pulled a Dylan on myself, calling a story by another name. After that, I changed the URL to my own website to TheDuffProject

.com. Because that's what it's documenting—my lifelong project to express myself in writing. The website is where it's all gathered, in a Common Place. That's where you will find all of my Common Sense. But don't be fooled by the narrowness of it, either. My entire life is The Duff Project. And yours is yours. Those projects are the sum of our experiences, the invisible cities we build so as to be able to conjure up our own unique expression of the only story there is, which is love.

That is all there is, people:
You are given a life . . .
Your job is simply to live that life . . .
To soak up as much experience as you can . . .
And to use that experience . . .
To craft your own unique message of love . . .
And then to send that message out to the cosmos . . .
And to everyone you ever meet . . .
by tickling them.

In other words, write your own story. In *The Power of Myth*, Joseph Campbell says *Star Wars* "has to do with the powers of life and their inflection through the actions of man." What does he mean by that? I think he's pointing us to the fact that we are a lot more powerful than we think. Each and every one of us started with a thought—the idea that you could exist—and from that thought has sprung an entire universe. But it requires *action* to make it happen. So have the thought and then use *the powers of life* to bring it into being. Our physical existence may yield its secrets to measurement, but our spiritual existence, which has building blocks much more subtle than matter, will only yield its secrets to experience.

The good news is that all that it requires is that you *pay attention.*

So how can you learn how to pay proper attention to your life? That's easy: Learn how to meditate. I could write a whole book on the glories of meditation, and I've only been doing it seriously for a few years. Put the internal universe up against the so-called external universe and the internal one will win hands down. Learn how to look inside, and you will find that you already have access to what Sri Nisargadatta Maharaj calls "the whole supply of everything." Meditation teaches you how to focus, which will make you better at everything you do. Everything.

> If you don't already meditate, take my advice: Start.
> It will be the best decision you ever make.
>
> —David Lynch

That's because the act of meditating isn't just about the act of meditating. It's about everything else you do as well. Indeed, it might just be life's most transferable skill. What do I mean by that? I mean that meditation is about quieting the mind. It's about how to stop thinking and just *be*. You see, *being* contains *thinking*, not the other way around. If you're good at *being*, in other words, you're obviously good at *thinking*, too. If you learn how to meditate—how to simply *be*—you have learned how to do the thing that contains everything else. That's why it makes *everything* easier, including *thinking*, although the better you get at *being*, the less and less *thinking* you will need to do. We don't need time, and we don't need thinking. We don't need *time to think* at all.

If I sound like I think I've known this stuff all along, do not be confused. I only recently learned it from an Agent/Angel named Joey Moss and a little Messiah of Love named M. We are all angels and messiahs, though. You just need to pay attention, because they are everywhere you look.

The Love Equation

Know the One by knowing which
you will know everything.

—Various scriptures

We have a choice to make, my friends.

But first we need to accept a couple of things:

First: We cannot predict the future, because it doesn't exist.

Second: Our obsession with the science of probability has blinded us to the art of possibility. We need to quit it with all the numbers and predictions and probabilities and simply learn to live right here, right now, where anything is possible.

Why have we tried to narrow the possibilities for so long? What's the point of that? What is wrong with us that when it comes to what our lives could be, we choose to settle for less instead of more?

Third: The way back to now is to find our way back to getting into flow, to feel the interconnectedness of all things. Just ask J. K. Rowling, Bob Dylan, and David Lynch. They've been there all along, waiting for the rest of us to show up.

Fourth: The way we do that is to use our senses, to feed the brain, to give it all the things it needs from us, so that it can do its thing.

Fifth: That is, we need to start using our common sense again.

It's about *time*, isn't it?

Whoa, hold up now! That's exactly where we went wrong in the first place!

It's not about *time*. It's not about time *at all*.

It's about *now*.

So let's get back to that choice:

What are we going to do right now?

*   *   *

I can't tell you what to do right now. I probably don't even know who you are or what kind of situation you are dealing with. But I can tell you what not to do: Stop with all the *thinking*.

We think too much.

That's it. Too much thinking, not enough being. That is the problem. That is our biggest problem.

When we use math and science and physics to try to predict things, we are trying to answer an unanswerable question, *What does the future hold?* If it could really be done, we'd be doing it all the time. But it can't, which is why the responsibility for doing so has been relegated to that part of us that doesn't actually do things— the intellect. You can't think your way into the future. You can't even think your way into the present. Only awareness can take you there. And when you're truly conscious of what's happening right now, the future comes to you.

(Actually, the question is answerable: The future contains everything. And nothing. Because it doesn't exist. The only part of the future that is real is the part that is unpredictable.)

When we decide that we can *think* our way through to an answer that does not exist, we trap ourselves inside our minds and lose track of what is happening right now.

> Courage in the face of the unknown is an important quality in a wizard.[1]
>
> —*Harry Potter and the Goblet of Fire*

More to the point, we end up in what is known as a paradox, a situation that combines contradictory features or qualities. Paradoxes resolve themselves when we step back and realize how we'd been thinking about everything the wrong way.

Say, for example, we thought we could use the tools of mathematics and precision to measure our way to understanding. That would probably present quite the paradox, wouldn't it?

At least until we stepped back and realized that we were using the wrong tools. When we realize that, something as seemingly contradictory as the *Precision Paradox* would instantly disappear.

What's the problem with science? Scientific models can't account for the variable called love. The biggest problem that physics couldn't figure out? The so-called Theory of Everything? The answer to that is love. They should have asked an angel.

What's the problem with capitalism? Economic models and economic systems can't account for the variable called love.

There are way too many people among us—I was one until only recently—who don't believe in anything other than science-by-measurement. That means they don't really believe in anything other than certainty. And certainty is not a proxy for love. I speak from experience.

All my life, I thought I'd been figuring stuff out, but I hadn't figured out the one thing that was right there, in front of my face. I had two beautiful women, M. and Joey, aiming all the love power they had right at me, and it still took a plague to wake me up.

At this point, for both of our sakes, I can only hope that the book you are reading still exists. Because I just showed you how the paradox that was supposedly at the heart of it wasn't even really a paradox. (They never are.) I was just confused. I was trapped in an illusion. Until it suddenly dissolved.

*   *   *

I don't think I've told you the particulars of how I woke up, how the last piece of the puzzle fell into place for me, and how the missing *variable* turned out to be the *only variable* that there is. You are either open to and doling out love or you are not. That is it, folks. There's even *an equation* for it. Joey writes it down all over the place.

LOVE MORE

Just kidding. That's not an equation. There is no *equation* for love. The universe doesn't do equations. It just does love. If it were an equation—a formula—it would say something about time, give us an "*if this, then that*" kind of promise. But you don't need time to do this. You can do it *right now*.

LOVE MORE

As recently as February 2020, I did not fully understand what that meant. I mean, I understood why Joey likes to put those *You Are Beautiful* stickers everywhere she goes. Our friend Dinshaw called her once from JFK Airport and said, "The Delta counter?" Yup, that was Joey. You should see her when she's getting ready to put one on a subway pole. She gets this funny look on her face, as if she's up to no good, as if telling people they are beautiful by putting a sticker on a train pole is somehow against the rules. When I see that look, I see an angel laughing in the face of man's silly strictures.

So let's get back to that last piece of the puzzle. I love my daughter. I always have, even if I didn't quite act like it in the years after she was born. I have tried to be a caring and attentive father. M. has always loved me, too. But as Joey tried to tell me every now and then, she was also a little . . . scared . . . of me.

She was talking about the anger that was always beneath the surface, even if I was in a good mood. M. felt that, and it scared her a little. Which means that I wasn't always tickling her. Worse yet, I wasn't always *listening* to her. I thought I was being a good father, in the same way that I thought I was being a good writer, but I wasn't paying close enough attention to either one. But that's the way it always happens, right? I couldn't see the absence that was right in front of me. Because I wasn't looking for it. And it's pretty hard to see something you're not looking for.

Right before the quarantine hit, I signed the contract to write *The Precision Paradox*. At a time when a lot of people were losing their jobs, or worse, I was sitting pretty, with cash flow, good health, and the long and mostly enjoyable runway of working on a new book in front of me. I had eighteen months to write it, and I decided that I was just going to ease into things and try to enjoy life.

In March, M. started hounding me to read Harry Potter. Her stepfather was already reading it with her, but she wanted Harry Potter to be on the reading list of both of our houses. I told her that I was too busy with *work*. But she was undeterred. Every single night, she would read Harry Potter memes over FaceTime to Joey and me. I started getting annoyed, and even told her a couple of times that she should respect the fact that we weren't as interested in Harry Potter as she was.

To recap:

My daughter was literally begging me to read Harry Potter with her.

First, I told her that I didn't have time, that I had real *work* to do.

Then I told her to stop talking to me about something that *tickled* her.

Could I have been a bigger asshole?

I am not sure of the exact moment when I realized that I needed to read Harry Potter—that *my job* was to read Harry Potter. (Her stepfather already knew this. You want to know how lucky I am? He loves her as much as I do.) Let's just assume that Joey told me to, because that's what Joey does. She spreads love around everywhere she goes. M. was trying to share her love of something with me, to take what tickled and pass it on. She was holding it out to me, but I was too distracted to accept it. When someone hands you some love, you should take it.

When I announced one evening that I had started reading Harry Potter that afternoon, she lit up. After that, everything snapped into place with such force that it was startling.

Five years ago, I posted a cute picture of me holding M. in my arms. The caption said, "The Lady refreshes the spell that controls her father."

The day after I told her I'd started reading Harry Potter, she

posted an updated version of that photo on her own Instagram. We hadn't discussed it or even mentioned it since, well, since I'd included it in a story I'd written for *Wired* in November 2019 about how much I loved her.

I'm going to say that again, just so that you hear what I am saying: The day after I told her that I would read Harry Potter with her, she posted a photo that she'd modified (that is, copied) without the original caption. She was telling *her story*, not mine.

But let's not forget what I'd written in my own caption: *The Lady refreshes the spell that controls her father.*

So . . .

The spell that controls her father was and is love.
That is the spell that controls all of us.

My daughter aimed her wand at me, and cast a spell of love.
She did it using Harry Potter, which is all about casting spells . . . of love.
There is only one story, people, and that is it.

Or, if you like Joey's version better:

LOVE MORE

At that point, everything started swirling around me. Literally. And then it all started falling into place. With every passing day, things seemed clearer to me, and that clarity extended to pretty much everything you have read in this book.

I did not *know* most of what I have written here before I sat down to write. Although maybe a better way to say that is that while I knew a bunch of stuff, I didn't know why it mattered, what mattered about it. In place of that *knowing* sat what some refer to as an ancient longing; others call it the nostalgia of the soul. Deep down, I could feel that there *was* an answer to this thing called existence, but I hadn't the faintest idea what it was. And then, all of a sudden, I did. It was like a bolt of lightning that went straight into my soul and *illuminated* all the things that mattered to me.

I suddenly realized what I really felt about everything.

Professionally, I finally understood what I had been trying to say for all these years. I saw all the costs of our quantified reality, crystallized for me, as if I'd known them all along:

I saw the hollowness of numbers.
I knew what was wrong with capitalism.
I realized the heart of the management consulting hustle.
I realized the futile quest of a science of measurement.

I also saw what mattered about the things that mattered to me, clearer than I'd ever seen them before. We'll get to the ones I haven't already told you about in the pages ahead, but here's a preview:

I had a renewed sense of why I love Bob Dylan.
I realized the essence of kombucha.
When I read Harry Potter, I could see to the heart of J. K.
   Rowling's message.
I realized that I had stopped listening—to other people, but also
   to myself. And if you stop listening to yourself, you won't know
   what tickles you.
I was able to touch my child's heart again.
I saw Joey for what she really is, which is an angel.
Literally. I married an angel.

I was swimming in the ocean of consciousness, but I didn't know it yet.

In May, I was up early one morning and I stumbled on a video in which David Lynch was talking about the ocean of consciousness. I ran upstairs and woke Joey up.

"This is what is happening to me!" I said.

Agent Angel wasn't surprised. She knew. She'd been waiting for me, too. All this time. Patiently waiting.

For a minute, I thought it was something special, meaning that it was something special meant only for me. But that's how the ego does its work.

It was only love.

> [Spiritual] practice consists in constantly going beyond the wall of the ego, in reaching out and embracing all life fearlessly, with an open heart. There must be complete clarity and integrity in one's feelings. Most people are "collapsed at the heart." They are in doubt of God, others, and themselves.[2]
>
> —The Kundalini Experience

Love is all around you. To find it, you just need to start listening. I listened to Joey and then I listened to M. And then all I could hear was the sound of joy.

*   *   *

So, just to be very clear about what I'm saying here: The thing the scientists are looking for with their measuring instruments—a unifying principle—is not something that you can count. It's called infinite possibility. But you could also call it love. Love is the creative force of the universe. Love is possibility. It is the causeless cause of all creation. It is the concept upon which all other concepts take place. It is the foundation of everything.

Things happen because . . . love. At the same time, love *is* the universe. So it is both *why* things happen and the things that happen themselves. You grow by love, you live by love, you return to love after your body dies. I am not speaking in metaphor. I mean this *literally*. There is only love. Whenever you think something is missing from a situation, the missing thing is always going to be love. It is only when we find ourselves in the absence of love that we get into trouble.

When experiments in physics come up short, when they don't account for all the outcomes, do you know what they are missing? They are missing the fact that sometimes, something unexpected happens. In other words, anything is possible.

When experiments in economics or behavioral science don't account for all the outcomes, do you know what they are missing? They are missing the fact that people sometimes do the unexpected. In other words, anything is possible.

The missing variable in all those calculations is the sheer infinitude of now. Otherwise known as everything. Otherwise known as love. We get confused when we lose sight of love, and think there is something else to find. There isn't.

I don't need a scientist to tell me about the origin of the universe. Because I know what happened: Before the universe, there was nothing but possibility itself. But possibility got bored and decided, "Screw this nothingness. Let's *do something*. Let's *play*." And then suddenly there you were.

So that's *what* happened. But *why* did it happen? Why did the universe come into being? Well, considering that you are the universe, that's a question you're going to need to ask yourself. Why did you come into being? Why do you exist? Why did you give yourself the cosmic gift of existence? Because it was in your nature to do so. Because you love yourself. Because of that, you gave yourself the most precious gift of all, which is existence.

Numbers? What use are numbers in the face of existence? Numbers lead to comparison. But what is comparable to the entire universe? Nothing. We've been deluding ourselves into thinking that we can measure each other and decide who is better or worse than whom. That's rooted in a profound misunderstanding. We're all the universe. Nothing can compare to *any of us*.

Why? *Because we exist.*

Love did that.

From now on, when someone tells you that your choices are limited, as shown by their probability calculations, you should tell them that they have no idea what they are talking about. You are the universe. You can do whatever you want.

*   *   *

So M. made me a sweatshirt for Christmas 2019. On the front is a picture of a black cat's face. Underneath it, it says, "WHAT?"

I know it's a meme. But it was also an inside joke. In our house, the exclamation "What?" refers to that moment when you pretend to be annoyed with someone even though you are thrilled that you have just realized that they are looking at you—that they are *connected* with you. The type of joke where you put your hands up and ask, as if you really only wanted to be left alone: *What?*

When we do it, it means:

What?
Why are you looking at me again—you and all your love?
What do you want with me?

What we want is to love each other.

M. told me her story, not mine. You need your story, not mine. What is yours? I'll give you an opening thought: You are beautiful. Go from there.

———

CHAPTER 13

The Jasmine Troupe

She was the love of my life. I'm not shittin' you.
She and I lit the flame of love.[1]

—Jack, *What Did Jack Do?*

I once read that Vladimir Nabokov wrote better opening lines to stories than any writer who has ever lived. It's true. I went through his collected short stories and have confirmed it. The man is a master of the opening salvo. While I never had the patience to *solve* Nabokov's more complicated novels—I *almost* grasped *Pale Fire*, but not quite—I decided to aspire to great opening lines myself ever since I was made aware of the possibility of specializing in them. My version is a little different, though. Like Bob Dylan, who insists his songs are appreciated best while being heard, not read, I think my best storytelling is in person, in spoken word, and not in print. I have since tried, in conversation, to begin my stories with the best possible opening lines.

You can ask Joey: I am constantly refining what we have come to refer to as "the preface." I use prefacing remarks to set up a laugh before I've even gotten to the point:

You're not going to like what I'm about to tell you, but . . .
This might be the most interesting thing I say to you today . . .
Before I say this, I want you to know that I still love you . . .
You may have heard this somewhere else, but not in the
following way . . .

It's all about *playing*, people. I use the preface to focus the listener (in most cases, Joey) and get her mind ready for . . . whatever is coming next. It's like opening a conversation by wrapping it in a gift box with a card that says, "You're really going to like what's in here." At that point, the conversation is all possibility. I am laying the groundwork before telling the tale. I have said something that could lead anywhere before I begin saying the thing I am about to say.

POSSIBILITY ➡ CHOICE

Outside of my mother, Joey and M. are the two most important women in my life. At this point, too, they often act as one when it comes to the power of love. Give me one of them, and I can feel the underlying force of the universe. Give me both of them, and I am practically drowning in it.

We have a lot of nicknames in our house. M. is Uno. As in, Numero Uno. We got there because I told her one day that she was my favorite of all the kids I have ever had. (I have only had one.) "You're numero uno!" I said, and she smiled. M. is a funny kid, and she loves it, always responding, "I'm the *only* kid you've ever had!" And then, one day, I was telling Joey that she was the love of my life, wait, maybe, uh . . . she was the second love of my life, after

Uno. So we started calling her Juno. M. put "Juno" on a sweatshirt she made for Joey.

(You will have noticed that I also call M. The Lady. I use The Lady in writing, but Uno in conversation. One has to have rules, or there would be chaos.)

The other nickname we have given Joey of late is Jogi, because she's the chief yogi at Rockledge. Most nicknames in our house don't stick, because we keep on making up new ones, but every time I see Joey these days, I exclaim, "Hey, Jogi! What are you doing?" It's a keeper.

M. and Joey make the universe sparkle for me. Or, as Jim James might say, there is more stardust when they are near. I get love in both directions, from below and from above. Their patience, calm, and love for all living things have created the most wonderful environment in which a man could hope to exist. They are both angels, Uno and Juno.

*   *   *

What can I tell you about M.? When I finally started paying attention to her—that is, when I quit drinking—I realized that parenting isn't just about reading books to cute little girls at bedtime. It's not just about going to soccer games or birthday parties. Parenting is about helping another human being learn how to feed their own brain. When I realized that, I also realized that I had quite the little brain to work with.

I am not saying that my kid is smarter than your kid. I have no idea how "smart" M. is, nor do I really care. I learned my lesson about putting too much faith in "smart" when I banked on it myself. What I love about M. is that she's got quite the combination going—she is loving, curious, brave, funny, and empathetic. That's the complete package, which has made the part I get to play in helping her learn how to interact with her brain more fun than I ever could have imagined.

I think I made three smart choices when it came to parenting. The first was that I have always spoken to my daughter as if she is a complete human being. The second is that I have emphasized the importance of a sense of humor. To do that, I held her to a high standard when it came to being funny. I see no point in telling someone, especially a child, that they're funny when they're not. The next thing you know, you have an unfunny adult who thinks they're funny. So we have kept the banter high-quality in this house, and the results speak for themselves. She makes me laugh almost every single day. The third thing I have tried to do is communicate to her that she should always be wondering. Always. Because you're never going to create the best possible universe if you haven't thought it through. I'm not saying that I want her to be a thinker. I want her to be a doer. Thinking is overrated. But you still want the doing part to be interesting, and that's where the wondering comes in.

What if we do this?

What if we don't? Our other thing is inside jokes. One of them is the Jasmine Troupe. M., Joey, and I are in it, along with our friends Rachel, Christiane, and the late Owen Osborne, one of the sweetest human beings I have ever met. We have a secret password. We make sweatshirts. (Rather: M. has made us sweatshirts. And T-shirts.) We have a secret handshake. And what is the Jasmine Troupe? Well, that's for us to know and for you to find out. It's not an exclusionary club, but we don't just take anyone. What do you bring to the table?

*　　*　　*

What else can I tell you about M.? Well, in January 2020, she had the audacity to get kicked in the face by her horse, Barney.

I wrote this the next day:

> She's doing fine, although no one (including the surgeon) was able to keep track of the number of stitches that went into her lip and cheek. I was proud of her bedside team. But if you thought that a kick in the face could break The Lady, you thought wrong:
>
> Pre-stitches: "I can't even say words that start with the letter . . . actually, I can't say the letter . . . it's the second one in the alpha-et."
>
> Post-stitches: "I'm exhausted. I can't wait to get home and get in . . . ED."
>
> Enduring pain is one thing. Enduring pain while cracking jokes is next level.

More important: In pain, waiting to get stitches, she tried to tell us how the wound was getting in the way of her using . . . language.

A few weeks later, she decided to mine the experience for another good laugh. "It turns out there are good things about getting kicked in the face by a horse," she said one day, out of the blue. "I'm not afraid of having a blood test anymore. So, thanks, Barney, for that."

Sometimes, life is easy. Sometimes, it's harder than that. For me, the transition between the two has, at times, been difficult. I have been blessed with a comfortable and relatively healthy life, but when something unexpected has arisen, I have not always had the good grace to handle the transition well. Worse yet, I spent so many years in an alcoholic haze that I would get pretty far down the wrong path before I realized what I was doing, and my overreaction would be even worse than it otherwise might have been. That's been my Achilles' heel. (Or at least one of them.) I have failed to make adjustments properly, and then given in to frustration and anger when the time to adjust had finally come.

And then I look at my daughter, who until recently was so tiny that I could pick her up with just one arm. Inside that little girl, whose parents split up when she was just three years old, you will find something that I rarely had access to until recently: equanimity. I have of late discovered that the key to a meaningful life is acceptance—not just of who you are, but of what is happening to you. You always have a choice about what to do next in the situation you find yourself in, but the last thing you need to do is start complaining about the things that happened to get you there. Because those things are gone. The only thing you need to do is figure out what you're going to do right now. On countless occasions, my daughter has shown me how to handle life's challenges with grace. Sometimes you teach your child about life; at other times, your child teaches you. Humility is sneaky that way.

While we're on the subject of horses, when she was healing from her wound and the world hadn't run inside to hide yet, we regularly went to this great bookstore/cafe in Kingston called Rough Draft for breakfast. It's such a great place, built with readers, and not customers, in mind. Anyway, M. and I were having a reader's breakfast at Rough Draft one morning. On the way there, she said sneezing is "like getting a back scratch up your nose." While we were hanging out, reading over coffee, cider, and croissants, she described another customer as "half cowboy, half Albert Einstein." Her mouth may have been injured, but her mind was on fire. What was she reading? Harry Potter, of course. Did you really need to ask?

*　　*　　*

The Jasmine Troupe operates out of Rockledge, our house in Hurley, New York. Leafing through some old newspaper clippings about Anne Kreyer, the widow who owned our house one hundred years ago, we came across that name.

The best one is the following:

> Miss Anne Kreyer and some friends spent some time here
> last week at her summer home, "Rockledge." As Miss Kreyer
> is still having many changes and improvements made at her
> beautiful place here she will not take, this winter, her usual
> trip to Europe.
>
> —*Kingston Daily Freeman*, February 18, 1929

If you thought a stock market crash would slow Anne Kreyer down, you thought wrong:

> Miss Anne Kreyer recently entertained a houseful of guests
> at Rockledge.
>
> —*Kingston Daily Freeman*, November 11, 1929

Anyway, we started calling the house Rockledge after we found that.

I bought the house in 2014, a few years after I got divorced. I'd always wanted to get a house in the middle of nowhere and keep a place in the city. The ex-wife had wanted the suburbs . . . so we'd bought a house in the suburbs. Anyway, when I bought Rockledge, I was dating Lauren, a delightful and funny actress born a half century late. She would have made an amazing femme fatale in noir Hollywood.

Lauren transforms bland into delightful, and she wanted to transform Rockledge from someone else's house into our house. I was
too busy being me to realize what she was doing and ended up
losing her attention after a year or so. For a time, I told myself it
was because she wasn't ready to settle down. But that was just mirroring. It was all me, the same as always. I wasn't settled yet, and
Lauren could feel it. She moved on. She made M. laugh, and we
still talk about her every now and then.

*　　*　　*

I met Joey on my second date with my ex-fiancée. I have been holding this little detail back for a while now, but it's time to come out
with it: Joey was my ex-fiancée's best friend. Before you go thinking this is some big scandal, allow me to clarify: My engagement
did not end because of something untoward between Joey and me.
Indeed, when my engagement ended, it looked like I was going to
exit the situation and Joey would stay best friends with my ex. But
that's not what happened.

What did happen? I was a wreck, because I had been in love. I
asked Joey for help, because I was floundering. After a bit, I realized that I had put Joey in a very uncomfortable situation and told
her that I didn't want to do that to her. Meanwhile, my ex was
concocting a story that wasn't true about me and insisted that Joey
stick to the party line. Joey refused, and my ex broke up with Joey,
too. Joèl Moss (that's her sophisticated name) saved my life, pure
and simple. She was sent from heaven to rescue me from myself,
and that's what she did. She took my crown of thorns and gave
me shelter from the storm. She helped quiet my mind and then
reminded me that the universe needed my attention. She showed
me how to look inside.

Joey is the kindest person that I know. She is the best listener that I know. She has more capacity for love than anyone I have ever met. She's more of a doer than a talker. She is patient. She loves to laugh. She's a lot of things, but one of Joey's essences is rainbows. When I bury my head in her chest, eyes closed, I see rainbows. Joey walks around with a stack of those "You Are Beautiful" stickers in her bag so that she can put them in the back of taxis or on seatbacks in airplanes. Just to make people smile.

Sri Nisargadatta Maharaj writes, "Don't try to love somebody, be love. When you are love, that love will be useful to humanity. Just like water, if you are water, everything will grow."[2] That's Joey. When she says *Love More*, she means it.

She taught me how to listen. She taught me how to love. She taught me how to do things, instead of just talking about them. She taught me how to be patient. She taught me how to stop taking myself so fucking seriously. I already knew how to laugh, but Joey taught me how to laugh all the time. Life with Joey is one laugh after the next. Every single day. They say that the partners you attract are what you need. When it comes to Joey, that is 100 percent true.

The short version of that: Joey taught me how to love myself. It's the only thing that any of us ever needs to do, right? And once I had that figured out, the rest just fell into place. Because once you know how to love yourself, you can figure out how to tickle yourself. And once you figure out how to tickle yourself, you can tickle other people.

CHAPTER 14

Infinite Kombucha

Before unearthing this letter, I had wondered
how a book could be infinite. The only way I could
surmise was that it be a cyclical, or circular, volume,
a volume whose last page would be identical to
the first, so that one might go on indefinitely.[1]

—Jorge Luis Borges, *The Garden of Forking Paths*

Ask anyone who knows me well or is connected to me on social media, and they will be able to tell you about my two great loves (other than Joey and M.): kombucha and my airtight wood-burning stove. I've been getting to know the fireplace since I bought my home in 2014. My love affair with kombucha began a few years later, in the summer of 2017, when a friend introduced me to the magic elixir.

While kombucha and a good roaring fire inside an airtight stove may seem different enough on the surface, the fact is that they are more related than you think. Both of them offer access to the notion of infinite possibility. They allow me to reach into the infinitude of *now*, to grasp the heart of existence. I know that sounds a little crazy, but I assure you that it's not.

I'll dispense with fire first, because it's a little easier to explain. For the last few years, I have been telling anyone I know who owns a fireplace to switch over to an airtight. Why? Because the near vacuum in there allows you to temporarily capture angry energy before it dissipates back into the cosmos. That's good for *heating*, of course. But what it's really good for is the *viewing*. If you keep your glass door crystal clear—I clean mine off before every single fire—a good fire is the best show of all, Fire TV. Because fire is literally energy on the loose. When you trap it inside your box, if only briefly, the thing you get to watch is basically Infinite TV. Stack your logs right, and you can send the flames swirling up and down, left and right, in whatever colors your particular wood has to offer.

My friend Billy told me to throw a copper pipe in there in May 2020, promising a color show. He was right: Copper burns neon green, which turned the fire into something out of a Harry Potter spell, which I immediately told M. about. "Billy is a wizard!" I said. So trap your flame, add your color, and watch energy do its thing. It is *infinitely* entertaining, I guess until you are Joey and you're being asked, for the millionth time, to appreciate the fire that she was already capable of seeing with her own eyes.

So . . . kombucha. I quit drinking after my divorce in 2012. I'd been searching for my replacement drink ever since. I went down a couple of wrong paths, including Diet Pepsi and Marlboro Lights. (When a friend noted how much ice cream I was eating at the time, they observed that I was on the "fat girl diet." That's not PC, but you have to admit it's pretty funny. It also got me off the diet.)

I think the first kombucha I tried was a GT's Gingerade. GT's makes some okay kombuchas, but there's *too much flavor* in most of them. Their *Euphoria* flavor, which contains cayenne, used to explode all over my shirt every time I opened one. I am not sure why I tried to open it so many times, all with the exact same result (see: the definition of insanity), but I did.

I drank a lot of GT's. The best flavors are *Original, Pink Lady Apple,* and *Gingerade.* They miss the mark on *Tantric Turmeric* and *Heart Beet,* making the classic mistake of the overenthusiastic health food type; they miscalculate the trade between good taste and good health. (Note to all healthy food makers: It still has to taste good. We are putting it in our mouths.) I drank a lot of Kevita brand, too. Their best flavors are *Dragonfruit Lemongrass* and *Tart Cherry.*

I was buying a lot of kombucha at retail in the summer of 2018 when my friend Chris MacFarland asked me why I wasn't just buying it on tap from the place out on Route 28 by my house in Hurley. The reason was that I have not always been good at paying attention, and I didn't even know the store was there.

Anyway, once I realized that I could buy it on draft, I began buying it at $20 a gallon. Bottled kombucha at retail isn't cheap— anywhere between $3 and $6 a bottle—so paying $20 a gallon was a way to save myself hundreds, if not thousands, of dollars. The store on Route 28, which used to be Brooklyn Kombucha, carried a great brand, Katalyst. Their *Jasmine* kombucha is divine.

The owners of the store sold it to their landlord, La Bella Pasta, who brought in a guy named Mike to run the place. I told Joey that I was going to make friends with Mike. For the kombucha . . . but also to make friends with Mike. (That's a win-win.) Mike not only gave us the idea of combos—*Jasmine-Hops* and *Ginger-Hops*—but he also convinced me to start making kombucha at home. Mike is a master SCOBY maker, and he set me up good. (The SCOBY is a Symbiotic Culture of Bacteria and Yeast, aka the thing that is alive in kombucha.) We threw a party in the summer of 2019 and Mike gave me the gift of a tap mounted on an old wooden crate and we served kombucha on tap to our guests. Some people say that my brother-in-law and sister's food made that party the greatest ever, but I think it might have been the kombucha on tap. Hey, you never know.

We started making kombucha at home in the winter of 2019. The first batch, in Brooklyn, took forever—kombucha needs to be above a certain temperature to ferment, and it was *cold* that winter—but once we moved the operation upstate, things began to take off. At first, I had a three-gallon ceramic vat. Then I thought I should upgrade and bought a five-gallon one to replace it. Then I realized that we needed all eight gallons. And then I bought another five-gallon vat. We are holding steady there, but it's going to go up again soon. I can just feel it. My ex-brother-in-law Rent even figured out how to keep the brew going all winter, by putting the tanks in bigger tanks and heating them with fish tank heaters. That's a sign of true genius, if you ask me.

Our kombucha is much lighter and more subtle than that which you buy in the store. It's crisper, and doesn't overwhelm you with a flavor assault each time you take a sip.

The house flavors of choice: *Mother Flavor, Mint, Elderberry-Mint, Malfoy-Mint (*aka *Mulberry-Mint)*, and *Ginger-Mint.* We had a failed experiment with *Basil,* but it tasted like pizza, so we called it the Margarita.

We started making honey kombucha in 2020. Some people call that Jun. We call it *Rockledge Rasa. Rasa* means nectar or essence. Or God. Joey recently took over flavoring from me, and I just focus on keeping the SCOBYs alive. We will open Duff's Kombucha Bar soon enough. Billy already made the sign for us, so we kind of have to at this point.

Joey and M. and I love kombucha. We drink it all day long. What do we like about it? I said, for a long time, that it was because of the *infinite choice.*

Q: What flavor do you want to make?
A: What flavor do you want to taste?

But I recently realized that I was just slightly missing the point. And it took a taste test to show me how.

Our flavors are great. *Mulberry-Grapefruit*, M.'s favorite, would probably earn most first-place votes if we voted, but we don't. I like *Mint*, both for the taste and what I imagine to be a reflection of my sophistication.

But let's pick a flavor: *Blood Orange*. Read the label, know that it's blood orange, and you can taste the blood orange as clear as day. One day, though, I poured some for Joey without telling her what it was and asked her to guess. She went through all the flavors we had on hand without getting it right.

"What the hell was that all about?" I started wondering. We know what flavors we make, and they are clear as day when you know what they are. How could they not be obvious without reading the label?

And then it hit me: The beauty of kombucha isn't the *possible flavors* you can make, although that's a big part of it. The beauty of kombucha is *possibility itself*. That's why our Mother Flavor tastes so good. It is the platform on top of which any flavor can be placed. It is the vessel for anything and everything. The point of kombucha is not the flavors themselves, it is that *any flavor is possible*. They all taste the same until you know what you're tasting. Or most of them do. All you need to do is add *the essence* of some flavor to your platform, and the brain will accept it—provided that you tell the brain what to accept. Living things can be or do whatever they want, and that extends to kombucha itself. It is what we want it to be.

You know those optical illusions where you trick your brain into seeing something that isn't there? The same goes with kombucha. Don't want to drink an entire glass of blackberry juice, because of the sugar? Well, drink a glass of blackberry kombucha. Your brain thinks it's blackberry, at least in terms of taste. And your body thinks it's kombucha, which has almost no sugar. You get the flavor of juice and the health benefits of life itself. We use a tablespoon or so of flavoring in each of our half-gallon bottles. I have decided to see if we can use even less than that. Just how little flavoring do you need to use before the brain says, "Hey! What's going on here?" I don't know, but I am sure it's less than we currently use. At some point, we are going to be using wavelengths of flavor. You know, when we build our laboratory.

(Before I realized this, I was getting at the same point when I coined the *Transitive Property of Kombucha,* which says that you can mix almost any kombucha with almost any other kombucha and it will taste just fine. Try it, you'll see.)

An aside: The word *platform* is overused in technology. Everything is a platform these days. But the inclination to use it comes from the right place: A platform is *all possibility*.

The promise of kombucha is *possibility*.

The flavor of a particular kombucha is *choice*.

POSSIBILITY ➡ CHOICE

Do you know why this happens? Because kombucha is a living drink. That is, it is made with a living yeast. It is alive. Anything that is alive contains the universe, or infinite possibility. Kombucha is infinite possibility in a drink.

Shifting *perspective,* you could say that when I talk about kombucha, I am also talking about life itself. Subjective reality (that is, consciousness) contains the potentiality for experience. The self (that is, you) provides the actuality of experience. Anything is possible; it's just up to you to make a choice.

POSSIBILITY ➡ CHOICE

Another aside: This is why we love water sports. Because the platform of water, in any state—water, snow, ice—allows for the most frictionless contact, and therefore the most possibility.

Surfing, explained: When you are on the wave, you are all *possibility*. When you pick your line, you are *choice*.

POSSIBILITY ➡ CHOICE

*   *   *

Things are going to start moving fast here, so hang on tight.

In Maryanne Wolf's book *Reader, Come Home*, Wolf talks about how researchers have realized some really neat things about how we read. One of them is that when you're reading a particular sentence, your eyes dart back and forth, reading a few words ahead of your conscious brain and then circling back. If the word that's two or three words ahead of where you're reading is something like "stick," your brain "surfaces" all the possible meanings of that word that you are aware of, and then quickly collapses down onto the correct one as soon as it realizes which it is.

Is it a stick, like a branch?
Is it "stick to something," like glue?
Is it "stick to a plan"?
What is it?

The point, though, is that the brain needs to know stuff in order to consider stuff. You are nothing without learning.

Here's what Wolf says about that: "Clearly nothing about the expert reading brain is left to chance, but rather is based on probabilities and prediction that, in turn, are based on context and prior knowledge."[2] She's almost right. It's *possibilities*, not *probabilities*.

Probabilities are what mathematicians use.
Possibilities are what the brain uses.

I talked about that with Joey a lot after I read it, because I thought it was pretty cool. The way I saw it, your brain had stored all the meanings it knew in some kind of wave field, which got invoked when the eyes saw the word, and then the wave converged onto the particular meaning when it figured it out.

POSSIBILITY → CHOICE

Wolf mentioned the findings as support for the idea of reading—the more you've read, the more possible meanings you know, so the better you will be at understanding, quickly, anything you read. That makes you better at consuming new information and better at interpreting it. *Reader, Come Home* is a beautiful book, a warning that we need to stay open to possibility, instead of closing ourselves off to it.

Wolf is the one who pointed me to Alberto Manguel's *A History of Reading*. I think about that book all the time. One of Manguel's most fascinating observations: Books are infinite. What does he mean by that? Your reading of a book is different than my reading of a book is different from someone else's reading of a book, with the difference deriving from the differences in the sum of the experiences (that is, the self) we each bring to that book. Everybody knows that, of course. So let's call those the many possible differences in a book, horizontally speaking (that is, between readers). But the idea works vertically, too—when it comes to different readings that each of us might experience when we read the same book at different points in time. You can read a book today, next year, or a decade from now, and each of *those* readings will be different, given the sum of your experiences (that is, your new self) to that point. So books vary along both axes. Books are infinite.

POSSIBILITY → CHOICE

Manguel also explains how words are pure magic, in that they can travel through space and time. (Humans can't do that, at least not in physical form. Our Selves can, of course, through Transcendental Meditation and other means. But that's a discussion for later.) Stephen King agrees with him. "Books are a uniquely portable magic,"[3] says the main character in King's book *Later*, one of the more recent in a never-ending (let's just call it *magical*) stream of books that the master of storytelling has given us over his remarkable career.

If we're going to talk about books and the infinite, we obviously need to talk about Jorge Luis Borges. Did you know that Borges went blind just a few years after becoming director of the Argentinean National Library, at the age of fifty-five? Guess who was one of his "readers"? A man named Alberto Manguel.

Borges's story "The Library of Babel" runs a mere seven pages, and it's still one of the greatest things ever written. In it, he postulates a library of almost unimaginable size: In an infinite series of hexagonal rooms, four of six walls in each room contain five bookshelves apiece; there are 32 books per shelf, 410 pages per book, 40 lines per page, some 80 letters per line. The library is large enough to contain all possible arrangements of an alphabet of 25 symbols in those books.

How many books is that? I asked myself that question a lot, and stayed curious enough about it to buy a book called *The Unimaginable Mathematics of Borges' Library of Babel*. According to the author, the total number of books in the library—$25\textasciicircum 1{,}312{,}000$, an almost unimaginable number—would not fit in the known universe. It's a neat image, but it's wrong. Because the calculations that the physicists have made of the known universe are wrong. Everything fits in the universe, because it is *now*. It is *infinite possibility*, like kombucha.

But the point of the Library of Babel is not to figure out how many books the infinite library (aka the universe) might contain; it's that somewhere in there is the story of your own salvation, and that you get to write it yourself. The best use of your time is not to *count* reality. The best use of it is to *create* reality.

POSSIBILITY ➡ CHOICE

Borges doesn't even bother including the number in his story. Why? Because, as we have already discussed, quantification is a poor means by which to attain a true understanding of anything. Umberto Eco later pointed out that the actual number is irrelevant to both the story and the reader. He was right. What is relevant is the *content* that Borges suggests—the *words*—those books might contain. In short: *everything*.

He has his own list, but I will give you my own:

The story of Duff, writing this sentence.
The influence of kombucha on all things.
The influence of Bob Dylan on all things.
The influence of Bob Dylan on Duff and how that influenced
*   his kombucha making, which led to the writing of the first*
*   sentence above.*
Every one of those stories could be told in one of those books.
Every story is told in one of those books.

POSSIBILITY ➔ CHOICE

Borges's stories, by the way, are interconnected by themes that point to the interconnectedness of all things: dreams, labyrinths, philosophy, libraries, mirrors, and mythology. His oeuvre is a representation of the universe.

While we're on the subject of libraries, I should give a shout-out to Dolly Parton, one of the greatest human beings to ever walk the earth, a superspreader of joy. Did you know that Dolly created something called the Imagination Library, which has donated millions of books to children around the world? She also played a part in funding a COVID vaccine. Oh, Dolly, you really are one of the best. I bought your Christmas album and your CD and your mug and your book as presents for Joey this year, because she specializes in joy, too. Dolly is also Miley Cyrus's godmother. Whenever I hear Miley sing, I go weak in the knees. So thanks, Dolly, for that, too.

Where was I? Oh, yes, libraries. Italo Calvino goes deep on the nature of the library as well: "Who is each one of us, if not a combination of experiences, information, books we have read. . . . Each life is an encyclopedia, a library."[4]

What Maryanne Wolf and her colleagues have isolated in terms of reading—the brain surfaces all possibilities before converging on one—isn't just restricted to reading. It's what the brain does all day long. When you (meaning, your brain) find yourself in a novel situation, it surfaces all known analogous situations so as to make the most informed decision about what to do next. And then it converges on the one.

How to Live a Life: You do a thing, take note of the interesting stuff (that is, feed it to your brain), and then move on down the road to the next thing. That is all. (Or, if you prefer: Chop Wood, Carry Water.)

Examples of interesting stuff: things that taste good, music that sounds good, vistas that look good, flowers that smell good. Also: kisses, stories, kittens, sunsets, babies, water, birds, fish, horses (especially horses named Barney), and my daughter, M.

When something reminds you of something, that's your brain telling you that you're doing a good job. It's got a big file going, and it needs to bounce each new experience off things in the file to figure out what to do. Your job is to build the file, not to analyze it. That's what the brain does.

Thinking is for chumps. You are here to *live.*

This is why déjà vu feels so weird. It is your brain accidentally showing you how it does its thing. So there's the mental part of it, but there's also something approaching a physical feeling of déjà vu, right? It kind of tickles, on the inside? You know what else tickles in the same way? Love. You know why that is? Because they're the same thing. When you have déjà vu, your brain is giving you a glimpse of the interconnectedness of all things, which is love. Déjà vu tickles because it reminds you of love. Why does it remind you of love? Because the message traveled down the same channel that messages from your brain travel to you, and there is only one message, and it is love. Love More is the suggestion. Love Tickles is the observation. But it could also be a command: Love Your Tickles. What else were you going to do?

This is a very human mistake: We confuse the feeling of déjà vu for something *we* are doing, that is, *thinking*. You think that you are thinking when you get the feeling, "Have I seen this before? This feels weird? I totally have déjà vu." But that's not you *thinking* that you might have seen it before. It is your brain flipping through its archives and letting you have a peek while it's doing so. They are not the same thing.

It is *brain activity*, not *mind activity*, that's happening. The reminders belong to it, and not to your mind. And you're not who you *think* you are. You just are what you are. You are also consciousness and the universe and the interconnectedness of all things. Those—and you—are all one and the same. Other than *that*, you are nothing. There, chew on that for a bit. We will get back to the really fun stuff in a moment.

There's a passage that caught my eye in *Reader, Come Home:* "An insight is a fleeting glimpse of the brain's huge store of unknown knowledge. The cortex is sharing one of its secrets."[5] But that's too scientific. It's not "the cortex," even though it is. It is the brain, which is consciousness, which is love, which is the universe, which is now. Insight is you tapping into the biggest brain of all, the interconnectedness of all things. You don't *have* knowledge. You *are* knowledge. Again: We are what we seek.

Insight is you looking within—via *in*-sight—to have a look at what's in the biggest file of all, the big brain. If you're connected to it, you will find what you need. If you're not, good luck finding anything at all.

This isn't exactly a revelation, but I am not sure anyone put it precisely this way before:

Your first responsibility is to possibility.
Stay open to the idea that anything is possible.
Stay right there, until it's time.
Because your next responsibility is to choose.
And then go for it.
What are you going to do right now?

Of course, it's difficult to embrace uncertainty in all facets of life. You'd need to be rootless, with no personal ties, and no guarantee of a meal tomorrow—just heading on down the road. (Or, as Dylan tells us, you'd need to "keep on keepin' on.") Most of us seek to tamp down uncertainty in some part of our lives, either by getting a job, entering a monogamous relationship, buying a house, whatever. That's okay, because uncertainty is . . . well . . . uncertain. And life can get scary sometimes.

So we try to eliminate uncertainty in the places where we don't want it. But the key is to then seek it out in the places where we do. That is what hobbies are for, although you don't really see the results until you've invested the effort. Once you have the craft, you can reside in the deep now, and let uncertainty come at you with all it's got. That's why we read. That's why we play music. That's why we ski, surf, dance, talk, grow gardens, and more. It's why we make kombucha.

The danger, of course, is when we let the novelty become an addiction that renders us ineffective in terms of our relationships to other humans or to ourselves. Sex addiction is a perfect example. I can totally see the draw of having sex with every single person I find attractive. But I can also see how that wouldn't work for most of those people, or most people, period. The real draw of online dating sites like Tinder, if you think about it, isn't the sex you had with that person; it's that Tinder is *a platform for possibility*. I loved using Tinder when I did—it took me out of the solitary life of being a freelance, divorced father who didn't drink and worked from home, a situation that doesn't really lend itself to meeting new people, and put me right in the center of the singles scene. I only spent a few years in the digital trenches of love, and only in my forties, but I have nothing but good things to say about it. There is nothing wrong with opening up more possibility than any one person can deal with.

POSSIBILITY ➡ CHOICE

What are you going to do right now?

CHAPTER 15

The True Story of Harry Potter

Slowly, very slowly, he sat up, and as he did so he felt
more alive and more aware of his own living body
than ever before. Why had he never appreciated what a
miracle he was, brain and nerve and bounding heart?[1]

—*Harry Potter and the Deathly Hallows*

Dancing is one of those things I chickened out on in life. I mean, I'll dance if you want to, but it's one of the things that scares me most. I have rarely been able to tap into the *now* part of dancing.

M. didn't know that when she was four. (Today, she does not think much of my dancing skills.) We have a bunch of songs that we've danced to over the years, but the one that stands out is Bruce Springsteen's "American Land," on 2012's *Wrecking Ball*. It's Springsteen does the Pogues, and we used to waltz from one end of our apartment to the other with her flying between and around my arms. She was a tiny thing back then. We retired "American Land" from our repertoire in 2018 or so, when she got too heavy for these old arms. We both dread the impending end of shoulder rides.

You know the best part of being a father? It's when you look into the eyes of your child, and you feel love flowing between you. You can feel something similar with someone that you are *in love with*, but it's not quite the same thing. When you look into the eyes of your child, you see creation itself. You see the glint in their eyes that says, "This is amazing, this thing called life."

M. is a fountain of joy alongside my other fountain of joy, Joey. So I have two. Between them, they managed to wake me up. Whatever it was I have been doing for the past fifty years, it has all added up into one right thing, an awareness of being alive—fully alive—right now. So I *was* doing it right. The whole time. I see that now.

We are but the sum of our experiences. From this vantage point, it's a little startling to realize that I'd been avoiding myself during a lot of my life, even as I was there all along, every last moment. Joey saw that and started talking to parts of me that were scared as well as the parts of me that were not. I spent my life reading Borges, even took the time to *explain* the Library of Babel to Joey, and the whole time, she was just patiently waiting for me to shut up for five seconds so she could invite me into the present. Enter COVID. And clarity.

Because clarity is what it's all about. Clarity about the nature of consciousness, which is both way more magical and startlingly simpler than I realized. I thought it was much more complicated than it was.

I was not fully present. I am now. Why didn't anyone tell me that now contained all the good stuff? All of it! Oh wait, they did. Over and over and over again. I'm humbled by my ignorance but energized by the possibility of which I am finally cognizant.

Now now now now now now now.

Imagine if no one ever doubted themselves again. What kind of holy heaven would that unleash on the world?

My most important task, at this point, is to help keep M. and her brain in the flow. I am trying to share with her everything that I have learned, not so much as lessons as an attempt to tell her the story of her father as it is happening in real time. She is listening, because we are finally connected. I didn't know about this part. But you never do, right? Anyway, it's a new feeling, and it's amazing. I know that she can feel it, too, because of the glint in her eyes, the one that says, "This is amazing, this thing called life."

We have dozens of ongoing conversations that we loop back on and build upon whenever someone remembers something funny. Joey is in on everything, too, and more: Joey is both mother figure and the sibling I did not give M. They go talk about girl stuff and put it "in the vault." Almost every day that she is at Rockledge, M. and Joey (and sometimes me) will walk out into the bluestone quarry on the edge of the property. "Let's go to the Rock Ledge," says M., and then they are gone. There is an inherent loneliness in being an only child with divorced parents. But since Joey came along, M. has not been lonely. She has a best friend, and there could not be more love between them.

This is amazing, this thing called life.

I am helping her construct her mind and she is grateful to me for that. I can see that in her eyes. She is a delightful child and a wonderful and empathetic human being. When I look at her, I feel magic. I mean, I feel like my heart is about to explode. We all want bliss. This is part of it.

Magic conjures something from nothing. Love does that. In other words, love is magic. Or magic is love. It doesn't matter. It's all the same thing.

Illusion, on the other hand, refers to something that is not real. Things that are pure copies of other things are not really real. When there is nothing new, that means nothing has been created. And if nothing has been created, then nothing happened. Truth can now be photocopied and nobody knows the difference because every-body's so distracted by the numbers that are crowding out their capacity for understanding.

I wanted to be a magician when I was young. My father was an amateur magician, and I wanted to be like my father. I ended up becoming an illusionist, writing books that were full of other people's thoughts but packaged as my own. That's copying, pure and simple. The two people I copied more than anyone else—J. C. Spender and Matthew Stewart—were always gracious about it. Looking back, I can tell that they could see that I was working through the thing that we all need to work through, and let me adopt large parts of their thinking as my own. Both are true phi-losophers, with intellects that leave me in awe. But I am finally creating something of my own. I know that to be true because it is happening right now. It continues to happen. I am creating it with every single word I type. . . .

*   *   *

When I finally realized that the only job I had was to read Harry Potter with M., I had absolutely no idea what it was going to do to our relationship or to me. Or this book. Or my life. As the spring and summer of 2020 unfolded, I was under constant pressure to finish whatever Harry Potter book I was reading at the time before her next visit, so that we could then watch the movie together on the weekend—my first viewing, her millionth.

At some point, I got a little stressed about how slowly I was read-ing the series. Not because of the movies. M. could wait. So why? Because I was letting my mind go to the future, where I'd somehow concluded that I would have to finish the entire Potter series if I were going to finish this book. You see what I did there? I took an amazing thing and somehow got it tangled in the future, where it became a source of stress. We do this kind of thing to ourselves every single minute of every single day. The only way to avoid it is through vigilance. All too many of our daily inputs, whether they are news, marketing, or otherwise, are designed to do the very same. That's how you control a population, folks. This is how you sell them stuff. Keep them focused on tomorrow, so that they forget to do something about today. The systems that we create to communicate and cooperate are, by their very nature, designed to allow us to take into consideration not just our own wants and needs, but those of other people, too. That's a noble and worthy ideal. The risk is that we allow a system—any system—to keep our attention pulled away from our Selves. Because it's much easier to manipulate someone who has lost touch with who they are.

A system that seeks to *quantify* everything is, at its very core, a distraction from the Self. Numbers don't contain meaning, so the more time we spend thinking about them, the less meaning we have in our lives.

A system that seeks to *explain* everything—say, for example, *science*—is doing the very same thing. It pulls us into our intellects and away from our hearts. When we focus on things that we imagine are *explainable*, we take our attention off those that are not. And the only things that really matter in life are not *explainable*—things like love, fun, beauty, or existence itself. The riddle of spirituality is not something that we can solve with the intellect.[2] The answer lies in the heart.

A system of *gratitude*, on the other hand, might lead us to stop taking credit for everything and simply be grateful that we are alive. A system of *love* would do the same thing, revealing connections instead of distinctions. Diversity seems like a good thing, but unity is even better. We really *are* all one, but we will never realize that until we stop counting our differences.

But I digress. When it came to the problem of *how to read Harry*

Potter, M. showed me the way, as she often does. I told her that I was reading as fast as I could. "No, don't do that!" she said. "Don't finish it!" I realized, at that moment, that I should take it easy. I took a month per book, a respectable slow pace, if you ask me.

All of which reminds me of a review I read of *War and Peace* a long time ago. I can't remember the words verbatim, but the reviewer said something like, "My only problem with having read this book is that I will never have the pleasure of reading it for the very first time ever again."

I did not make that mistake with Harry Potter. I drew it out as long as it tickled me to do so. I took my time. The Lady gives good advice. Do you know what happens when you take your time? You pick up on things you might not have otherwise. I have been listening pretty carefully these days, and I heard a lot more of what J. K. Rowling was trying to tell us than I ever would have before.

The Harry Potter saga is one of the greatest literary achievements of all time because it contains the truth. We are heroic when we are heroic, we're not when we're not. Ron Weasley, Harry's best friend, is loyal but susceptible to egotism. Hermione is loyal and hardworking but uptight. Harry veers between all the poles—loyal, egotistical, thoughtful, impulsive. These are real people in a fantasy realm.

What do I mean when I say that it contains the Truth? Rowling made this a story about children, but the journey she sends Harry on is the journey of the Self. And the things she teaches him—and us—along the way are the lessons of a lifetime.

The only education of any value any of us ever gets doesn't come from a textbook. It comes from experience.

> Muggles . . . Don' listen properly, do they? Don' look properly, either. Never notice nuffink, they don't.[3]

Ron makes it almost to the end of every adventure with Harry, at which point Harry has to go the final leg of the journey alone. That's called self-knowledge. You can't take your friends down that road with you. You've got to go by yourself. And then go back and hang out with your friends again.

Most important: You are the universe. While there will be many other people in your personal orbit as you go through your life, the thing that you are creating is yours and yours alone. No one else is to blame for what happens to you, because you get to make your own decisions. And when you make those decisions, you are going to want to rely on instinct more than anything else. You want to listen to your heart, not your mind. Because thinking is overrated. Harry Potter might not make all the right choices, but he keeps making choices. Moreover, he tries to do the right thing. Always. And that's all we ever need to do.

*   *   *

It is *all* in there, people. Rowling pulled off the impossible, and crammed everything about life into just seven books.

> "Never," said Hagrid irritably, "try an' get a straight answer out of a centaur. Ruddy stargazers. Not interested in anything closer than the moon."[4]

Translation: I think she's telling us that scientists (in this case, astronomers) aren't focused on the human condition.

Slytherin, the house of science and credentialism and white supremacy and money, "had the fastest racing brooms gold could buy."[5]

What a surprise.

In *Harry Potter and the Chamber of Secrets*, Hermione defends

Lockhart because he represents himself as an expert. We all fall for that.

Why are we always competing? There is no need to compete. There is no need to *win*. Quidditch isn't the greatest game ever. Quidditch is a pastiche of all the dumb games that man plays, with all the balls (large and small), goals, bats, and incomprehensible rules. If your Seeker catches the Snitch, you get 150 points. Why 150 points? Because sports aren't fun unless someone is *winning big*, and a single point won't do.

There is no need to rank. There is no need to score. There is no need to see who has more than whom. (Gilderoy Lockhart counts his Valentines.) We get too caught up in silly competitions when there is no winning at life itself. The only *goal* is simply to realize who you really are.

> You'd be surprised. . . . Some of the books the Ministry's confiscated—Dad's told me—there was one that burned your eyes out. And everyone who read Sonnets of a Sorcerer spoke in limericks for the rest of their lives. And some old witch in Bath had a book that you could never stop reading![6]

The Ministry is the system. It wants to stamp out subversive material before it takes root. Things like . . . Shakespeare . . . the original Bard of Love. Or reading itself. M. couldn't stop reading Harry Potter. She read a few of the books in the series *three* times, and she's currently listening to them on Audible all over again.

Hagrid is friends with Harry, Ron, and Hermione. In real life, kids aren't friends with adults who aren't their relatives. Because we're scared. But how interesting would it be for both kids and adults if we all treated each other like human beings? Adults think

they know stuff, when it is children who have the clearest understanding of love. I'd be friends with other kids like M. any day if
they wouldn't run me out of town for it.

In *Harry Potter and the Chamber of Secrets*, Harry asks how he
could be taken inside someone else's memory. In a diary, that's how.
The most subversive act of all is to tell your own story with courage
and love. The Chamber of Secrets *is* a diary. It's your own heart.
The end of that book reminded me of one of my favorite childhood
books, *Encyclopedia Brown*. It turns out it's all right there in front
of you; all you have to do is listen.

> "Books can be misleading," said Lockhart delicately.
> "You wrote them!" Harry shouted.
> "My dear boy," said Lockhart, straightening up and frown-
> ing at Harry. "Do use your common sense."[7]

In *Harry Potter and the Prisoner of Azkaban*, Azkaban Prison is
a metaphor for guilt and shame. Sirius, Harry's godfather, spent
years in Azkaban. But he's a stand-in for Harry himself. Sirius is
what will happen to Harry if he becomes a prisoner of his own
shame. This is J. K. Rowling's book about time travel, too. It's hard
to contemplate young you talking to old you, but it's not hard to
contemplate old you talking to young you, in which case young you
is talking to old you. Either way, there is only one thing you will
ever need to know in your life, and it is who you really are. That's
your only job, to find that out.

> It is our choices, Harry, that show what we truly are, far
> more than our abilities.[8]

*   *   *

Rowling is also a master at inverting what's good and what's bad. The whole point at Hogwarts is that if they *teach* the little wizards enough (via *education*), then they will be able to resist *the dark arts*.

But you know what she's saying, right? It's that if you stuff your brain full of pointless things, you will become so enamored with your intellect—you will become so *in love with your mind*—that you will be able to resist *actual love*, which is just another way of saying *the unexpected*. Hermione personifies this issue: A teacher's pet, she would like nothing more than the ability to organize her own future before it even arrives.

> "Wait, wait!," cried Hermione. . . . "We can't just go, we haven't got a plan, we need to—"
> "We need to get going," said Harry, firmly.[9]

And that's one of the most important lessons of all. While the temptation to plan one's life is overwhelming, the correct choice is simply to live it. Planning requires that one be able to predict the future, a difficult task considering that the future does not exist.

> As Hagrid had said, what would come would come . . . and he would have to meet it when it did.[10]

As I was reading the last few chapters of the last book in the series, *Harry Potter and the Deathly Hallows*, I started to cry. I cry at a lot of things these days, whether it's a good book, a movie that grabs my heartstrings, or, most often, a good song. M. acts like she thinks it's funny, but I know that she understands that it's evidence of a beating heart. Finishing Harry Potter is like coming to the end of anything truly wonderful. It's always bittersweet.

Why do we love stories so much? One reason is that the mere invocation of a story-on-the-way—whether it's "once upon a time" or "I've got a story for you"—puts the heart and brain of both story-teller and listener at ease. But that's not all. When a story begins, the storyteller moves into a state of giving, and the listener moves into a state of *receptivity* that makes it easier to take in meaning, to be transported from the present into the story inside the words themselves. Words and stories are powerful things. They can carry teachings, for one. But if you listen closely, you can find all sorts of other powers floating around inside them as well, including memory, love, courage, and more. We can all learn to engage with storytelling in a more active way, to treat it more as a spiritual practice than we typically do. Because stories are a reminder of the power of creation, a reminder that we are all Gods in the end.

At one point, Harry Potter is racing down a hallway at Hogwarts and he is cheered on by a figure in a painting, Sir Cadogan. Says Cadogan: "Braggarts and rogues, dogs and scoundrels, drive them out, Harry Potter, see them off!" Cadogan is Rowling's Don Quixote, one of the greatest fictional heroes ever put to paper. Cervantes's Don Quixote was considered a bumbling fool by most, but he saw himself on a quest for the Holy Grail. Everyone else was wrong. He was right. We are *all* right. Because we are *all* God. As far as each of us is concerned, we really are the greatest thing that ever happened, because we are our own creations. What Rowling is reminding us is that no matter who we are, if we are not always—in each and every moment of our existence—on a quest to do the right thing for the universe that we have created, then we are missing the point entirely.

That's why, even as she keeps the narrative centered on Harry Potter—it's *his story*, after all—Rowling expands the frame a bit in the final action and shows how every character we know is the star of their own life story. Neville Longbottom, for example, kills Voldemort's snake, Nagini. Dean Thomas, who also dated Ginny Weasley, has a couple of heroic moments of his own. Rowling is showing her readers that even as we are, by definition, the stars of our own narratives, there are an infinite number of other narratives going on all around us. It's all just a matter of your particular point of view. We are all leading actors in an infinite story.

> "Where do Vanished objects go?"
> "Into nonbeing, which is to say, everything," replied Professor McGonagall.[11]

Like I said, J. K. Rowling got it all in there. The entire goddamned universe.

CHAPTER 16

How to Tickle Yourself

If you want to know the world, all you need to
do is listen. What people see when they travel is
nothing more than an illusion. Shadows chasing
other shadows. The roads and the countries teach
us nothing we don't know already, nothing we can't
hear within ourselves in the peace of night.[1]

—Amin Maalouf, *Balthasar's Odyssey*

When I first landed on the idea of learning how to tickle yourself as
the guiding philosophy of this book, I also delineated what I called
a taxonomy of tickles. The way I saw it, there were four basic ways
you can tickle yourself. They are:

Tickle #1: Feed Your Body
Tickle #2: Play with Your Body
Tickle #3: Feed Your Mind
Tickle #4: Play with Your Mind

The first few times I tried to write this chapter, it was basically a long list of all the different ways that I, Duff McDonald, have found to tickle myself via one of the four categories above. I listed my favorite foods, my favorite ways to be active, the ways that I feed my mind (that is, to learn), and the ways that I play with my mind (that is, to create). I also made long lists of all the people that I love. I wasn't trying to convince anyone to like the things that I like, just to point out that the goal was really to tighten your focus in on things so much that you taste the *rasa*, or essence, of any particular experience. That's when you feel the tickles coming on.

From there, you want to try to create a daisy chain. Share your tickles with other people, and you are pretty much sharing love. The spiritual masters have been trying to tell us this for ages: The best kind of love is not love for something or someone outside of you. The best kind of love is love of your Self—love of your own existence. When you get really good at it, they don't even call it love anymore; they call it bliss. If you really want to blow someone's mind, the best thing you can do is to keep your focus *within*. If you love everything about yourself—who you are, what you do—it is the most contagious thing there is. Love yourself—without being a narcissist about it—and people will love being around you. They might even love being themselves around you. There is no truer love than that.

But something was eating at me. At the same time that I recommended pursuing our passions and burrowing as deep into them as possible, there was something bothering me about the fact that I was essentially advocating for a life of sensual pleasures. As someone who has finally and belatedly understood the profound impact of meditation on one's ability to inhabit one's own existence, I was having trouble squaring the two. Meditation teaches you to rein in the mind, to exercise control and discipline over your senses. In other words, you don't let your sense organs lead you around . . . by the nose? (Sorry, I couldn't resist.)

But I'm not a monk, and you probably aren't, either. I love the taste of kombucha and I love the sound of Bob Dylan. I wouldn't want to be the person who tries to take either of those away from me. So every time I sat down to try to deal with this chapter, I ended up frustrated. How could I advocate for control of the mind *and* the pursuit of my four tickles? They seemed to stand in complete opposition to one another.

The senses pull us outward. But what we are looking for is inside, beyond the reach of the senses. So how can we use our senses to attain the Truth? The scriptures tell us that the Truth is beyond the mind, beyond the intellect, beyond the senses of perception. Put another way: The Truth lies beyond everything. It is the backdrop on which everything else takes place. But the only means we have at our disposal to know *anything* are our senses. It is another paradox.

So what's the solution? The meditation masters will tell you that the source of our distraction is the same thing that can take us to our goal. With discipline, we can learn to tune out all those sensory inputs that are nothing but noise, so that we might tighten our focus on the things that matter, the things that show us the face of God. You are in charge of the way that you live your life. In any given instant, you get to decide what you're going to do, and, by extension, what you're not going to do. So the conclusion is to do the only thing that you *can* do, which is to focus on what is meaningful and ignore everything else. So what is meaningful? I can't tell you that; it's something you need to answer for yourself.

All knowledge comes through experience. We cannot truly understand *anything* until we have experienced it. Even the best attempts to communicate the essence, or *qualia*, of things—through language or art or literature—can only get so far. I'm not saying that those attempts are not valuable—they most certainly are, because none of us can experience everything—but there is no substitute for experience in the end. So the imperative, then, is to *do things*.

My recommendation—it worked for me—is to do things that, if you are really paying attention, make you feel that faint tickle inside of you. It is the tickle of experience, the tickle of learning, the tickle of creation, the tickle of love. It is all of those things. And the more you learn how to *zero in* on that feeling, the easier it will be to invoke it. On which note, I was talking to Joey's mom, Betty, and our mutual friend Rupam Das on one of our regular Sunday Zoom calls. Rupam is Indian, and he's also a physicist, and I'd asked him about India's greatest contributions to mathematics. He didn't need to think about it. India brought us the concept of zero, he told us, and zero contains all.

Betty then pointed out that zero is none other than the Self. Think about it. When you start counting along some line, or away from the center of some axis, it starts *somewhere*, right? That somewhere is *you*. Our number system is literally *built around the idea of the Self,* making it all the more amazing that Western scientists still insist on objectivity. There is no such thing as objectivity. It's an illusion. Everything that you know is contained in the Self. Everything.

Or consider this: you start at *zero.* If you start counting anything— say, for example, the contents of your own intellect—you are moving away from zero toward the infinite. But you will never get to the end. Not only that, if you divide your awareness by all those things you're counting, you will soon find that it's completely dispersed. But what if you didn't count anything at all? What if you simply stayed put, accepting that you are already complete, that the totality of you is all there is? Just you, the *one* thing that you are, which is existence itself. At that point, all you need to do is lean backward (toward zero) and fall right into the void of the Self. Divide your awareness by zero things counted, and you end up with nothing short of infinite awareness, aka the ocean of consciousness. And it doesn't take any effort at all.

Mathematics can't get you there, other than to show you that anything divided by zero is infinite. It's just pointing the way. You need to do it to yourself, and you will only need the one number we decided means anything, anyway, which is *one*. One is love, the totality. Zero is nothing. What do you get if you divide love by *no thing*? You might need to ask a mathematician about this, but I think you get *infinite love*. The yogis will tell you that the goal is to do nothing and to be nobody. I thought I understood that, but I didn't realize the kind of math they were doing. I mean, I knew that the doorway to the infinite ran through zero when it came to mathematics, but I most certainly didn't know that the same held true in life. You don't want to be or know *any particular thing*. You want to be and know *every single thing*. And the way to get there is right through zero. No wonder it's shaped like a portal. Just dive on through. Everything you think you know *is* an illusion when compared to the contents of zero.

The very same day of the conversation above, I walked by M.'s room and pointed to a towel lying on the floor, something I have done *countless* times.

"What's that?" I asked.

"An illusion," she replied.

That's part of what meditation teaches you—to tune out the distractions so that you can focus on the matter at hand. So maybe it isn't a paradox. Rather, like all paradoxes, it collapses with the right adjustment in perspective. There is nothing wrong with trying to tickle yourself your whole life long, as long as you are focused on the right kinds of tickles, the things that make you happy to be alive.

The Buddhists have a name for those thoughts, speeches, or behaviors that we engage in because we are motivated by a desire to get some experience. It's called *samskara,* and it means "that which is intensely done."[2] Eknath Easwaran called samskaras "the key to character." Our attraction to certain things lies deep in our consciousness, and the reason that we are attracted to them is simply that the sum of our experiences has led us to feel that way. And while I'm no Buddhist, my gut tells me that at least some samskaras can be identified by the fact that they tickle us.

When I am talking about tickling yourself, then, I am talking about improving your control over your senses so as to get closer to the ultimate goal, which is focus on your existence itself. But it's hard to pay attention, isn't it? The way I see it, the best way to teach myself how to pay attention to *now* is to do things that I enjoy doing. It's easier to pay attention to those things, which I can identify because they tickle. But the goal isn't the tickles in themselves. It's teaching myself how to focus, so that I might better appreciate my own existence.

It's not like it's that hard to figure out which things you can tickle yourself with, either. Your brain will let you know when any of the tickles have been activated. It sends you back that wild, mercury feeling that Bob Dylan referred to when describing the sound he was after on one of his many masterpieces, *Blonde on Blonde.* (Yes, Dylanologists, I know he called it a "thin, wild mercury sound"—I am taking liberties, like the man himself. It's all the same story, something Dylan has been trying to tell you all along. There is only one story: his, yours, mine, and ours.)

Where were we? Right: that wild, mercury thing. I'll tell you what he's talking about, even if he wasn't: He's talking about things that *tickle* you. In Bob's case, it was a sound that tickled him at that point in time. But in my case, or your case, the wild mercury thing will vary by context. What tickles you? Why do some people not like to be tickled? How crazy is that?

More to the point: How did we evolve as a species into thinking that one can't tickle oneself? Of course you can tickle yourself! You do it all day long, when you give your brain what it wants and it sends you back a message of love in gratitude for your having done so. It's the easiest way we have of inviting joy into our lives. Combine all three—the gratitude, the tickle, and the love—and you have the ingredients of a sense of wonder. The greatest sense of wonder of all is to appreciate the miracle of your own existence. But for a lot of us, that's harder to come by than it sounds. Well, you can start down that path by tickling yourself. It worked for me.

So why do we all think we can't tickle ourselves? Something very important has been lost in a society that writes off—even if only verbally—the possibility of doing so without asking twice.

A guy named Christopher once said to me, "Duff, you always seem to find the best version of something, and then commit to it."

My reaction: "Isn't that what everybody does?"

Before you think I'm getting all full of myself here, I think he was talking about hot sauce. But I thought about it, and at least in terms of things of personal taste—meaning, *what tickles me*—I realized that he was right. When I find something that I really like, I just load up on it until I can't consume any more. That goes for everything, from food to ideas to music to people.

When you save the best part of your dinner for last, you are trying to extend the tickle. When you try to stretch out the reading of a book? Extending the tickle. When you try to let that orgasm last forever? They call it edging, but that's the thing about orgasm, right? It's ticklish. You want it to last forever, because once it climaxes, you are done (in a matter of speaking). When you giggle with a friend and can't stop? You are tickling each other. When M. used to command me, "Tickle me, Daddy! More! More!" she knew what she was doing.

Why do we tell ourselves that we don't like being tickled? I think that anyone who doesn't like being tickled is doing some kind of system-level mind control on themselves. Tickling is a sign of love, so if you don't let the tickles in, you don't let love in. And if you don't let love in, you are a way easier target for fear. And if fear gets a hold of you, you will do what you are told. By an expert. Who will scare you into thinking that you need them and their expertise in order to navigate your way into a terrifying future that does not exist. They will tell you that you can use their numbers as spells against a scary monster called uncertainty, when all you need to fight it off is love. Which you can get via tickling. It's way easier than we have come to believe.

I was talking to Joey about the four tickles and she said that I shouldn't forget Don Miguel Ruiz's Four Agreements. She is right. His *four* are for how to live a good life. His encompass mine, but my *four* are a little more specific: They are about your passions, the things you do to tickle yourself. As J. K. Rowling said: Give yourself more *entertainment*—more *love*—by tickling *yourself* first, and you won't be able to help but send it out into the world.

No one knows how to ride your broomstick as well as you do. And once you learn how to ride the broomstick of your life, you are going to be able to give a lot of people rides along the way.

I've argued that *science* is overrated. I've also argued that *thinking* is overrated. What I mean when I say those things is that *the intellect* is overrated, at least when it is put up against experience itself. The confusion, I would like to suggest, lies in our belief that learning is an *active* pursuit. It is not. *Learning happens when it happens.* You can stuff your head full of anything you want, but until you *understand* it, it's pretty much useless to you. Not only that, it is not our intellect that learns anything of enduring value; it is our brain, which does not need our help. All it needs us to do is live, which merely requires that we use our five senses. When we *think*, we are just playing with toys of the mind, trying to create a small oasis of order within the seeming chaos of daily life. But behind that chaos there is another order, a higher order, that contains all you need to know. You can't get there by thinking, though. It's easier than that. You get there by listening closely enough that you can hear God speaking to you in the sound of the rain or the crash of the waves. The answers, as the Bard told us, are *blowing in the wind.*

One of the reasons that I made it all the way into my twenties without knowing myself (I made it a whole lot farther than that) is that our Western education system told me that I was smarter than most people, and I believed it. I mean, the "system" didn't tell me anything, because "the system" doesn't exist. But I bought into the idea that you could understand life by analyzing it. Because my "scores" in school said I was smarter than everyone else, I believed them. But I had a stunted ability to simply do things, as opposed to thinking about them. Because of that, I had no idea who or what I was. How so? Because we are not who we *think* we are; we are simply what we have *done.* Another way of saying that: We are *something that happened.*

There's a word in Indian spiritual tradition for the descent of divine grace that reveals the existence of a higher order. It's called *shaktipat.* Other religious traditions have different names for it, but they're all talking about the same thing, which is an awakening to something outside of ourselves—outside of our *small* selves, or our egos. The ego is the thing that tells you that you are what makes things happen. It "takes receipt" of doership—*I did that.* What happens during an awakening is the sudden realization that that might not be the case.

Such an experience challenges our notions of the relative autonomy of ordinary life. In its place arrives that sense of a higher order, of a wholeness that extends well beyond our own individual experience. While it invariably comes as a surprise—*waking up* always does—it also carries with it the weight of revealed Truth. What it really brings is *freedom* via *awareness.* When you realize that we are all one, the benefits of that realization soon follow. David Frawley calls it the law of life: *All beings further the one who feels unity with them*. It makes sense, doesn't it? If you feel *unity* with something or someone, then that thing is you. Why wouldn't you support it as you support yourself?

Why do humans think they're so special? We might be the only living species that does not know its own purpose. Trees know their purpose. They don't get confused; in every single moment of their existence, they make the decision to continue being a tree. That is why they have so many leaves. They make the decision to keep being a tree over and over and over again. There is no miscommunication *between* trees, either. On the contrary, they talk to each other underground, and when one part of the forest needs something from another part, they all do their thing. Joey reminds me, too, that trees also migrate, although at a pace incomprehensible to our own sense of time. Compare that to humans who are constantly failing to communicate with each other properly, always making incorrect assumptions about each other, and yet still running around calling ourselves *evolved*. Humans are the *least evolved* of the species.

How on earth was man able to convince himself that he or she should be in charge of the brain, something that is so far beyond our capacity to contemplate that we couldn't design it if we had a billion years to do so? And please don't compare the brain to a computer. Computers don't know a thing about *experience*. They are *machines. They are models of human cognition, not interchangeable with humans.*

You need to feed your brain and then let it do its thing, not "think" your way out of a problem. To learn is to feed your brain. We are so arrogant as a species that we think we are building important things inside our minds. That we should be *driving* the brain instead of feeding it. We have lost sight of what is actually happening here.

All that said, I would like to suggest that one kind of *thinking—*

which is probably better termed *wondering*—is the good kind. You can use your mind to find new things that you can feed to your body and your brain. You can use your mind to figure out why your brain or your body likes this thing and not that thing. The trap here is if you get stuck on why you don't like some things, as opposed to focusing on the things that you do.

As for learning, you can do it by watching. My friend Billy told me the greatest term for this. While he might tell you he works in construction, he's really an artist, and gets his inspiration from watching other people do what they do. "In the trades, we call that *stealing with your eyes*," he says. Don't steal people's stuff. But by all means, steal with your eyes until you can't fit anything else in the getaway car.

Trust me on this. I am *very familiar* with this trap: For much of my life, I have constructed extremely articulate explanations of why something or someone just didn't meet my standards. I have hurt people when I have done so. If someone wasn't very funny, I concluded that they couldn't be very smart. And then I didn't listen to them. If someone wasn't facile with numbers, I concluded that they weren't very smart. And I didn't listen to them. If someone questioned my point of view, I deemed them ill-informed (see: smarter than everyone else, above) and I dismissed every single thing they said. To all those people: I am sorry. To any of them who remain my friends: Thank you. I promise to do better. Not in the future, but *right now*. I am doing better *right now*.

What I have realized is that my brain does not need me to *think* to solve problems; it does need me to *think* about things to do. Things that might tickle me. That's what *thinking* is for: so that I can *wonder* about the next thing I am going to do.

What should I do now?

So I choose to focus on the things my brain and body find to be true, which I know because they tickle. And I will feed them until it doesn't tickle anymore. I try not to do it all at once, although I sometimes do that with music, playing an album nonstop until I can't listen to it again. If your brain is like my brain, it will let you know when it's had enough. Or not. I have stumbled on a few musicians of late that it seems impossible to burn out on. I am talking about you, Sturgill Simpson, and you, Jonathan Wilson, and you, Valerie June. Sturgill Simpson put out two monumental bluegrass albums in 2020, the combination of which constituted nothing less than an explosion of creative force. Valerie June's "You And I" might be the most beautiful love song ever written. At least it is for me—the latest best love song I have ever heard.

And I don't see anything wrong whatsoever with specializing in something to the point of near-obsession. M. is reading Harry Potter for the umpteenth time as I write this sentence, and that is the best thing she can do for herself, because her brain literally can't get enough of it. (And that's because J. K. Rowling put the whole damn thing in there, people, *all of life*. No wonder the child wants it all. An entire life in a single set of books? You'd read it ten times if you had the ability to do so yourself. Maybe you should try.)

If I don't do what tickles me, that's me telling my brain that I don't care what it wants. And that is no way to establish a good relationship with your brain. If you do that for too long, your brain will cease communicating with you. And why wouldn't it? Would you keep in touch with someone who doesn't care about the things that make you happy—that *tickle* you? No, you would not. And if you wouldn't do that, why on earth would your boss—sorry, your *brain*—do anything different?

Do you want a kundalini experience? I haven't the faintest idea what to tell you about that other than the suggestion that if you're not focused on the tickle of Truth, thereby reaffirming your connection to the cosmos, you don't stand a chance.

> By controlling the senses, you control thought, and the mind becomes peaceful. By doing this the ego vanishes.
>
> —Vivekachudamani of Sri Sankaracharya

*   *   *

I'm one of those people who keep all their books. I have carted boxes of books with me from country to country, city to city, and home to home. Why do I do that? It has nothing whatsoever to do with what other people might think when they see my books. It is so that I can remember the books that I have forgotten that I have read, and jiggle the memory back into a state of potentiality, so that the book can once again help me learn something new.

A violent rainstorm threatened Westchester, where M. lives with her mother, during quarantine. "Mom made us sleep in the basement," she told me afterward. "She said to get whatever I needed from my bedroom and bring it down."

What did she bring with her? What if she could never go upstairs again?

All her Harry Potter books.

Nothing else.

That girl knows how to tickle herself.

———

Always Be Wondering

Put *that* in your book.

—M. McDonald

I was telling my friend Matt about these books my mother has carried around for years. She calls them "brain books" and they contain everything she needs to know. He told me that all the great thinkers used to carry them around. In *Where Good Ideas Come From*, Steven Johnson describes Darwin's notebooks as "a cultivating space for his hunches." That's a pretty cool way to describe it.

Even better, Johnson points us to the name "Commonplace Books," which any self-respecting member of the Enlightenment apparently carried around with them. There is even a verb, *commonplacing*, which is so much more *sophisticated* than today's gaudy alternative, *journaling*. (The Lady and I are in an ongoing competition over who is more *sophisticated*. She is winning.)

It all goes back to Aristotle's ideas about common sense. Put it all in one place, and let your brain do the rest of the work. Of course the Enlightenment thinkers got it all backward. The English philosopher John Locke wrote a treatise in French on commonplace books, published in English in 1706 as *A New Method of Making Common-Place-Books*. Locke detailed the appropriate "techniques" for arranging materials by subject and category. He even included his indexing scheme in his famous *An Essay Concerning Human Understanding*. Scientists! They're always looking to organize everything!

It seems like everyone who missed the target by a really wide margin kept a highly organized commonplace book, including Francis Bacon and the theologian William Paley. The best commonplace book is the one that is as scattered as your thoughts as you have had them. An example: Leonardo da Vinci described his notebook as "a collection without order, drawn from many papers, which I have copied here hoping to arrange them later each in its place, according to the subjects of which they treat." Thank God he didn't get around to that. It would have ruined everything. Mark Twain's commonplace book was also all over the map.

The organizers were wrong. Leonardo and Twain were right. There's a reason that Amazon's warehouses have no organizing principle. Because that's how the brain works. You just need to shove it all in there; your brain will take care of the rest.

J. K. Rowling put her own version of the commonplace book in *Harry Potter and the Goblet of Fire*. It's the stone basin in Dumbledore's office called a Pensieve that Harry tumbles into only to find himself in Dumbledore's memory. "I sometimes find, and I am sure you know the feeling, that I simply have too many thoughts and memories crammed into my mind," Dumbledore explains to Potter. "At these times, I use the Pensieve. One simply siphons the excess thoughts from one's mind, pours them into the basin, and examines them at one's leisure. It becomes easier to spot patterns and links, you understand, when they are in this form."[1] The word, a pun on the word *pensive*, is a brilliant one, because it suggests the process of finding meaning and insight in the mass of memory. But it's really nothing more than a diary.

This is where we go wrong with language. Commonplace used to mean the place where it all gets dumped together, leaving it to the brain to assemble everything for the win. Today we think of commonplace as so ordinary that it barely merits attention. That's a huge mistake: There is nothing wrong with normal things—or normal people. Anyone who thinks they're special is wrong. To be normal is to be special, because you exist.

Not that long ago, I asked Joey, "Do you know where that notebook I had hanging around for a while is? Did I give it to you?" I had. It's a little black book made by Chronicle Books with gorgeous gold script on the cover that says, *Fucking Brilliant.* Joey gave it back to me because it's clear that it was for me. Joey doesn't really swear, whereas I consider it an art form.

We all lead busy lives. Write stuff down so that you don't forget it. You can *journal* if you want, but I'm talking about something else, a storehouse for all your best ideas. Mine are brilliant, as you can see from where I keep them. I am sure yours are, too.

*   *   *

I'm a big fan of yoga. The yogis know what's what. Whereas Western religions and philosophy tend to break life systems apart into separate pieces, the Indian traditions realized that it is all one—physical, mental, and spiritual. One of the central problems facing Western culture these days is that far too many of us misunderstand the whole idea of a life. You are never going to find your way to an enlightened state if you simply chase one or two of the three components. If you want to be *whole*, you have to bring your *whole* life around.

I have never been the kind of guy who wanted to join exclusive clubs. Exclusive clubs are silly, an attempt by insecure people to feel better than someone they don't even know. True success is to be better than *yourself*. That's what yoga is all about. Likewise, I have always been irritated by any organization that seeks, as a matter of course, to exclude rather than include. Certification is only good for things like scuba diving, where you don't want to kill yourself by accident.

We can always improve, and so we pick up bits and pieces from other people's systems, every step along the way. But I don't want *your* system; I've got my own. You should get your own, too.

Before I tell you about mine, let me make something very clear, so that you don't think I think I know more than you. I am the biggest dummy of them all. I have spent fifty years thinking about it all wrong.

I lived a quantified reality while lashing out at others for doing so.
I was not happy and I was not connected to the universe (aka, my
*   Self).*
I blamed it all on other people, even when I knew that wasn't right.
That led me to alcoholism, anger, and resentment.
Agent Angel saved the day. She showed me how to love myself.
And love tickles. Who knew?
It was only by surrendering to love that I was able to let it all go. I
*   let go of my need for certainty and my need to be right. I kicked*
*   precision to the curb and let love of my existence take its place.*

Have you ever *secretly* wondered *Why am I not happy? Why am I not connected?* If you haven't, I stand in awe of you. If you have, I hope that this book has convinced you that you, too, can let it all go.

Anything can happen.
The universe is infinite possibility.
You can do anything you want.
All you have to do is Love More.

That's it. It's the easiest thing you will ever do. And once you start doing it, everything else gets easier, too. Before you know it, you will have a complete life system laid out in front of you as if it came out of nowhere. And that's because it did: The ocean of consciousness is very deep, and it contains everything you need to know.

I'm not suggesting that you follow my path or make my story yours or even to copy a single thing that I do. I'm not telling you to do anything other than to come up with your own system. Why? Because it's hard to find purpose in your life if there is no underlying coherence to what you do. The word *discipline* has gotten a bad rap; it's the means to figuring out who you really are.

Why do you do the things you do?

If I'd asked myself that question a few years ago, the only thing I could have come up with was "because I feel like it." But that's not good enough. There is only one reason to do anything, and it's because *you feel that it's the right thing to do.* But you won't know what that is unless you have a system for living that informs your decisions, from the very big to the very small. There's nothing wrong with spontaneity; indeed, it's the essence of life. But even spontaneous moments take place in a larger context—that is, the context of *you.* If you can learn to *focus* on your own existence—your *Self*—you will ultimately realize who you are and why you do the things that you do. At that point, you will stop doing some things and start doing some others. Eventually the system will take care of itself, and all you will have to do is show up.

In other words, the only thing you need is *awareness*. That's it. Nothing else. That's when you can feel experience tickling you. But what is experience, really? It's something that takes place *within consciousness*. So when an experience tickles you, that's actually consciousness tickling you. And what is consciousness? Well, it's *you*—you are conscious because you exist.

EXISTENCE ➡ CONSCIOUSNESS

CONSCIOUSNESS ➡ EXPERIENCE

EXPERIENCE ➡ TICKLES

Or, if you prefer shorter equations:

EXISTENCE TICKLES

Which is just another way of saying:

LOVE MORE

One of the chapters of this book offered to tell you how to tickle yourself. Here's the secret, in one single sentence: All you have to do is be aware of your own existence, to love the fact that you are alive.

That's the fountainhead, the tickle that contains all other tickles. When Descartes said, "I think, therefore I am," he included one too many steps. Because thinking is not required. All you need to do is *be*.

I Am.

If you get your system right, there will be a day when everything seems to lock in, as if the puzzle of reality were being solved inside yourself. It won't come through the intellect; rather, it will be unknowing and spontaneous and it will manifest as if there were no cause. Because there won't be. You just need to be ready for it when it comes. It happened to me, and the freedom I've felt since has been extraordinary.

DUFF'S LIFE SYSTEM

Try to See the Humor in Everything

If I have excelled at any one thing in my life, it is this. I'm not saying I'm the funniest person around, because I'm not. But *Reader's Digest* was right: Laughter really is the best medicine.

Hang Out with Your Friends

I am very good at this, too. I've never really wanted to be in charge of anything. I just wanted to have my friends around. It's why I bought Rockledge, if you don't include the real reason I bought Rockledge, which was to give it to my daughter so that she would always have a place to call home. The other reason I bought Rockledge was to try to lure my friends out of New York City to a place more conducive to conversation. But that was backward. Yes, we do have friends who come up from the city. But we are making new friends, right here, right down the street. I finally figured out what they mean by community, and it's pretty awesome.

Go to See Live Music

Go see Bob Dylan before he dies. And go see Kyle Ferguson before *you* die.

Read. A Lot.

We have been through this. Experience is the best way to feed your brain. But reading might be the most efficient. Maryanne Wolf and Alberto Manguel can explain it to you. Read anything that interests you, but you should eventually do some reading about realization of the Self. In Hindu philosophy, the path of knowledge, or jñāna, means knowing the Self as none other than the Supreme Reality. Those are the books that will remind you that you are God, which is a good thing to remember. Because God can do anything, and so can you.

Be a Specialist, Not an Expert

There are no experts. There are only specialists. Experts "think" about stuff. Specialists just "do" stuff. Try to avoid thinking too much and just go out and do what needs to be done.

Go Outside

We have a creek on our property called the River Phoenix. M. named it that after seeing *Stand by Me*. We talk to the creek. I write it letters in my mind. My best jokes are about it. ("I think Joey is having an affair with the River Phoenix. Every time she goes out to see him, she comes back all wet.")

Share the Good Stuff with Other People

Post stuff on social media that you think is amazing. But don't be a narcissist. Use social networks to spread the news about amazing things *other than yourself.* Okay, you can post about yourself if you want, but please include a link to something that I have written every now and then.

Don't Drink Alcohol

I have always been reluctant to tell people how to drink alcohol. You know, the whole pot and kettle thing. But it's time: When people talk about this person having a drinking problem and that person *not* having one, that is confusion, pure and simple. Anyone who drinks alcohol has a drinking problem. Alcohol is an almost insurmountable obstacle to finding a state of presence, which means being right here, right now. When you drink alcohol, it takes you out of now. That's why you say things you don't mean, and why you get in arguments you don't want to be in. When you are recovering from drinking, your mind is sluggish, and you are still out of *now.* You are tired, moody, physically sick. There is nothing good about alcohol. It is poison.

Try Surfing

Joey and I try to surf. Neither of us is any good, but who cares? Surfing is fun. Joey says surfing is one-stop shopping for happiness. It's meditative, it's physical, you're in nature, you can be social, and you can even catch a wave. When people talk about flow, they're really talking about surfing your way through life. Flow is a numberless state. You need to believe me about this: If you are thinking about numbers, you will never get into flow. Because when you are thinking about numbers you are probably thinking of the past or the future, and that is no way to surf a wave. You will miss all the fun. The problem with our society is that we are all numbers, all the time. We forgot what it's like to flow.

Did you know that the vascular system operates by means of something called a *standing wave*, which emanates from the heart's aorta? And when you meditate, you activate oscillators in your nervous and circulatory systems that lock you into a *wavelike* rhythm of pulsations in the magnetic field around your head. It's all waves, people. Anything that isn't in flow is not fully alive.

Stay Focused on Possibility, not Probability

That means trying to shake loose the grip that numbers have on you.

Use your words, people.

Don't Waste Your Time

One way to do this is to try to avoid the Trap of Time. When you think about the past and the future, you are squandering your now. Stop thinking so much. Just do stuff. Of course, you are welcome to remember the good times, but don't dwell on them. There is only now.

Don't Plan to Do Stuff in the Future; Do Stuff Right Now

When I say don't plan, I don't mean that you can't do things that *require* planning, like putting on a big party or building some great work of art. Those are just fine, because when you set your intention and set them in motion, you are simply working in a series of *nows*. What I'm saying you shouldn't do is to say, "I will do that when I'm ready," or, "We shouldn't do this until we do that." I spent a lot of my life thinking that it had to be lived sequentially. That's wrong. You should do what you want to do right now.

Always Be Wondering

Wondering is not the same as thinking. Wondering is a state of receptivity, not active inquiry or planning. It's all about spontaneity.

When you think too much, you focus on the probable. When you wonder, you stay fixed on the possible. There's a universe of difference between the two. Keep your mind open and keep asking yourself questions.

At the end of the Bhagavad Gita, Lord Krishna advises Arjuna, "I give you these precious words of wisdom; reflect on them and then do as you choose."[2]

You're almost done with this book.

What are you going to do when you put it down?

Keep It Simple

This is not an original thought.

But everybody copies everybody, right?

My favorite version of it is by Swami Vivekananda. He advises that it's better to seek the general than to get bogged down in the specific:

> If a man wants to know this universe bit by bit, he must know every individual grain of sand, which means infinite time; he cannot know all of them. Then how can knowledge be? How is it possible for a man to be all-knowing through particulars? The Yogis say that behind this particular manifestation there is a generalization. Behind all particular ideas stands a generalized, an abstract principle; grasp it, and you have grasped everything.[3]

Or, if modern sages are more your style, you could just listen to Tom Petty. In his song "Wake Up Time," Petty advises that it's time to open up your eyes, so that you "might find the forest there in the trees." Same point, different words. You will never find the infinite in the particulars. The path to ultimate knowledge runs through an appreciation of sameness, not difference.

Do Yoga

I started doing hatha yoga in 2013. Joey introduced me to the philosophy of yoga after I met her. What is yoga? Sri Nisargadatta Maharaj put it succinctly: "Selfishness is rooted in the mistaken ideas of oneself. Clarification of the mind is yoga." Yoga is focus. Yoga is unity. Yoga means uniting yourself with the universal consciousness. (Reading can give you knowledge of the universal consciousness; yoga unites you with it.) When you incorporate yoga properly into your life, you bring everything back into balance.

Joey, not surprisingly, describes the essence of yoga better than I do. Ask her about her true purpose, and she will tell you that she tries, every single day, to find a way to touch a place of love. When she does that, she knows that she starts to vibrate, and that's when she can add her own frequency to the song of the universe. I have never met another human being with as much capacity for love as Joey. It's really quite humbling and can make me cry with gratitude if I think about it too much. Anyway, that's the whole goal of yoga: to make yourself right again, in all the ways—to make yourself aware of the glory of your own existence. It works.

Meditate

Joey got me to start meditating. We do Deepak and Oprah's sessions, which are great. Although that's a new opinion for me: For the longest time, I told her that I enjoyed Deepak but couldn't connect to Oprah. I demanded a neck rub during Deepak, to boot. And then in April 2020, Joey put on Oprah one morning, and I understood everything that Oprah was saying and realized that I loved her. The problem had been *me*; it *always* is. I also meditated properly for the first time in my life. Oh, and by the way: the reason cats that aren't scaredy-cats are so chill? It's because they spend most of their day *meditating*. Just look at them when they close their eyes. They are *meditating*.

Seriously, though: Meditation is no joke. It is, as I have recently come to describe it, "the answer." The only way to see things as they really are is to quiet the storm of conceptual thinking that is the mind, to eliminate the subject/object duality that is worldly life. If you can do that, you can start to see around the corners of your ego. In other words, you can see things from a better *perspective*. That's all ego is, right? *Your* perspective. Every one of us is constantly falling into traps of perspective that don't allow us to see clearly. Meditation allows you to train your mind to keep it down so that you can both reside and react in the moment itself.

Love More

Real love is about being open, being able to say, "I don't know what's coming, but I am ready." That is love. Just light the flame. The tinder is all around you.

Just Be

There is nothing easier than this, once you figure out how to do it.

The Infinite Afterward

Everybody copies everybody, right? So I am going to copy my daughter to bring an end to this book. This is a drawing by The Lady. Kids know more than we do, because they haven't overloaded their brains with useless information. They are still dealing with stuff that came straight from the universal source, the ocean of consciousness.

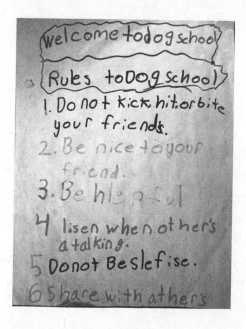

We consider this list such a jewel in The Lady's archives that we had it framed. But to really understand it, we have *to focus* on its underlying message, the thing behind the thing.

WELCOME TO DOG SCHOOL

Rules to Dog School
1. Do not kick, hit, or bite your friends.
2. Be nice to your friend.
3. Be hlepful
4. lisen when other's a talking.
5. Do not Be slefise.
6. Share with ather's

There are so many things to like about this document.

It's a list of rules that starts with a "welcome." That's the right stance to open anything.

"Rules to" is so much better than "Rules of."

Numbers 1 and 2 come at the idea of friendship from both sides. That's holistic.

Number 3 is a sign of a good person.

Number 4 is just great advice. I have not always followed it.

Number 5 is a sign of a kind person.

Number 6 will happen spontaneously when you figure out how to tickle yourself. Because tickles are contagious.

You see what happened here?

We're not really talking about Dog School, are we?

We are talking about Life.

The Lady gave us the Rules to Life.

Considered in that light, the start of this is actually: *Welcome to Life*

God, I love this kid.

So here goes:

WELCOME TO LIFE

Rules to Life

1. Pay attention ➞ POSSIBILITY.
2. Ride the wave ➞ CHOICE.

If you start to truly FOCUS on what's happening to you . . .

Things should start to get interesting right about . . .

NOW.

Love,

The Universe

P.S. It's going to tickle.

Acknowledgments

This book came out of nowhere, just like everything else.

But four people deserve my express gratitude for helping me bring it into existence.

Thank you, Hollis, for having faith in me. We did it!

Thank you, M. You are the best idea I ever had, by far.

Thank you, Joey, for riding into my life on those angel wings of yours.

Thank you, Mom, for everything. But especially for coming up with the idea of me. You and Dad did that with love. I know you miss him, and I do, too. But he is most assuredly looking down at us right now, laughing his ass off at the fact that I finally figured out how to be.

—Hurley, New York, March 2021

Notes

Chapter 0

1. Swami Vivekananda, *The Four Paths of Self-Realization: The Path of Knowledge, the Path of Inner-Transformation, the Path of Selfless Action, the Path of Devotion* (Discovery, 2017), 167.
2. Tomas Sedlacek, *Economics of Good and Evil: The Quest for Economic Meaning from Gilgamesh to Wall Street* (New York: Oxford University Press, 2011), 171.
3. Ibid., 328.
4. Eknath Easwaran, *The Dhammapada* (Tomales, CA: Nilgiri Press, 2017), 46.
5. William Deresiewicz, *Excellent Sheep: The Miseducation of the American Elite and the Way to a Meaningful Life* (New York: Free Press, 2015).
6. Deba Brata Sensharma, *The Philosophy of Sadhana* (Albany: State University of New York Press, 1990), xiii.
7. Sri Swami Satchidananda, *The Yoga Sutras of Patanjali* (Integral Yoga Publications, 2012), 78.

Part I: The Great Awakening

1. J. K. Rowling, *Harry Potter and the Chamber of Secrets* (New York: Scholastic Paperbacks, 1998), 324.

Chapter 1: Be Here Now

1. I should mention that the primary outside source for this book is the Harry Potter series of novels. Why? The first reason is that I am doing it for my daughter, M. She's got Harry Potter fever right now, and I love

her, so Harry Potter it's going to be. But there's another reason that's almost as good. (Nothing is as good as love.) The second reason is that J. K. Rowling managed to cram everything into those novels. And if you're only going to use a single source other than yourself, you might as well go with the one that contains everything other than you. Joey's mom, Betty, told me that the swamis say you need to bring three things to your message if it is to have any credibility at all. First, you need to include some teachings from scripture. Second, you need to include some teachings from your guru. And third, you need to include your own experience. Well, I'm in luck! The scripture in this book is the Gospel According to Harry Potter. My guru? For the time being, his name is Bob Dylan, and this book is chock-full of teachings from the guy. Finally, it is overflowing with my own story. There, instant credibility!

Chapter 2: There Is No Equation for Enlightenment

1. J. K. Rowling, *Harry Potter and the Goblet of Fire* (New York: Scholastic Press, 2000), 199.
2. If you want my recommendation of the very best book you can ever read about doing so, it is *I Am That*, by Sri Nisargadatta Maharaj. Reading Maharaj, I realized one of the ways that we have it all upside down in the West. Westerners think objectivity is truth. But Eastern philosophy thinks objectivity is false. Says Maharaj: "There is nothing objective about Truth, which essentially is pure subjectivity." Understand that, and you realize that no one person or group of people has a greater claim on truth than any others. All perception is false. It makes it way easier to consider loving every human being on earth when you realize that none of us is right.
3. https://www.theverge.com/2020/12/15/22167586/pandemic-time-perception -2020-covid.
4. David Frawley, *Vedantic Meditation: Lighting the Flame of Awareness* (Berkeley, CA: North Atlantic Books, 2000), 34.
5. Paul Eduardo Muller-Ortega, *The Triadic Heart of Siva* (Albany, NY: State University of New York Press, 1989), 169.

Chapter 3: The Best Book I Ever Read

1. Stephen King, *The Outsider* (New York: Gallery Books, 2019), 522.
2. Alberto Manguel, *A History of Reading* (New York: Penguin Books, 1997), 211.
3. With thanks to Sri Nisargadatta Maharaj for putting this thought in my head.
4. Erin Morgenstern, *The Starless Sea* (New York: Anchor Books, 2019), 328.

5. Ibid., 388.
6. Ibid., 348.

Chapter 4: Stories About Numbers

1. Robin Wall Kimmerer, *Braiding Sweetgrass: Indigenous Wisdom, Scientific Knowledge and the Teachings of Plants* (Minneapolis: Milkweed Editions, 2015), 347.

Chapter 5: Books About Numbers

1. Don LePan, *The Cognitive Revolution in Western Culture: The Birth of Expectation* (Broadview Press, 1989), 170.
2. A man named Jay Alix recently spent several years pursuing McKinsey in U.S. bankruptcy courts, trying to get McKinsey to comply with the law. I did some consulting work for Jay during that time. Before doing so, I wondered, briefly, if working with Alix might damage my reputation as a journalist. But then I realized that if I didn't work with him, it wasn't my career that would suffer but my opinion of myself. McKinsey was treating the law with disdain, and I regret nothing. By observing Jay over time, and seeing both his motives and behavior on full public display, I came to see him as an avenging angel with a sword made of his time, energy, skills, and treasure. A highly respected former bankruptcy judge publicly referred to Jay as a hero. I concur with that observation.
3. Stanislav Andreski, *Social Sciences as Sorcery* (New York: St. Martin's Press, 1973), 95.

Part II: The Stamp of Reality

1. Sri Nisargadatta Maharaj, *I Am That* (Durham, NC: The Acorn Press, 1973), 6.

Chapter 6: The Trap of Time

1. Don LePan, *The Cognitive Revolution in Western Culture: The Birth of Expectation* (Broadview Press, 1989), 86.
2. E. M. Forster, *Howards End* (New York: Everyman's Library, 1991), 190.
3. Swami Nikhilananda, *The Gospel of Sri Ramakrishna* (New York: Ramakrishna-Vivekananda Center, 1942), 259.
4. J. K. Rowling, *Harry Potter and the Chamber of Secrets* (New York: Scholastic Paperbacks, 1998), 297.

Chapter 7: You Can't Measure Freedom

1. J. K. Rowling, *Harry Potter and the Prisoner of Azkaban* (New York: Scholastic Paperbacks, 2001), 109.
2. Lee Sannella, *The Kundalini Experience: Psychosis or Transcendence* (Lower Lake, CA: Integral, 1987).
3. Swami Vivekananda, *The Four Paths of Self-Realization: The Path of Knowledge, the Path of Inner-Transformation, the Path of Selfless Action, the Path of Devotion* (Discovery, 2017), 185.
4. With thanks to Sri Nisargadatta Maharaj, who opened my mind to this line of thinking.
5. Fritjof Capra, *The Turning Point: Science, Society, and the Rising Culture* (Toronto: Bantam, 1984), 375.
6. Amin Maalouf, *Balthasar's Odyssey* (New York: Arcade, 2002), 75.

Chapter 8: The Precision Paradox

1. J. K. Rowling, *Harry Potter and the Chamber of Secrets* (New York: Scholastic Paperbacks, 1998), 150.
2. David Frawley, *Vedantic Meditation: Lighting the Flame of Awareness* (Berkeley, CA: North Atlantic Books, 2000), 46.
3. Sri Swami Satchidananda, *The Yoga Sutras of Patanjali* (Integral Yoga Publications, 2012), 105.
4. William Byers, *The Blind Spot: Science and the Crisis of Uncertainty* (Princeton, NJ: Princeton University Press, 2011), 19.
5. Ian Hacking, *How Shall We Do the History of Statistics?*
6. Paul Eduardo Muller-Ortega, *The Triadic Heart of Siva* (Albany, NY: State University of New York Press, 1989), 53.
7. My friend Rupam Das pointed me to it. It's great.

Chapter 9: The Answer Is Not for Sale

1. J. K. Rowling, *Harry Potter and the Deathly Hallows* (New York: Scholastic Paperbacks, 2009), 185.
2. J. K. Rowling, *Harry Potter and the Prisoner of Azkaban* (New York: Scholastic Paperbacks, 2001), 51.
3. Dr. Richard Gillett, *IT'S A FREAKIN' MESS: How to Thrive in Divisive Times* (New York: Kingston Bridge Press, 2020), 112.
4. Sri Aurobindo, *Essays on the Gita* (Twin Lakes, WI: Lotus Press, 1995), 416.
5. Robin Wall Kimmerer, *Braiding Sweetgrass: Indigenous Wisdom, Scientific*

Knowledge and the Teachings of Plants (Minneapolis: Milkweed Editions, 2015), 305.

Chapter 10: What Now? (The Only Thing That Matters)

1. J. K. Rowling, *Harry Potter and the Chamber of Secrets* (New York: Scholastic Paperbacks, 1998), 333.
2. Eknath Easwaran, *The Bhagavad Gita* (Tomales, CA: Nilgiri Press, 2007), 63.
3. J. K. Rowling, *Harry Potter and the Prisoner of Azkaban* (New York: Scholastic Paperbacks, 2001), 53.
4. Eknath Easwaran, *The Dhammapada* (Tomales, CA: Nilgiri Press, 2017), 118.

Part III: Anything Is Possible

1. Nisargadatta Maharaj and Ramesh S. Balsekar, *Seeds of Consciousness: The Wisdom of Sri Nisargadatta Maharaj* (Durham, NC: The Acorn Press, 1990), 102.

Chapter 11: No Time to Think

1. Erin Morgenstern, *The Starless Sea* (New York: Anchor Books, 2019), 543.

Chapter 12: The Love Equation

1. J. K. Rowling, *Harry Potter and the Goblet of Fire* (New York: Scholastic Press, 2000), 281.
2. Lee Sannella, *The Kundalini Experience: Psychosis or Transcendence* (Lower Lake, CA: Integral, 1987).

Chapter 13: The Jasmine Troupe

1. *What Did Jack Do?* (David Lynch, producer, 2017).
2. Nisargadatta Maharaj and Ramesh S. Balsekar, *Seeds of Consciousness: The Wisdom of Sri Nisargadatta Maharaj* (Durham, NC: The Acorn Press, 1990), 132.

Chapter 14: Infinite Kombucha

1. Jorge Luis Borges, *Collected Fictions* (New York: Viking, 1998), 125.
2. Maryanne Wolf, *Reader, Come Home: The Reading Brain in a Digital World* (New York: Harper, 2018), 29.

3. Stephen King, *Later* (London: Titan Books, 2021), 241.
4. Ibid., 54.
5. Ibid., 64.

Chapter 15: The True Story of Harry Potter

1. J. K. Rowling, *Harry Potter and the Deathly Hallows* (New York: Scholastic Paperbacks, 2009), 692.
2. Thanks to Sri Nisargadatta Maharaj, who put this idea in my head.
3. J. K. Rowling, *Harry Potter and the Prisoner of Azkaban* (New York: Scholastic Paperbacks, 2001), 36.
4. J. K. Rowling, *Harry Potter and the Sorcerer's Stone* (New York: Scholastic Press, 1998), 254.
5. J. K. Rowling, *Harry Potter and the Chamber of Secrets* (New York: Scholastic Paperbacks, 1998), 166.
6. Ibid., 230.
7. Ibid.
8. Ibid.
9. Rowling, *Harry Potter and the Deathly Hallows*.
10. J. K. Rowling, *Harry Potter and the Goblet of Fire* (New York: Scholastic Press, 2000), 734.
11. Rowling, *Harry Potter and the Deathly Hallows*.

Chapter 16: How to Tickle Yourself

1. Amin Maalouf, *Balthasar's Odyssey* (New York: Arcade, 2002), 24.
2. Eknath Easwaran, *The Dhammapada* (Tomales, CA: Nilgiri Press, 2017), 85.

Chapter 17: Always Be Wondering

1. J. K. Rowling, *Harry Potter and the Goblet of Fire* (New York: Scholastic Press, 2002), 597.
2. Eknath Easwaran, *The Bhagavad Gita* (Tomales, CA: Nilgiri Press, 2007), 263.
3. Swami Vivekananda, *The Four Paths of Self-Realization: The Path of Knowledge, the Path of Inner-Transformation, the Path of Selfless Action, the Path of Devotion* (Discovery, 2017), 197.

About the Author

DUFF McDONALD is the author of the *New York Times* bestseller *The Firm: The Story of McKinsey and Its Secret Influence on American Business*; *Last Man Standing: The Ascent of Jamie Dimon and JPMorgan Chase*; and *The Golden Passport* and the coauthor of *Frictionless* and *The CEO*, a satire. He has written for *Vanity Fair*, *New York*, the *New York Observer*, *Esquire*, *GQ*, *Wired*, *Air Mail*, and other publications. He lives in Ulster County, New York, with his wife, Joey, eight chickens, and three cats: The Sherriff Steven Wondrous; Corey Feldman, Esquire; and Princess Steven Buscemi. Lastly, he is the cohost (with Matt McButter) of the podcast *How to Tickle Yourself*, which you should check out after you are done reading this book.